D1458379

THINKER, SAILOR, SHEPHERD, SPY?

James D G Davidson

ATHENA PRESS
LONDON

THINKER, SAILOR, SHEPHERD, SPY?
Copyright © James D G Davidson 2009

All Rights Reserved

ISBN: 978 1 84748 424 6

Every effort has been made to trace the copyright holders of
works quoted within this book and obtain permission. The
publisher apologises for any omission and is happy to make
necessary changes in subsequent print runs.

First published 2009 by
ATHENA PRESS
Queen's House, 2 Holly Road
Twickenham TW1 4EG
United Kingdom

Printed for Athena Press

To my wife Janet, to my sons and daughters – Sandy, Ros, Polly and Calum – and to all my grandchildren; to my sisters and their families – and to my first wife, Kit, to whom fate gave a raw deal.

Contents

Prologue

We were not far from our destination when the air raid sirens started their ominous, undulating wail. The train pulled into a suburban station and we were all herded out, across the unroofed platform towards a nearby air raid shelter. Overhead the sun shone brightly and the drone of countless aircraft filled the blue sky. Once in the gloomy concrete shelter, we heard the intermittent crump of falling bombs – some distant, some seeming quite close.

My father was on convoy duty in the North Sea, so my mother was taking me to London to catch the express from Paddington to Dartmouth, to begin life as a Naval Cadet. The brand new cadet's uniform was itchy, the collar of the white shirt uncomfortable. At thirteen, I felt very self-conscious. Following the last muffled explosion, there was a prolonged silence. My heart sank as my mother announced loudly and proudly to our fellow passengers, 'My son has just joined the Navy!' A ripple of subdued laughter ran round the shelter and I wished that one of the bombs had fallen right on top of me.

With a father who had served in a destroyer at Jutland, and a mother who thought the Services were the only respectable life for a man, I had always wanted to join the Navy, but three experiences – one inspirational, one aspirational and one which filled me with irrational envy – had their effect, too.

In 1938, on a summer holiday at my grandmother's house in Nairn overlooking the Moray Firth, I was playing on the beach below the house, exploring rock pools, when I looked up to see a thrilling sight – the battleships *Nelson* and *Rodney* and the battlecruiser *Hood* emerging from the Sutors, the cleft in the red cliffs which is the entrance to the Cromarty Firth, four miles away. I sat on a rock for more than an hour watching them until they disappeared beneath the eastern horizon. It affected me deeply.

Later that summer I was taken to Inverness to see my first Technicolor film: *Sons of the Sea*, in which a young Dartmouth cadet marched proudly up a ramp beneath a fluttering White Ensign, to the strains of a Royal Marine band, and whizzed round the Devonshire lanes in a little red sports car, accompanied by a pretty blonde. I was dazzled.

Then, late in 1939, I met a cadet who was already at Dartmouth. He had been issued with a proper Services gas mask, not just a silly civilian one like half a school satchel. My decision was made. I took the entrance examination and passed, then steeled myself for the interview and medical examination at the Admiralty.

My mother's father, F W Osborne, had been known as Red Fred. He had had red hair and an aggressive moustache, neither of which matched his disposition, which was sunny and good-tempered. When I knew him, what was left of his hair was white. His chief loves were sport, his grandchildren and reading the *Australasian*, a thick broadsheet in a pink cover, full of photographs of cricketers and prize-winning sheep. During the Boer War he had served as a colonel with the Royal Australian Horse Artillery. My maternal grandmother, by the time I knew her, was completely crippled by rheumatoid arthritis – I never saw her walk. She bore constant pain with fortitude and patience and the help of her Christian Science faith. They had come to this country from Australia when my mother and father were married. Their only son had been killed in the final days of the First World War.

Jim Osborne was badly wounded and Mentioned in Despatches at Gallipoli – that appalling graveyard for young men – for 'gallant and distinguished services in the field,' after he had risked his own life to pick up and fling away a hand grenade which landed among his men in a trench. Badly wounded, he was invalided out of the Australian army and although he had been a captain at the age of only twenty-three, they would not take him back. His very strong sense of loyalty to the Old Country led him to join the Argyll and Sutherland Highlanders as a private. He was killed in France in July 1918.

Despite the loss of her beloved elder brother, and many young men among her contemporaries, my mother, Valentine, known as

Val, towards the end of her life spoke only of the happy times she had in Australia – riding in the outback, watching sheep-shearing, attending house parties and playing with her pet wallaby. She lived with her parents at Queenscliff, Victoria, where her father was stationed. She met my father, Alastair Davidson, when he was seconded to the Royal Australian Navy in the 1920s.

My father was the third son in a family of six boys and two girls. As in many families at that time, two children had died young. Although their home was in Nairn, my grandfather was a housemaster at Harrow for a time, with Winston Churchill among his charges. It was my grandfather who wrote the famous letter to Winston's mother, quoted in full in Randolph Churchill's biography of his father:

> After a good deal of hesitation and discussion with his form-master, I have decided to allow Winston to have his exeunt; but I must own that he has not deserved it. I do not think, nor does Mr Somervell, that he is in any way wilfully troublesome, but his forgetfulness, carelessness, unpunctuality and irregularity in every way have really been so serious that I write to ask you when he is at home to speak very gravely to him on the subject.

He concluded:

> Winston, I am sorry to say, has, if anything, got worse as the term has passed. Constantly late for school, losing his books and papers … He is so regular in his irregularity that I really don't know what to do and sometimes think he cannot help it … As far as ability goes, he ought to be at the top of his form, whereas he is at the bottom. He is a remarkable boy in many ways and it would be a thousand pities if such good abilities were made useless by habitual negligence. I ought not to close without telling you that I am very much pleased with some history work he has done for me.

Perhaps Winston was shown the letter and it had some effect!

My paternal grandmother claimed to be a Robertson of Struan but was brought up in the south-west of Scotland among the rich farmlands that fringe the north coast of the Solway Firth.

Of my father Alastair's brothers, Duncan, the eldest, served in the Cameron Highlanders in the First World War. He was very badly wounded and, after the war, farmed between Nairn and Inverness. Malcolm, the second, trained as an opera singer and was a published composer. He, too, served in the Cameron Highlanders in the First World War and was shot through the head. He recovered despite being unconscious for six weeks, but his self-confidence was badly affected. Fluent in German and Italian, he quietly helped a number of musicians and friends escape from Germany and Austria during the Nazi years and, after service as an intelligence officer in the Second World War, ended up as an examiner for the Royal Academy of Music. He was immensely kind to me as a boy and had a talent I deeply envied – he could swallow green peas and blow them out through his nose. Very late in life he married a lady from Skye with whom he never seemed to spend any time.

A younger brother, Angus, served in the Highland Light Infantry towards the end of the First World War but spent the Second World War in Intelligence. He was a highly regarded translator from the Italian and worked regularly with Alberto de Moravia. He also had two books published: a biography of Edward Lear and *Miss Douglas of New York*, about a distant relative. The youngest brother, Douglas, was a painter who had some association with the Bloomsbury Set.

There were also twin sisters, Olive and Marjorie, of whom only the former survived to marry and produce a family. It was to her home in Sussex that we were invited when war was declared in 1939 and my father was recalled to the Navy from his job as personnel officer in an engineering works. We were able to see him there sometimes, between east coast convoys from London to Newcastle and back. Such was the background I sought not to disgrace.

Naval Cadet

The interview at the Admiralty in London was alarming. Candidates were seated, in turn, at the end of a table round which were grouped half a dozen formidable admirals, and subjected to questioning for twenty minutes. The whole of my future, it seemed to me then, depended on the answers I gave.

More than sixty years on, I only remember one of the questions – the one I answered most successfully. On a big wall hung a physical map of the world. I was asked to point out the parts of the British Empire. In those days it included the self-governing Dominions of Australia, Canada, New Zealand and South Africa as well as many islands and colonies over which the Union Jack held sway in both hemispheres. This was information which had been drummed into me and I started by pointing out all the main Dominions and most of the bigger colonies, then continued with the islands and smaller places like Gibraltar and Aden. As I pointed my finger at the tiny island of Socotra in the Gulf of Aden, one of the Admirals said kindly, 'That'll do Davidson, you may sit down again.'

That evening, on leave between convoys, my father took me out to a slap-up meal and asked me how it had gone. I thought I had done pretty well and said so. In fact I passed in eighth out of the thirty applicants chosen from 750.

My first weeks at Dartmouth were a blur of drills, parades, swimming baths, classrooms, playing fields, the gym, the Sandquay Engineering Works... and running, running, running. We had to run everywhere. The routine was exacting. Moments of leisure were brief and closely supervised. Even our going to bed – 'turning in' as it was called – was a ritual. Clothes had to be meticulously folded on top of a sea chest, to a preordained pattern. Cadets had to lie at attention on their backs on the hard beds, under white coverlets with navy blue rugs woven with their initials in red for identification across their feet, while Officers'

Rounds were passing. A Cadet Captain who was in charge of my dormitory had the initials R.I.P. In the morning, we were woken by the shrill blast of the bosun's call and had to run, naked, carrying a towel, to take a cold plunge in a white-tiled communal bath with a dozen other pink bodies – first in, first out.

I do not recall a single case of bullying during my eleven terms at the college. Although the cane was used frequently by cadet captains, its use was strictly regulated – one or two cuts for minor misdemeanours like talking out of turn, wearing your lanyard too long or having shoes unpolished. 'Official Cuts', delivered by a sergeant of the Royal Marines in the presence of an officer and the Surgeon Commander, were decreed only for such heinous offences as smoking or drinking beer.

I was naturally a conformist and never deliberately broke rules, but I crossed the line on one or two occasions. The most serious punishment I received was a 2B Drill, consisting of an hour facing a pillar on the Quarterdeck, where I could be observed by every passing officer, schoolmaster or cadet; then an hour of bunny-hops holding a .303 rifle above the head. This literally punishing regime was repeated on two consecutive days. My offence had hardly been criminal: I had imitated the laugh of one of the masters in his hearing. Mr Bullock took us for Naval History. He had a strange sense of humour and an even stranger laugh. He would make jokes which none of us understood, then guffaw long and loud, shoulders heaving, with alarming intakes of breath. I quite liked the man and my imitation was spontaneous – almost unconscious. In one horrible second his face changed from amiable enjoyment to cyclonic wrath. 'Get out!' he spat. 'Out!' As he passed me at the end of the period, he looked icily at me and said, 'I am awarding you a 2B Drill.'

The teaching staff at Dartmouth was a mixture of naval officers and some civilian schoolmasters, many of them pensioners who had volunteered to come back out of retirement for the war. One or two had taught my father, among them P T Harrison, our maths teacher, who was rumoured to have been an English rugby international in the 1890s. PTH was tall and snowy-haired, with aquiline features and a severe expression, but all the time his blue eyes twinkled. His hands were shaky but

I have never met anyone quicker at mental arithmetic. He demanded complete silence and absolute attention. Those who did not comply were treated to a ritual apparently unchanged in forty years. Seen for the first time, it was awe-inspiring. The whole class froze in fear. Seen for the third or fourth time – so long as you were not the object of his attention – it was sheer entertainment. He would fix the offending cadet with a penetrating stare, raise his right arm horizontally and point his forefinger at the miscreant. 'Stand out, boy, stand out!' he would say in a quavering voice, dramatically exaggerated. There would follow fifteen to thirty seconds of complete silence and stillness, with every eye fixed on PTH. Then, in a crescendo rising from a deep bass to alto, he would repeat, very slowly, the familiar words, 'Remember, I have only to clap my hands, and a squad of Royal Marines will come and carry you away!' His voice would fade as if across a vast chasm. After a few more seconds of silence, the finger would be lowered, the boy told to sit down and the class would continue. PTH never needed to mete out punishments.

He once called me a sentimental donkey after he had reduced me to tears of frustration during one of his classes, then some hours later rewarded me with a penny because I had won my fight against a boy a year older than myself and a few pounds heavier in the finals of the college boxing championships. 'You did well, boy!' he said, 'do not spend it all at once.' It was intended as a joke, but in those days a penny could buy a small bar of chocolate, a bag of sherbet, a tube of liquorice or a few ounces of sweets from a glass jar at the college canteen.

We were very much aware of the war and read the newspapers avidly. We had to carry our gas masks and tin hats everywhere and there were frequent exercises and air raid drills. Even the thirteen-year-olds were given instruction in the use of rifles and bayonets and throwing hand grenades. At that age we still had a romantic idea of war and were excited at the thought of the Germans landing and our having to fight them off.

We saw a badly damaged destroyer, *Kelly*, commanded by Captain (later Admiral) Lord Mountbatten limping into Dartmouth harbour. Later Captain Philip Vian, my father's friend and my godfather, invited me on board *Cossack* soon after the famous rescue of British seamen from the German prison ship *Altmark*, anchored in a Norwegian fjord. Philip Vian was knighted after prodigious war service in the Atlantic, Mediterranean and Pacific and became an Admiral of the Fleet. I remember him as a man with a lethal sense of humour, huge bushy eyebrows and an aura of unremitting drive. I have read and re-read his fascinating memoir of those times: *Action This Day*.

When an air attack was made on the RN College Dartmouth in September 1942, we were fortuitously all on leave. We had, for some unknown reason, been given an extra week's holiday. The college was bombed on the very day we would normally have returned after seven weeks' absence. The six German aircraft came in low from the Channel, following the course of the River Dart where it joined the sea between wooded headlands. Two of them targeted the MTB base in the harbour, two attacked the Engineering Works and two scored direct hits on the college buildings.

We were all given yet more leave while the authorities searched for somewhere else to send us. Eventually the senior four terms of cadets were allowed back to the undamaged part of the college. The rest of us were sent for one term to Bristol. This was a strange decision. Not only was Bristol the target of numerous German air raids – because of the Bristol Aircraft Works and other factories – but there were no facilities in our proposed quarters for seamanship training.

I have always felt sorry for orphans but never more so than during that winter term in Muller's Orphanage. It was situated in an ugly part of the city, surrounded by high walls with broken glass along the top. The buildings were early Victorian, cold and grey with stone-flagged passages and nothing in the way of modern conveniences. The only redeeming factor was an extensive area of playing fields. As seventh-termers, we were among the oldest cadets there and some of us were made temporary cadet captains. This promotion and the privileges which went with it made life just about bearable. We were allowed to stay up an hour later and to do some elementary cooking in our cadet captains' 'cabin'.

I was, of course, by then interested in the idea of love and sex, but our opportunities to see girls were very limited. During the holidays, I carried out a rough survey and came to the conclusion that I found one in five of all girls and women between the age of puberty and forty attractive.

The headmaster at my prep school had believed in preparing boys for the outside world before they left. One by one, we were sent for, to be told the facts of life. He appeared acutely embarrassed. The personalised lecture went something like this:

> When you leave here, you will probably find that older boys want to talk about sex [cough] and having babies, [cough] and so on. [Cough, cough.] Tell them you know all about it and you don't want to listen. [Cough, cough.] When a man and a woman are married, they come together in a wonderful way and through love, [cough] a baby is conceived and born nine months later. [Cough, cough.] Now if anybody tries to tell you unnecessary details, [cough] just tell them you've been told about it already.

Fortunately for me my father, who was away at sea, had written to one of the married masters and asked him to speak to me on the subject. I was given a full, factual and unembarrassed explanation which filled me with wonder and astonishment.

The system employed for keeping cadets' minds off sex was constant movement, close supervision and practically no spare time. However, we had weekly film shows and after the college had been evacuated from Bristol to Chester, there were WRNS stewardesses serving in the dining room. The effect they had, particularly during the summer months, was disturbing. They wore white cotton blouses with black skirts and black stockings, sometimes nylons. Stringent precautions were taken to prevent any contact and there were serious consequences for any cadet found consorting with a Wren.

On summer holiday I saw a girl playing in a tennis foursome with her mother and two other older women. My mother, eager to encourage any romance, told me who she was – and that she was nearly a year older than me – a devastating blow in my adolescent mind. When the foursome finished, the group came to sit near us and my mother introduced me. The girl's name was Jeanne and close up she was devastating. Tiny beads of perspiration shone on her forehead. I asked her if she would like me to get her a glass of orange squash from the club house and, with a melting smile, she accepted. I was grateful that the other three refused. My pocket money was embarrassingly limited.

This was the start of a year-long relationship, holidays only – passionate on my side, gently restrained and tolerant on hers – and totally innocent. I got a morning job in a local timber yard, cutting the bark off newly felled trees with an adze, so that I had money to take her out – more tennis, the cinema, Saturday evening dances at the local hotel.

At the end of my summer leave, back at Dartmouth, I wrote her ardent letters but when I got home again at Christmas she told me she was going to join the Women's Auxiliary Air Force. She was already nearly eighteen. A few months later, I was shattered to learn that she had become engaged to someone else.

In March 1944, just before I joined my first ship as a midshipman, I called to see her, wearing my uniform. She had had a baby, but the marriage had already broken up. She was sad, distant and clearly not happy. Nor was I, but I was only seventeen and about to win the war. I never saw her again.

One evening, my House Officer came into the dormitory for his customary chat before lights out, accompanied by Mr Fawkes, the college chaplain, and a young man in the uniform of an RNVR lieutenant with Fleet Air Arm pilot's wings on his right sleeve above his wavy gold stripes. As Cadet Captain, I went with them as they moved around the dormitory, pausing to talk to different boys. Naval fliers were the glamour boys of the Service and this one was very much the centre of attention. It was soon established that he flew Seafires, a naval version of the famous Spitfire which had played such a prominent part in the Battle of Britain. Wide-eyed, the lads asked him all sorts of questions about the aircraft: its landing speed, what the deck of an aircraft carrier looked like from above and whether he had shot down any German aircraft. The answers were modest and unassuming. I saw the Reverend Fawkes, a popular figure with a permanent smile and a skein of fair hair falling across his left eye, looking slightly startled at one or two of the replies, but thought nothing of it at the time. When the round of the dormitory was over I turned off the lights and went along the passage to the cabin I shared with three other cadet captains, to cook cheese on toast.

A couple of evenings later, my House Officer, Lieutenant Commander Robertson, came round the dormitory again, this time unaccompanied. He was asked if the Fleet Air Arm pilot had gone back to his ship. We were told the surprising news that the young man had been an impostor – a deserter. He was a Naval Aircraftman, but he had never flown an aircraft in his life. He had bought an officer's uniform and travelled from one Naval establishment to another, all over the south of England, repeating the story that his aircraft had developed engine trouble and was grounded at the nearest airfield. He had got away with this for weeks and had been wined and dined in wardrooms all over the country. It was the Reverend Fawkes who had eventually bowled him out. As a qualified pilot, he noticed that the self-styled Seafire pilot had given the wrong landing speed for that particular aircraft. A simple phone call had established that there was no Seafire with engine trouble at a nearby RAF station. He had been taken under escort to Plymouth Naval Detention Quarters.

Sunday Divisions was the great occasion of the week – or it had been at Dartmouth. We were inspected before marching up the ramp from the parade ground to the music of a brass band and dispersing for church. At Dartmouth it had been a Royal Marine band. At Eaton Hall, near Chester, the home of the Duke of Westminster, where we were sent after our year at Muller's Orphanage, the band consisted of gallant pensioners, and we paraded on a square of hardcore. In my years as a cadet, I was inspected at Sunday Divisions by King George VI, Winston Churchill, General de Gaulle, General Sikorsky, Field-Marshal Montgomery, Admiral Sir Bruce Fraser and Admiral Lord Mountbatten, among others.

At the beginning of my final year I took a decision that was to have far-reaching, though unforeseen, consequences. Cadets in the top French class were allowed to take another language – either German or Russian. One day, without warning, a list was circulated round the class and we were invited to put a tick against the language of our choice. I was sitting next to a friend and asked him what he was going to do. 'Let's try Russian,' he suggested.

Impressed by stories of the courage of the Arctic convoys to Murmansk and the Soviet army at Stalingrad, I agreed.

My status during my final year was much enhanced by my elder sister, Penelope, known as Pen. She was doing a season with the Robert Atkins Shakespearean Company before becoming a nurse. The company appeared in Chester, with Pen in the role of Rosalind in *As You Like It*. By chance it was the play we were studying in English class at the time. I suggested to Mr Eustace, our English teacher, that the whole class should go to see the Company's performance. To my surprise and delight, he agreed. Mr Eustace was an excellent teacher of those who paid close attention to him and his methods. Those who did not suffered an alarming but relatively harmless form of torture. The offender was made to stand in front of the class and read from a book of poetry held between both hands. Mr Eustace would stand two or three yards in front of the victim holding a billiard cue by the thin end. In time with the rhythm of the poem he would swing the cue upwards. With unerring accuracy the thick end hit the spine of the book:

> In Xanadu did Kubla Khan [thump!]
> A stately pleasure dome decree [thump!]
> Where Alph the sacred river ran [thump]…

Few boys allowed their attention to lapse once they had experienced a billiard cue poetry recital.

Pen was a sensation as Rosalind and for weeks I basked in the glory of her appearance. Even my House Officer was so impressed that when, some months later, Pen had a series of roles in radio plays performed by the BBC repertory company, he invited me along to hear them on his radio.

At last, in March 1944, we sat our final examinations. I passed out fifth of the thirty cadets in my term, with prizes in English and History. We were allowed to state the type of ship and the station where we wished to serve – and the names of any friends we would like to have as shipmates. I asked to be appointed to a cruiser on the West Indies Station along with Mike Higgs and two other friends. In the event, Mike Higgs and I received appointments to the battleship *Anson* and were ordered to join her at Scapa Flow in the Orkney Islands.

Bulbs and Bullets

I spent the summer of 1943, my last before I joined *Anson*, with my family on the island of Arran. My father had just come back from a voyage convoying ships round the world in command of an armed merchant cruiser, *Ascania*. She was a Cunarder of about 14,000 tons. Her conversion had consisted of a coat of grey paint, with a couple of six-inch guns and a few anti-aircraft weapons mounted on her upper deck. Such ships stood little chance against submarine or air attack and even less if confronted by a heavily armed German pocket battleship or cruiser protected by thick armour plate. Cunard liners were very well built, but their thin hulls were not designed to withstand any form of explosive attack. My father was fortunate to have returned sunburned but unscathed. While *Ascania* was acting as part of the protective force escorting one convoy through the Caribbean, seven ships had gone down in the night, sunk by U-boats. My father was now commanding the old cruiser, *Cardiff*, training RNVR officers in the Clyde and off the Irish coast. At weekends the ship anchored in Lamlash Bay, off Holy Island.

The family took the White House, a dilapidated lodge at the end of a beech avenue set back from the village and seashore by a rough paddock. That holiday was one of the happiest of my life. Arran had an abundance of game and a climate in which soft fruit could grow. It seemed to be largely insulated from wartime rationing. I was taken shooting for the first time by an officer from my father's ship, coming home with a rabbit and a snipe, and the ship's doctor introduced me to rock climbing. It was a time when I got on particularly well with both my sisters. Pen was only two years older than me, but until that summer she had always seemed much more grown-up and mature. Now I was able to talk to her almost as an equal and we spent a lot of time together, going for long walks and talking about life.

Although the climate on Arran was mild, it was also wet. I

took piping lessons from Mr Middleton, a fine piper and exponent of pibroch, the classical music of the bagpipe, despite having hands gnarled by the heavy work of laying bricks and mixing cement.

I returned from his home in the village one evening to find our own household in turmoil. Pen had not come back from a walk and was now more than an hour overdue. I had an idea where she might have gone and set off to look for her. I walked over the hill, down the other side, on to the String Road and back, but saw no sign of her. When I got back, although worried to find she still had not returned, I was also soaked to the skin and chilled to the bone. I wondered whether I would be considered callous for taking a hot bath if some terrible accident had befallen her. While I was debating the point, Pen turned up, as wet and cold as I was. She had got lost in a wood on the way down. My relief was tempered by the fact that she was given priority in the bathroom and by the time my turn came there was no hot water left.

Some months later Pen became a VAD (Voluntary Aid Detachment – a nurse) and joined the Royal Naval Hospital at Haslar in Portsmouth. She volunteered for the unglamorous TB ward, while other girls of her age were nursing the wounded returning from the D-Day landings. After the war she returned for a short time to repertory theatre before marrying and living in South Africa where her husband's company had sent him. Within weeks of their marriage he fell ill with leukaemia. She nursed him until his death and then stayed on in South Africa, unable to leave the place where they had been so happy for such a brief time. A year or two later she came back to Britain and married John Owen, a tea merchant. They had two children, a boy then a girl, but Pen died of cancer when her daughter was only two years old. Everyone remembers her as a wonderful person. She was beautiful, warm-hearted, generous, intelligent and full of fun. Her early death makes it difficult for me to believe that life is anything but a lottery.

My younger sister Julia and I always got on well. Perhaps that is because I am three years older and very determined, whereas she is diplomatic and good-natured. I sometimes led her into trouble. One day in the summer of 1937 we had decided to cook for ourselves at the bottom of the garden. We took some potatoes from a sack and found some onions in a box in the garden shed. We built a fire out of sight of the house and boiled the onions and potatoes together in an old saucepan, then sat down on a log to eat the mixture with spoons borrowed from the kitchen. It tasted horrible. Julia only had a couple of mouthfuls but I would not admit that there was anything wrong with our cooking and ate most of the contents of the blackened pan. Half an hour later Julia was spectacularly sick. A great fuss was made – although she had the talent of being able to vomit at will which she used effectively from time to time as a bargaining tool. An hour later I began to feel appallingly ill and I, too, was violently sick. This caused a bit of a sensation because I had only been sick about three times in my life, the most recent occasion being at Christmas dinner – but in that instance I had overeaten. I was closely questioned and admitted to cooking vegetables in the garden, but nobody asked exactly what the ingredients were.

Some weeks later my father read in the paper that two children had died after eating daffodil bulbs. He asked me again about our meal that day. I should have known that onions are not usually kept in a box on the floor of the garden shed...

In the summer of 1940 the Battle of Britain had dominated the blue skies above the sunlit countryside between the English Channel and London. From my aunt's house in Sussex, we had a ringside seat. A number of incendiary bombs had been dropped on the roof and several smallish bombs, probably 500-pounders, had fallen in fields not far away. We saw many aircraft shot down – Heinkels, Dorniers and Messerschmitts, as well as our own Hurricanes and Spitfires. One Heinkel crashed a few miles from the house. I saw it go past very low with smoke billowing from the tail. We could even distinguish the pilot's head, a black knob in the middle of the Perspex cockpit cover. Before anybody could stop me, I grabbed my airgun and bicycle and sped off in the direction of the stricken plane. I had visions of myself proudly marching the pilot to the nearest police station with my airgun stuck in the small of his back. I heard the thud as the plane hit the ground, but by the time I got there, the Home Guard had cordoned off the area and the pilot was dead.

Julia played the leading role in one domestic drama that summer. There had been a dogfight in the skies above the wooded countryside, between ME-109s, escorting the German bombers, and Hurricanes and Spitfires of the RAF. We had been made to come in out of the sunshine and take shelter in a dark passage in the centre of the house. Eventually the all clear sounded and we were summoned to the living room for tea. I was the first to notice a small, neat, circular hole high up in a window pane, obviously made by a spent bullet emanating from thousands of feet overhead. All of us, my sisters, three cousins, their old nanny, some evacuees, my aunt, my mother and I – got down on our hands and knees to search for it. No lost diamond or gold coin was ever sought more thoroughly, but no bullet was found and the incident remained a mystery.

Many years later, in a moment of great candour, Julia made a confession to me. Earlier that afternoon, she had been playing with the long wooden-handled window opener – the sort with a brass hook for pulling down the upper casement. Her small hands had not been able to control it and she had punched a neat hole in the glass. Terrified of her aunt, who considered her to be a bit spoilt, Julia was dreading the moment of discovery. The idea of the spent bullet came as a godsend. None of us searched the floor more assiduously than Julia, who still blushes at her deception.

One day, a week before I was due to leave Arran and return to the RN College, I put on an old suit of brown check plus fours belonging to my father, a leather waistcoat and hobnailed boots, and set off by bicycle for the stalker's house overlooking the bay, half a mile from Brodick Castle. I had been given the opportunity of a day or two of deerstalking. I had been warned that Alec Fraser, the Duchess of Montrose's Head Stalker, did not suffer fools gladly and expected guests to do what they were told. Above all, he disapproved of unnecessary talk.

I found the hobnailed boots were not ideal for riding a bike, but arrived safely and knocked on the door. Alec Fraser – it couldn't be anyone else – filled the doorway. He was about six feet tall, very broad, with massive legs encased in hand-knit stockings. I was relieved to see that he too wore a plus-four suit. He looked at me critically.

'You'll be Mr Davidson,' he growled in a voice from the northern Highlands.

'Yes – James Davidson.'

'Where is your hat?'

'I haven't got a hat.'

He regarded me sceptically. 'I doubt your head will get very wet.'

I said nothing. There was nothing to say. He turned and disappeared into the house, reappearing a minute later with a spyglass in a leather case and a canvas cover in the shape of a rifle. He was now wearing a deerstalker's hat with the flaps tied on the crown of his head.

'Follow me,' he said. He crossed the road and opened the gate into a field below the house. We walked in silence to the bottom of the field, which merged into a piece of rough ground covered in clumps of heather and stone outcrops. There, the imposing figure stopped and methodically pulled the rifle from its case. It was a heavy calibre Mannlicher.

'Lie down,' he ordered and as I did so he loaded the rifle with a silver-coloured bullet projecting from a brass cartridge.

'Fire at yon white stone,' he said, handing me the gun and pointing at a small but distinctive outcrop at least 200 yards away. Carefully, I cupped the foresight in the notch of the backsight, took aim and squeezed the trigger as I had been taught by the Chief Petty Officer on the firing range at Dartmouth. The bullet hit the rock with a satisfying smack. Alec Fraser grunted. Apparently I had passed the test.

We drove north along the coast road in an old van. I sat in the front and the young under-stalker, Robert Davidson (no relation), in the back. We got out at the bottom of Glen Sannox and climbed two or three hundred feet up the hillside to a knoll. I was not allowed to carry anything except the small rucksack with my sandwiches and a Thermos flask. As we approached our target, I was deprived even of that, so I would be ready to fire without encumbrance. For more than an hour we moved steadily upwards, making a great detour across the mountainside. We picked our way over heather slopes, peat hags, watercourses and scree. I was given only one word of advice: 'Silence.'

As we turned east towards the sea, Alec Fraser dropped on to all fours. He took the rifle from the under-stalker and slipped it out of its case. Holding it well clear of the ground to keep it dry, he wormed his way forward. We crawled fully fifty yards. At the time I did not notice that my plus fours were soaked. Inch by inch we approached the top of the ridge. Miraculously, before us, about 150 yards away, was a stag with half a dozen hinds, grazing unconcernedly. Fraser handed me the rifle, pointed to the stag, lifted the safety catch and nodded. He had told me as we drove along to aim for the neck. I was intensely excited, but knew what to do. I aimed carefully and squeezed the trigger. The tremendous kick against my shoulder coincided with an ear-splitting report. Within seconds, all the deer, including the stag, were bounding away across the heather and scree and over a ridge. I was bitterly disappointed at having missed. I turned to Alec Fraser forlornly: 'I'm very sorry.'

'You hit him in the neck,' he replied. 'He'll be lying dead.'

Sure enough, we found him 200 yards further on, stone dead. The keeper gralloched the beast with his sheath knife and Robert Davidson tied a rope round its antlers, ready to drag the carcass down to the roadside. We moved to a nearby knoll to eat our sandwiches and drink hot soup from the flasks. To my embarrassment, I found I was expected to sit separately from the two stalkers – a form of social distinction which I ignored on subsequent occasions.

It took nearly two hours to drag the carcass down. I was only permitted to help haul on the rope over particularly difficult ground and even then my help was accepted reluctantly. While Robert Davidson walked the mile or two to fetch the van, I sat and waited with Alec Fraser. He lit a pipe and for a long time nothing was said. So far, I had done all that was expected of me and I felt that an attempt at conversation might be permitted.

While I was wondering what to say, he spoke. 'So you're in the Royal Navy then?'

I explained that I was still under training but would be going to sea in the following spring. Then I took the plunge. 'Were you in the Cameron Highlanders in the last war?' I had guessed he came from Inverness-shire.

'I followed my Chief,' he replied, a touch indignantly.

'Ah,' I said, 'the Lovat Scouts!' I was on target and from that moment, although conversation was sparse, I was put on his approved list. The Lovat Scouts was a unit of sharpshooters and snipers raised by Lord Lovat, hereditary chief of the Clan Fraser.

I had two or three more days' stalking and at that time I felt that I could happily have spent my life as a stalker. It was with considerable reluctance that I left to return to Eaton Hall, Chester.

Scapa Flow to Alexandria

Mike Higgs and I left from Scrabster for Scapa Flow in an MFV – a Motor Fishing Vessel converted as a Naval tender. Everyone was seasick except the crew, who were fishermen of the Naval Reserve. The sight of the Home Fleet at anchor in Scapa Flow was enormously impressive: three aircraft carriers; three modern battleships of the King George V class, one of which was *Anson*; the battleships *Nelson* and *Rodney*, which I had last seen from the beach at Nairn; some even older battleships of the *Royal Sovereign* class; a dozen cruisers and more than fifty destroyers and smaller vessels.

The two principal roles of the Home Fleet at Scapa Flow were to prevent German warships emerging from the Baltic Sea into the Atlantic and to provide long-range cover for the convoys taking munitions and supplies round the north coast of Norway and through the Arctic to the only Russian port with direct access to the Atlantic – Murmansk. Early in 1944 the Russians were still hard-pressed by the Germans although the tide had begun to turn. As a midshipman in a great battleship I had very little idea of what the ship was supposed to be doing.

It was a strange sensation to have a vast warship as a floating home. It was several weeks before I settled down and felt myself to be part of the huge ship's company. As midshipmen we lived by routine, kept watches, ran the picket boats and closed up at our action stations when the alarm sounded and the order came over the loudspeakers.

My action station was in the Transmitting Station, down in the bowels of the ship. It was a technological nightmare – dials, pipes, telephones and handles. The centrepiece was a rudimentary computer into which all the data was fed to enable the ship's fourteen-inch guns to be pointed in the right direction, whether at another ship or at a shore target. My job was to listen on a headset and to feed certain information into the computer by winding two handles.

The job I enjoyed most was being in charge of a big picket boat. There were various types and we had to handle them all, but the most fun were the big two-engined powerboats. They had a cabin fore and aft with the engine room amidships, just forward of the bridge. These boats carried a crew of four – two able seamen, an engine room artificer and a petty officer or leading seaman. They could take about fifty passengers. A midshipman was in charge and took the controls – the steering wheel on the bridge and two big throttles, one for each engine, forward or reverse, which made the boats extremely manoeuvrable. Probably the most demanding situation was when the Captain had to be taken alongside another ship in rough weather – a not infrequent situation in Scapa Flow.

Once, I had to take my Captain ashore at Lyness. The weather was calm. Neatly I brought the boat alongside – about a yard out from the jetty. The Captain stood, waiting to step ashore. In theory, I knew exactly what to do but on this occasion it just did not seem to work. A touch ahead with the port engine, a bit of port wheel and then a touch astern with the starboard engine to bring the stern into the jetty. I went back and forth several times, but could not get any closer. The Captain gave me a dirty look, attempted to jump the gap, lost his footing on the slippery wooden steps and barked his shin. I was lucky not to get into trouble and it took me a long time to live it down.

One night during the middle watch the alarms sounded. Then came the order: 'Away first and second picket boats. Midshipmen of the picket boats report to the Officer of the Watch!' Tersely I was told that there was an emergency. It was thought that enemy midget submarines had penetrated the defences and entered the anchorage with the objective of immobilising the battleships and aircraft carriers lying at anchor. I was ordered to bring the boat round to the gangway amidships and to embark an officer and a rating of the Torpedo Branch with some small depth charges.

For the next two hours, along with other boats, we patrolled back and forth, parallel to the ship's starboard side at a distance of two cables' lengths, dropping the charges at intervals of two to three minutes. We went at full throttle so that the boat was well clear by the time each charge exploded. In the middle of the Flow the destroyers were dropping full-scale depth charges. Every now and then, when the half-moon appeared between scudding clouds, we caught sight of a phosphorescent plume of water, forty feet high. By three o'clock in the morning, despite the flasks of hot cocoa thoughtfully provided by the Officer of the Watch, we were getting very cold. By five we were all frozen, bored and very tired, but just as we were recalled to *Anson*, we heard a deep thud. A 'W' class destroyer, about half a mile away from us, had reduced speed and was about to come to anchor. We saw the anchor splash into the water and heard the cable rattling out through the hawsepipe, then a great spout of water rose from beneath her stern. As it subsided we could see that her quarterdeck was angled down and her stern guardrails had disappeared beneath the surface.

On the destroyer's bridge, the captain had given the normal order for anchoring: 'Let go!' On the fo'c's'le the pin holding the cable slip had been knocked off and the anchor had splashed into the sea, but on the quarterdeck an inexperienced torpedo man had taken the order to mean, 'Let go a depth charge.' Several men lost their lives.

Life had its brighter moments. We visited friends in other ships. Occasionally there were games of rugby or hockey on the playing fields near Kirkwall, or dances at the WRNS base there. There was a canteen on Flotta with an unlimited supply of hard-boiled eggs and weak beer. On a long walk round the little island I saw a man ploughing a field with a single ox. It must have been one of the last ox-drawn ploughs in Britain. There were also large flocks of sheep. I wondered why, when one cruiser put to sea, sailors in the other ships lined the guardrails and bleated. It was explained that a sailor in the cruiser had been court-martialled for bestiality. According to legend his defence was that he thought a sheep was a Wren wearing a fur coat.

D-Day was a time of intense disappointment for those of us serving in the more modern battleships of the Home Fleet. The older ships all moved south to provide cover for the landings in Normandy. They acted as mobile and very accurate gun platforms, bombarding the German defences. The more modern ships, including *Anson*, patrolled the seas west of the Danish and

Norwegian coasts to prevent any remaining German warships from leaving the Baltic or the Norwegian fjords. We missed all the excitement and no warships came out to do battle with us.

Before *Anson* was sent to Liverpool for a long refit, we spent a day or two at Invergordon on the Cromarty Firth and I was given permission to go by train to Nairn to see my grandmother. The old lady was delighted to be visited by a grandson in naval uniform. She was sweet and round with snow-white hair, perfectly brushed. I spent Saturday night in the spotless guest room overlooking the Firth. Next morning, after a sumptuous breakfast, I was taken to church and shown off to her friends. We then had a lunch of roast chicken. I was in heaven when Granny suggested that we should go for a little drive. I asked if she had any petrol coupons. She had never heard of petrol coupons. 'When did you last have the car out?' She thought my Uncle Douglas, her youngest son, had driven it the previous summer, more than a year ago. I was not convinced we would be going for a drive, but a walk to the garage found a car in immaculate condition, with a half-full tank and a live battery. It was a black Austin 8. My grandmother had not asked me whether I could drive. She just assumed I could.

We set off at a dignified speed and drove through the beautiful autumn countryside south of Nairn, planning to return in time for tea. In the centre of the town, we were waved down by a large, elderly policeman. 'Do you know, sir, that your vehicle is not licensed?' My heart sank. I told him the car belonged to my grandmother. Recognising my grandmother through the passenger window, the policeman asked humorously, 'Is this your chauffeur?' He knew full well that my uniform was naval. My grandmother explained with dignity that I was on leave from a battleship. Despite this, the policeman felt bound to report the offence and insisted on driving the last few hundred yards to my grandmother's home. The incident cast a shadow over the rest of my stay, but when the legal summons came to me in *Anson* I wrote a polite letter of explanation and received a charming reply from the Fiscal telling me he had dismissed the case in view of my age and the fact that I was on active service.

One day on leave with my family, still in Sussex, I heard the ominous, unmistakable pulsating engine of a doodlebug, much louder than usual. It appeared above the trees, looking enormous, menacing and so near that I could see every detail if its fuselage and tailplane with torpedo-shaped protuberances on the ends. The engine cut out when it was very close above. I guessed it would fall beyond the house. As it disappeared from view, I threw myself flat. Seconds later, a huge explosion shook the ground. I got to my feet and tore up the road in the direction of a black cloud of smoke. It had landed less than half a mile away on Crowborough Golf Course and, by an appalling stroke of chance, it devastated a Canadian army camp – soldiers waiting to be embarked for France. I was turned back by the troops, who had formed a cordon round the scene.

I was in a sombre mood when I joined the cruiser *Newfoundland* on the Clyde as senior midshipman. It would be several weeks before she was ready to start working up for service with the British Pacific Fleet. Because I was the only snotty (the Royal Navy term for midshipman) on board, I lived in the wardroom with the officers, though unlike them I did not have a cabin. At night I slept between decks in a hammock. When the refit was completed, *Newfoundland* moved out of the dock and anchored off the Tail of the Bank, the broad reach of the Clyde opposite Greenock. I was now living in the gunroom with the other midshipmen and sub-lieutenants. Our routine was one of torpedo and gunnery exercises and speed trials by day. Soon night exercises were included. From time to time we were given shore leave. One week I managed to see three Gilbert and Sullivan operas performed by the D'Oyly Carte in Glasgow. It was then that my love of opera began to develop, although I had heard my Uncle Malcolm singing and we had old 78 rpm records of opera at home.

One night I found myself in a difficult situation due to an ill-judged decision by the Executive Officer, the Commander. The wardroom officers had a party on board, anchored out in the Clyde. While the party was in full swing, a gale warning was issued. The Commander should have sent all guests ashore immediately, but he allowed the party to continue for an hour or more. I was midshipman of the picket boat and by the time it was called away there was a heavy sea running, spray was being driven horizontally from the white crests of six-foot waves and it was getting dark. I pointed out to the Officer of the Watch that according to the orders issued by the Naval Officer in charge of the port, all boats should have been hoisted inboard. The Officer of the Watch was embarrassed but told me that he was acting on the Commander's orders.

The gangway of a warship at anchor consists of a platform at deck level with wooden steps down to another platform at water level. When I took the boat alongside, the sea was rising and falling by eight to ten feet. The difficult and even dangerous task was to embark a dozen or more guests, mostly Wren officers in various stages of inebriation, laughing and joking and occasionally squawking in alarm. My Leading Seaman thoroughly enjoyed himself. While I kept the boat alongside to the best of my ability, using the engines and aided by the seamen in the bow and stern hanging on one-armed with their boathooks, he grabbed each girl in turn as she negotiated the fluctuating gap between the gangway and the boat's side. The more experienced guests managed to step across when the boat's gunwhale was level with the platform. It was only by a combination of luck and skill that nobody was injured or fell into the surging water.

With relief I gave the order to let go and turned the boat towards the lights of the Greenock jetty, more than a mile away. Luckily my passengers were too drunk to be frightened. Every pitch and lurch of the boat was greeted by squeals and giggles. We shipped some water over the stern but not enough to be serious and eventually I brought the boat alongside in the lee of the Greenock jetty and the Leading Seaman handed the Wren officers ashore, one by one. Not one of them thanked me or answered my salute.

By this time it was dark enough to see the greenish-white phosphorescent tops of the waves. The spray was driving over the end of the jetty. I seriously doubted if we could make it back and if we did, whether the boat could be hoisted. I sent a Morse code signal to the ship asking permission to stay ashore until the storm abated. This was granted and I found accommodation for my crew and myself in the local YMCA.

Once back aboard ship, the following day, I learned that there had been a major row. The Captain, who had not been present at the party, had been unaware that it had continued after the gale warning. The Executive Officer was in the doghouse, but I was congratulated by the ship's Navigating Officer on my handling of the boat and my decision to remain inshore overnight.

At the beginning of December we sailed south through the Irish Sea, past Land's End and across the Bay of Biscay. The plan was to finish our working up in the kinder waters of the Mediterranean. We entered Gibraltar harbour on 23 December 1944 and the Captain informed the ship's company over the tannoy that we would be spending Christmas there. We were delighted. The air was balmy, the shops full of fruit (fresh and crystallised) chocolates and sweets, leather goods and many luxuries I had not seen for four years. Oranges were a particular treat. I ate far more of them than was good for me. After an enormous Christmas dinner, four of us walked up to the top of the Rock, or as far as we could get – the summit bristled with radar aerials. We sweated off some of the excessive eating and drinking of the past two days and made the acquaintance of the famous apes.

On Boxing Day we sailed east into the second-worst storm I have ever experienced. We had to steam at full speed because we were unescorted, and U-boats were still active in the Mediterranean. Watertight hatches on the fo'c's'le, each battened down with six heavy brass butterfly nuts, were ripped open by the seas and the screw threads sheared. Both metal ladders from the fo'c's'le to the gun deck, welded to the superstructure, were torn off. The weight of water crashing on to the anti-aircraft gun deck distorted it to an extent that was hardly visible to the human eye, but was sufficient to require a major realignment between the anti-aircraft guns and the control tower.

Between decks, all was chaotic. Anything that could, broke loose. Plates crashed, and hammocks fell from their stowage. The odd fire-fighting appliance broke free from its fixture. At least half the ship's company were seasick. At night we tried to sleep in spaces insulated from the outside elements, with lights dimmed or doused.

We were at 'cruising stations' – halfway between 'action

stations' and ordinary watch-keeping. This meant that one third of the ship's company was ready for instant action while the other two thirds were sleeping or performing the ordinary domestic tasks, as necessary in a ship as they are in a house, hotel or barracks.

My cruising station was as Surface Plot officer – a responsible job for a seventeen-year-old. I had to plot the movements of both friendly and enemy ships by radar bearing and distance from our own ship. The surface plot was immediately below the bridge. I wore a telephone headset by which information was passed up from the Operations Room to be reproduced on the bridge plot so that the Captain or Officer of the Watch could see what was going on within a range of twenty or thirty miles. Wearing a headset, drawing on a table in the superstructure of a ship rolling through an arc of 60 °, exacerbated seasickness. The bitter acid taste of regurgitated orange stayed with me for many days and it was three or four years before I could face a fresh one again.

After four days of appalling weather, we ran into calmer seas and finally entered the harbour at Alexandria where we were to be based while the ship was 'worked up' for the Pacific and the storm damage repaired.

Mediterranean

Mike Higgs and I almost got into serious trouble the first time we went ashore in Alexandria. Between the harbour and the smart cosmopolitan centre of the city lay a two-mile network of mean streets and slums. The sights, sounds and smells were astonishing to two very young men straight out of wartime Britain. We had been warned to be on the alert, never to walk alone and also to avoid certain notorious streets. We decided we could afford a taxi one way but not both. Being unfamiliar with the city, we decided to drive in and walk back. We had an excellent meal in a restaurant called L'Auberge – prawns in cheese sauce featured – and we managed a half-bottle of wine.

After an hour or so spent wandering round the shops, staring in amazement at the widest range of goods either of us had ever seen, we decided to head back on foot. Within minutes we had a small retinue of Egyptians round us, trying to sell us everything from cheap watches and dirty postcards to a shoeshine or a virgin. There was one particularly persistent youngster of about our own age who wanted to polish our shoes. Eventually he spat a huge blob of spittle, scarlet with betel juice, on to the instep of my right shoe. He expected me to pay him for cleaning it off. Instead I made a kick at his backside, partly in anger, but mainly to remove the offending spit. He retreated a few yards then whistled. Two other youths joined him and one suddenly produced a knife from his kaftan.

Mike and I had bought primitive coshes in the town – lumps of lead encased in plaited leather with a thong to go round the wrist. The situation was not amusing. We had nearly a mile to go through streets pocked with concealed entrances and dark side alleys. Mike said, 'Let's just keep moving. I'll navigate and you keep a watch over your shoulder.' Swinging the coshes at our sides, we set off. The three youths followed at a distance of about twenty yards. The mile seemed endless, but at last we sighted the jetty and the waiting picket boat, the white ensign fluttering reassuringly in the stern.

After that, we took taxis everywhere, though that had its perils too – drivers varied their charges at whim and on one occasion a child ran out in front of my taxi and was knocked down, though not badly hurt. It was in no way my driver's fault but we were immediately surrounded by a yelling, gesticulating crowd. There was only one way out of it – I told the driver to get going and promised him an extra 100 piastres if he got us to the ship safely. He did.

One sunny afternoon when I was duty midshipman of the picket boat, we were called away at the double. I reported to the Officer of the Watch, who pointed to a figure in a felucca disappearing among a group of dhows anchored about half a mile away. 'He's been on board, stealing – catch him and bring him back.'

Within minutes we set off at speed, but most of the feluccas we saw were tied astern of the dhows, or alongside them and none appeared to be manned.

Suddenly I saw one about fifty yards away, with two boys paddling furiously. I opened up the twin throttles and within seconds we were alongside. The bowman threw a grappling iron down into the bottom of the felucca while the two boys protested vociferously. We tied it alongside and I asked my coxswain to go down into the craft and search it. Never had I seen such a splendid show of injured innocence. There was much hand waving, protestation and even tears. The coxswain found nothing. 'Try under the bottom boards,' I suggested. Sure enough, there he found a dozen or more watches, knives, rings and other valuables including a silver cigarette case inscribed with the name of our ship's doctor.

These thieves worked in pairs. One boy would hold on to an open porthole while the second slipped through and grabbed what he could. I decided to tow the craft back to the ship, but while the coxswain was tying it astern, the boys dived overboard into the filthy water and swam off. I changed plans. We recovered all the valuables then cast the boat loose and returned to the ship. The ship's company were delighted to get their possessions back.

One of the highlights of our time in Alexandria was the visit of Mrs Barker's Girls. They were famous throughout the Middle East for their song and dance shows. How Mrs Barker managed to get together a troupe of such gorgeous-looking girls, nobody knew, but the mess decks hummed with anticipation for days before their appearance in HMS *Newfoundland*. A stage was erected in the ship's seaplane hangar. We were not disappointed. The girls' singing and dancing may have been of modest standard, but their beauty was breathtaking and their appearance certainly not modest. The makeshift stage was a shimmering kaleidoscope of shapely legs, swirling skirts, heaving bosoms and tossing curls. When the show ended the cheering, clapping, whistling and stamping erupted. Pity the poor lads who had been obliged to remain on watch!

Democracy was not practised in ships of the Royal Navy and when the show was over, the girls were taken to the wardroom to be entertained by officers of the rank of lieutenant and above. There was nothing the ordinary sailors could do about this, but the midshipmen and sub-lieutenants decided to take appropriate action. We waylaid two or three of the girls and invited them to the gunroom. We were, after all, very much nearer their age. In twos and threes most of the troupe found their way from the wardroom to the dancing, to gramophone records, and South African wine in the gunroom. I got on well with a small dark girl, Betty Moffat, who told me her father was Scottish and her mother Egyptian. Alas, a promising evening had a disappointing outcome. The Commander was furious and stopped all shore leave for midshipmen for a week. I tried to ring Betty but was only able to get her mother, who firmly said Betty could not come out with me. I had to give up.

Newfoundland had developed a particularly good rugby team for a ship of her size. The team included two or three players from first class clubs, a member of the Welsh national youth team, a professional league player from Yorkshire, a New Zealand midshipman and two of us who had been in the 1st XV at Dartmouth. A team was entered for the Alexandria Sporting Club Rugby Sevens. We were considered rank outsiders.

The whole South African army had stayed to garrison North

Africa when the war moved into Europe. Our first game, against the South African Army B team in January 1945, was unforgettable. Never before or since have I been subjected to such aggressive barracking. The touchlines were packed six or seven deep with South African soldiers, their khaki uniforms distinguished by orange tabs on the lapels. Their shouting was vicious. They did everything but actually run on to the field in support of their Seven. We caused a sensation, beating them by the narrowest of margins – one goal to one try: 5–3. When the final whistle blew we were roughly jostled and I thought we were going to be lynched. We survived until the semi-final when we were beaten in extra time by the Alexandria Sporting Club, a team with some top British club players and a Welsh International by the name of Hopkins. We were disappointed when they in turn were beaten in the final by the South African Army A team.

The Coastal Forces Base was situated just across the harbour and we got to know some of the junior officers from the torpedo boats and motor launches based there. Mike Higgs and I discovered that two RNVR sub-lieutenants were due to get leave but could not take it because there was nobody to relieve them. We volunteered to replace them temporarily for a trip up to the Aegean. To our intense pleasure, our services were accepted and in mid-February 1945, we left for Cyprus in two special service motor launches.

These MLs were fascinating miniature warships. Their armament consisted of a 40 mm Bofors, two 20 mm Oerlikens, four 20 mm cannon and four machine guns. They also carried anti-submarine equipment, depth charges and a generator for making smoke screens. They had a crew of two officers and twenty-one other ranks and were powered by two big petrol engines. ML842, of which I was now theoretically second in command, was a special service boat equipped to carry supplies to isolated groups of men in the Greek islands, to put agents ashore and for other clandestine duties. Half the islands in the Aegean were still occupied by the Germans.

In addition to the normal ship's company there were four passengers on board. Three were SAS officers wearing special uniform equipped with various gadgets. One of them showed me how his buttons unscrewed – inside were a compass and maps printed on to material so fine that when spread out, it covered half the wardroom table.

It took us less than twenty-four hours to reach Limassol in Cyprus. Although by day the sky was blue, the sea was choppy and we rolled continuously. I spent the whole time on the bridge to avoid seasickness. We stayed only a few hours at Limassol before setting off for Castellorizzo off the coast of Turkey. The island had been heavily bombed and deserted by its inhabitants. We went shooting partridges with .303 rifles and one of the army officers taught us to render landmines safe, a skill I have never had the opportunity to practise.

We bypassed Rhodes, which was occupied by Germans, and called in at Symi. Here, too, there was extensive bomb damage but the civilians were still there. Through worsening weather, we proceeded west and north, slipping at night through the two-mile-wide Kos Straits, with the German-occupied island on our port side and the coast of Turkey to starboard. We were at action stations, expecting to be engaged by the shore batteries, but discovered later that a landslide had destroyed the enemy gun platforms. Our destination was an inlet on the east coast of Chios, where we landed one unidentified passenger. It was now blowing a full gale and we were therefore held at Chios for nearly a week. It was too cold to contemplate much in the way of exploring.

I was transferred to the other motor launch and we sailed by night to Symi and on south, west of Rhodes. A few miles off the south-west corner of Rhodes, the ship we were escorting developed engine trouble. We had to tow her to Skarpanto, which was garrisoned by Indian troops. The officer in charge treated our unannounced visit with great suspicion. He came on board with a heavily armed escort and queried the white patches on the lapels of my midshipman's uniform. As the rest of the ship's company were dressed more or less like pirates, it took the captain half an hour to convince him that ML861 was indeed a vessel of the Royal Navy.

We were again stormbound off the coast of Skarpanto, eventually arriving back in Alexandria on 1 March. Mike and I carried an aura of mystery and adventure into the gunroom, which we exploited for many months.

Newfoundland weighed anchor on 25 March and we departed from the fleshpots of Alexandria. Leaving harbour, my station was on the fo'c's'le with the cable party. One memory of the city cannot be expunged: the stench of the blue-grey mud on the cable and anchor as the capstan heaved them inboard through the hawse pipe from the sea bottom. This was the accumulated residue of thousands of years of human occupation of the Nile delta. The passage of the centuries had not mellowed the vile concentration of smells. It was, with, one exception, the foulest odour which has ever assailed my nostrils. The very worst was the stink from the fish glue factory at Muscat. Closely in contention would be the knackery at Kintore in Aberdeenshire, but neither figured in my mind as we sailed through the night in gale force winds and arrived off Port Said early the following morning.

My stay in the Mediterranean had been eventful and in many ways enjoyable, but it does not stay in my mind as a place of idyllic weather and clear waters. While there, I received the tragic news that my cousin Duncan, the only son of my uncle Duncan, and just three years older than myself, had died of his wounds during the advance on Rangoon. I did not realise at that time the significance this would have for my own future.

Pacific

We passed uneventfully through the Suez Canal and the Red Sea and changed into tropical uniform. The temperature in the gunroom rose to nearly 100°F. I enjoyed my first glass of iced passion fruit juice during our brief stay in Ceylon. We were then told we were heading for Fremantle, stopping at the Cocos Islands to refuel some vessels there. Crossing the Line was observed with traditional ceremony and I was lathered, shaved and ducked with everyone else who had not crossed the Equator before. Neptune fulfilled his role well enough, but Aphrodite was unconvincing in a sack and two colanders.

When we left the Mediterranean, the news of the war in Europe was good and it seemed strange to be steaming in the opposite direction. However, the Japanese still occupied most of the islands in the North Pacific. Although they were in retreat in Burma and New Guinea, they still had huge undefeated land, naval and air forces at their disposal. Every hour on passage was filled with exercises of one sort or another: action stations, close range weapons, damage control and a dozen variations of night and day attacks – some offensive, some defensive.

The Cocos Islands were the first tropical archipelago I had seen. The main island appeared out of a squall of rain, and was a palm-covered atoll in the shape of a horseshoe. We attempted to anchor in the limpid lagoon within the horseshoe, in four or five fathoms of clear blue water, but when the anchor hit the bottom, it did not hold – the sea bed was too hard. We had to weigh again and as the anchor broke the surface, a lump of pink coral fell off the flukes back into the pellucid sea.

It took only eight hours to fuel and store the few small naval vessels based at the island and then we put to sea again. Our twenty-four-hour stay in Fremantle was just long enough to enjoy a huge steak with two eggs on top, in a dockside restaurant.

Our arrival in Sydney was both surprising and a cause for

some embarrassment. Instead of sunny beaches and sparkling surf, we found a place of torrential rain with visibility down to half a mile. We went alongside a jetty in Woolloomooloo Bay, passing several other warships on the way, among them HMAS *Australia*, severely damaged by five Japanese kamikaze suicide bombers. Any sailors we saw were sensibly dressed in khaki shirts and shorts with sandals. We were still in white tropical uniform and were paraded on the upper deck for entering harbour. Sailors' caps were blancoed for the occasion and, as the rain continued to fall in torrents, white rivulets streamed down their faces and necks. The popularity of the Commander, whose idea it had been to keep every available member of the ship's company on deck through the deluge, was not enhanced. We were all soaked to the skin, but fortunately most of the shore-based Australian naval ratings had taken shelter so our sailors escaped some of the ridicule their appearance would have attracted.

Once the sun began to shine we could appreciate the magnificence of Sydney harbour, but I noted in my logbook that there were thousands of houses with a perfect view of every ship passing through Sydney Heads. I wondered if there were any Japanese with radio sets concealed in the houses clustered round the bays.

We stayed in Sydney for about a fortnight, taking on board stores and ammunition and making final preparations to join the British Pacific Fleet. We were at four hours' notice for steam so although we were allowed ashore, one watch at a time, nobody was allowed more than twenty miles from the centre of the city. I had to turn down invitations from various relatives who lived up-country but I met some of my mother's friends and relatives who lived in the city. My godmother, Cecily Duncan, came all the way from Adelaide to see me. I found Sydney exciting but frustrating. I had no money. My mother's first cousin, Jim Dickson, whose family adopted me while I was there, asked one day if I wouldn't like to take a girl out to dinner or dancing. It had not occurred to him that midshipmen received no more than pocket money. He generously made good this deficiency and I was able to play tennis at the Royal Sydney Golf Club and take Joanna Forbes, the daughter of a friend of theirs, out to dinner at Romano's and Prince's.

We had a visit from Admiral Sir Bruce Fraser, Commander-in-Chief of the British Pacific Fleet, who stressed the importance of anti-aircraft efficiency in the operations we would be undertaking. Just before our departure two Americans joined the ship to act as liaison officers for operations with the US Navy.

In the first week of May we sailed out through the Sydney Heads into the Pacific. The Captain told us that we were bound for Manus in the Admiralty Islands and would be engaged in operations thereafter. We reached Manus on the very day Germany officially surrendered and the European war ended. The Captain ordered 'splice the main brace' and I drank more than I had ever drunk before – Australian champagne – and the evening became a blur. Fortunately, because of the heat we had been issued with camp beds and so did not have to sling hammocks. I woke the following morning to find my tropical uniform meticulously folded beside my sore head, evidence of my Dartmouth training.

Problems with the Commander came to a head while we were at Manus. The man had proven himself to be incompetent. He drank immoderately and had a fetish for old nautical terminology. For instance he would call a rope's end a 'Hanging Judas' and used obsolete names for many bits and pieces of ship's equipment. As a result he was frequently misunderstood. One day, he ordered Midshipman Benson to remove something from somewhere. Benson unwittingly removed the wrong thing from somewhere else. The Commander was furious and ordered him to the masthead – a punishment which had gone out of date not long after Trafalgar.

Midshipman Benson was no fool. He recognised this as an opportunity and he took it. The ship had been assigned duty as radar guard. When several ships were anchored close together, there was no purpose in each ship operating their radar independently, so one ship would be assigned the duty. The aerials of the long-distance warning radar sets rotated around the mastheads and if, for any reason, anyone had to go up the mast, it was a standing order that before he did so he had to draw the radar boards, thereby stopping the rotating aerials and immobilising the radar. This was a commonsense precaution to prevent anybody being knocked off the mast.

Midshipman Benson asked the Radar Petty Officer on duty to draw the boards. When challenged, he said that he was obeying the Commander's order. Very reluctantly the Petty Officer handed over the boards, but reported to the Navigating Officer what he had done. As the long distance warning radar stopped operating, the ships at anchor, all within range of Japanese aircraft, were left unprotected. Within minutes someone on the admiral's staff noticed and an angry signal was flashed across the water, while the Navigating Officer simultaneously informed the Captain. It was the only time I ever saw the Captain really angry. At first his fury was directed at the Officer of the Watch but then it arced with impressive voltage to the Commander. Within twenty-four hours, the Commander had been sent back to Australia, the Navigating Officer had been promoted to Acting Commander and a senior lieutenant took over as the ship's navigator.

Our first action in the Pacific was Operation Wewack, covering the landing of Australian troops on the north coast of New Guinea. We formed up in line ahead some miles out of range of the Japanese guns. There was no sign of enemy activity. Early in the afternoon, we closed to within about five miles of the enemy positions and began a bombardment. A Boomerang of the Royal Australian Air Force spotted for us and reported that *Newfoundland* had scored hits with eighty per cent of the rounds fired and all three targets were knocked out. For me, closed up at my action station in the operations room, we might as well have been carrying out an exercise in the Firth of Clyde.

Before nightfall, we withdrew but then returned at 7.15 a.m. The Australian troops were due to land at 8.30. We carried out a further bombardment and all targets were obliterated. Four waves of troops – each of about 1,000 men – were landed. They met some resistance at one end of the beach, but this was soon overcome. We withdrew, then closed for a further bombardment at 4 p.m. before leaving for Hollandia, which was in an area already occupied by American troops. We stayed there for about a week. The thought did occur to me, 'Is this what I have done all that training for?'

While cruising off Wewack I suffered what turned out to be

permanent damage to my right ear. I was in the cabin flat below B gun deck where we were allowed to set up our camp beds. I did not notice that one of the scuttles was not properly closed. It should have been screwed down tightly with butterfly clips. On the other side of the scuttle was a triple turret of 6" guns. Without warning, one of them fired – or it may have been all three. For a fraction of a second I thought I had been blown up then I picked myself up off the deck, badly shaken and with my head singing. Dazed, but following well-ingrained instructions, I frantically closed the scuttle and screwed up the butterfly clips, finishing just before another explosion. I then went to the heads and was violently sick. I looked at myself in the mirror but could see nothing obviously wrong, except that I was a bit pale. My head sang for days, or even weeks, but it was years before I discovered that I had sound-induced deafness in the middle range of my right ear. I never discovered exactly what happened. Secrecy was a fetish and midshipmen were given little information. I did not report the open scuttle for fear of getting someone into trouble. The ship had also been damaged – she had a cracked plate on the fo'c's'le. We had to go to Auckland for repairs.

Auckland was a quiet place compared with Sydney, but we were allowed a day trip to Rotorua, organised by the New Zealand government. A ferry transported us to the city side of the harbour, where a special train was waiting. The last forty miles of the 100-mile journey appealed to me – great stretches of grazing land for sheep and cattle, and hills reminiscent of Scotland. On arrival we were given a splendid lunch in the large Town Hall, then taken to see the Rainbow and Fairy springs where huge rainbow trout – eight-pounders or more – swam in astonishing numbers.

Later we were taken to the local Maori village where a guide, Rangi, took us in hand. She had rubbed noses with Eleanor Roosevelt and had taken King George VI and the Duke of Windsor on conducted tours, so we must have seemed small fry, but she did not show it. She had an irrepressible sense of humour and joked continuously as she showed us round, giving us an explanation of her tribe's ancestry and way of life. She showed us the famous boiling mud pools and the geysers which project spouts of boiling water and steam from the earth's bowels up to forty feet into the air. We saw a stream where a trout could be caught in one pool and cooked in another beside it, and the little steam holes in the mud, over which some families cooked their meals. As a finale, we watched a display of singing and dancing by a group of Maori girls. We were impressed both by their beautiful voices and their generously proportioned figures. Along with their own native songs, they gave a touching rendition of 'Annie Laurie'. I have never heard it sung better.

The repairs to the ship took exactly one week, then we headed north again to the Admiralty Islands, reaching Manus in time to join Operation Inmate, an attack on the Japanese stronghold of Truk in the Caroline Islands, 8° north of the Equator. It was the most important remaining enemy base in that part of the Pacific. The task force consisted of two aircraft carriers, four cruisers and five destroyers. The object was to carry out air strikes on the Japanese installations and to follow these up with a bombardment. The action began on 14 June, when six strikes of about a dozen planes each were flown off. They attacked Japanese positions on Uman and Moan Islands, destroying two enemy aircraft on the ground and damaging two others. Three of our aircraft – two Fireflies and one Avenger – were hit by flak but returned safely. Night raids hit the radio station, airstrip and anti-aircraft battery and damaged another aircraft on the ground. Our bombardment commenced early on the following morning. With an aircraft spotting for us we fired 250 shells at the airstrip and installations on Dubon. No Japanese aircraft took off. Either they had no fuel or the airstrip was too badly damaged. We lost two of our own aircraft and four crew before withdrawing at about noon.

Despite being at war, midshipmen had to pass examinations to qualify them to embark on sub-lieutenants' technical courses. Four of us had to take exams in seamanship, navigation, engineering and ship construction at Manus on our return there after Operation Inmate. A hastily convened examination board of captains and commanders – British, Canadian and New Zealand – put us through our paces. Despite having no time to swot, we all passed, though I was disappointed to be given a second-class pass, which slowed down my progress by two months.

Between passing these exams and starting sub-lieutenant courses in Portsmouth, midshipmen had to spend two or three months getting experience in small ships. Normally this would have been in destroyers, but there was apparently no room for us in the twenty or so destroyers with the British Pacific Fleet. A big operation was brewing. We were told we could be at sea continuously for at least six weeks for a combined operation with the US Pacific Fleet against the Japanese coast. After a week at sea we learned that we would be transferred to frigates, instead of destroyers, to do our three months' 'small ship time.'

On Friday, 13 July, a large audience of sailors, laughing and chaffing us, assembled to watch Mike and myself being transferred by bosun's chair – a seat slung on a wire stretched between two ships – to our new ships. He went to *Redpoll* and I to *Whimbrel*. They were hoping we would get a ducking, but the exercise went smoothly and I did not even get my feet wet.

Nuclear Shock

Whimbrel had the essential but tedious task of escorting the fleet train, a job she shared with seven other frigates and an old aircraft carrier. The fleet train comprised the oil tankers, store ships and repair ships which enabled a fleet to remain at sea for long periods. *Whimbrel* was a well-equipped modern frigate, armed with the latest anti-submarine and anti-aircraft weaponry. Day after day, we steamed up and down about 400 miles off the Japanese coast, somewhere between Okinawa and Kyushu while the big ships of the US and Commonwealth navies bombarded the coasts and flew air strikes against inland targets. Every five days or so, they came to the fleet train to refuel and re-store. We had no close contact with the ships other than by pipeline from a tanker when it was our turn to refuel. This process could take anything up to half an hour, during which not only did constant course and speed have to be maintained, whatever the weather, but the ships were particularly vulnerable to attack.

The weeks passed in the tedium of endless routine and boundless horizons. Occasionally a destroyer was detached to steam at high speed to Sydney and return with mail. Mail was transferred to each ship in turn, by Coston gun line. These were the red letter days punctuating the monotony of our existence. At one point, we were detached to escort a damaged destroyer to the atoll of Eniwetok in the Caroline Islands, later to be the site of a hydrogen bomb test by the Americans.

There was rarely more than one midshipman in any destroyer or frigate and *Whimbrel* was no exception. It was to be more than three months before Mike Higgs and I met again, and I missed the company of anybody of my own age and background. I was allocated the Captain's sea-cabin beneath the bridge. He slept in the chart room when not on the bridge or using his large day-cabin aft. Discipline was relaxed, and attitudes very casual. The gunnery officer was a splendid Australian with a great sense of humour who had been both a violinist and a rugby player.

I had my first experience of having to censor letters written home by the sailors. The purpose was to cut out any information which could be of use to the enemy. It quickly became a chore, though an illuminating one. Some of the letters seemed to be written as much to the ship's officers as to the folk at home. It was one way a sailor could make a complaint or offer an opinion to authority without getting into trouble. I came to the conclusion that the main difference between the officers and most of the ship's company was that the officers had a veneer of education which gave them confidence and perhaps a sense of superiority. Some of the letters were very moving, the more so for being partly illiterate.

The news that the first atomic bomb had been dropped some 500 miles from our position came on 7 August. You might expect that the attitude of the ship's company would have been vindictive satisfaction, but it was far from that. We considered that the Japanese were already beaten. Although we were unaware of the horrors of radiation, the predominant feeling in the ship was that this was not the way to finish them off. Even now, more than half a century later, I wonder about the morality of that terrible act of destruction. I do not have to be convinced that it may have been responsible for a net saving of human life: 90,000 Japanese civilians against the appalling casualties which the Allies, and the Japanese, would have sustained if it had become necessary to invade the Japanese mainland to win the war. But why no warning? Was it revenge for Pearl Harbour or simply military callousness on the part of General MacArthur? The Japanese could have been warned. The feeling on board HMS *Whimbrel* was that they should have been warned that unless they surrendered unconditionally, atomic bombs would be dropped on one or more of a dozen listed cities and that all civilians must immediately be evacuated from those cities. Had the Japanese refused to surrender then the responsibility would have been entirely theirs.

For three more weary weeks the fleets steamed up and down off the Japanese coast, then at last we set course for Tokyo. We steamed into Tokyo Bay at 5.30 p.m. on 2 September 1945, the day the Japanese were to sign the surrender document in the United States battleship *Missouri*. We were disappointed that the top of the famous volcano Fujiyama was shrouded in mist, as were many of the buildings round the harbour. The sky above us throbbed with allied aircraft and by mid-morning, I was able to count 250 aircraft in sight simultaneously. As we entered the inner harbour, Yokosuka Bay, we could see a vast assortment of American and British ships, all with ensigns fluttering at their mastheads. The sight was impressive to us. To the Japanese it must have been devastating.

Through binoculars, I could see many small Japanese warships grounded and abandoned. We passed close to a Japanese destroyer and a minelayer with all the guns of an accompanying American destroyer trained on them. I studied the Japanese sailors. They had the despairing expressions of beaten and disillusioned men. Some were sitting on the decks with their heads held in their hands or between their knees.

On the second day in harbour, an escort carrier, laden with liberated British prisoners of war, passed along the lines of ships so that we could cheer them. They were mostly soldiers and men of the Fleet Air Arm. One soldier was playing the bagpipes.

We were not allowed ashore. Only armed parties, mostly American, were. We left a few days later in company with six other small ships. Fujiyama was still shrouded in mist, but I was to disprove the legend that I would never return to Japan.*

We headed for Subic Bay in the Philippines, but had to take shelter in the lee of Okinawa when we got word of a typhoon ahead. Even there, a huge swell was running and the ship rolled through an arc of nearly 90 °. These swells were the outer ripples of a fearsome storm which, we learned later, caused several American destroyers to capsize and sink with the loss of all on board.

I never learned the purpose of our visit to the Philippines and saw very little of the place. We dropped anchor in a mist-shrouded bay with a shoreline of thickly forested hills rising to 2,000–3,000 feet. Before evening, we weighed anchor and left for

---

* The legend has it that if you visit Tokyo but fail to see Fujiyama, you will never return to Japan.

Hong Kong. It was raining hard and a heavy swell was still running.

The harbour entrance at Hong Kong was seething with junks and sampans, many of them flying the Chinese national flag. Hong Kong in 1945 was very different from the Hong Kong of the twenty-first century. There were no skyscrapers, no high-rise flats, no neon lights and few motor vehicles. The city looked dirty and dilapidated. Beyond it rose range upon range of dun-coloured hills – the real China. The air above the burnished surface of the water shimmered in the heat and was suffused with a constant murmur of voices. Around the battleships, aircraft carriers, cruisers and smaller ships, their awnings spread to ward off the heat, hundreds of sampans clustered like ants around slices of fruit. Between the ships, the water was studded with the brown sails of junks.

As soon as our anchor hit the bottom, we were surrounded. Miss Ah Sing came on board and handed a note to the Sub-Lieutenant: 'Dear Sirs, we are pleased to see you back again and much obliged for your patronage.' From the sampans, trinkets and looted valuables were offered at prices bearing no relation to their real value. Anything could be bought with cigarettes. Men showed their wares, gesticulating and grinning. Women fed, washed and smacked their babies, and waved and smiled. Boys dived for coins and bars of soap thrown by the sailors. Whole families seemed to live in one big sampan, from babes in arms to grandmothers. The women wore black cotton trousers and white smocks, many of them with blue pinstripes. It was impossible to tell their ages. They all seemed to be small, brown-faced and flat-chested with smooth black hair. One of the few differences was that the older men and women had wrinkles round their eyes and their teeth were discoloured from chewing betel nuts.

One sailor bought the gold cup of the Hong Kong Golf Club for a 1,000 cigarettes. Unfortunately for him, an officer saw him strike the bargain. The cup was confiscated, but he was given 2,000 cigarettes, and the cup was later handed back to a surviving official of the Club.

In the course of the next few days I met other midshipmen due to return to the UK for their sub-lieutenants' technical courses and struck up friendships with some of them. One day we walked across Hong Kong Island to Repulse Bay. We swam from the beautiful shady beach, amazed to have it to ourselves. The following day we learned why. During the Japanese occupation, any prisoners who died were thrown into Repulse Bay, which teemed with sharks. Fortunately for us, that day they had not been hungry, but the day before a man's leg had been bitten off. No one had thought of erecting a notice at the beach and no warning had been issued to the ships. I suppose it was unusual for anyone to walk from the harbour across the island and it had not occurred to the authorities to put the bay out of bounds. In any case, a shark would have found me an unsatisfactory meal. After six months in the tropics on a wretched diet, I was skin and bone and, although over six feet tall, weighed just over eleven stone.

My condition was good, however, compared with some of those who travelled on the troop ship from Australia which we eventually joined to return to the UK. Our fellow passengers were mostly former prisoners of war and civilians, returning home after months and, in some cases, years in Japanese camps where conditions had been abominable and where ill-treatment had been the norm and torture commonplace. None of them wanted to talk about it, but at night their sighs, snores, cries and even screams in their sleep were very disturbing. We slept in stifling heat in three-tier bunks in huge dormitories. Most of the older hands had been in the Far East for years before the Japanese assault on Hong Kong, Malaya and Singapore. They had common experiences it was not possible to share with teenagers such as myself.

It was a novel experience for me to be in a ship at sea with women on board. Sometimes in the evenings there were dances in the dining saloon after the last sitting of dinner had been cleared away. The competition for female partners was intense. There was an attractive girl, perhaps seven or eight years older than myself, whom I contrived to dance with several times, but my success was short-lived. An elimination waltz was announced. When the music stopped, people wearing white shoes, or those who had false teeth or had never been in an aeroplane, or whatever, had to leave the floor – a very small area of cleared deck between the tables. Eventually there were only about six couples left and I began to think my partner and I might win. The music stopped.

'Look at your partner's chest. If she isn't wearing a brassiere or he hasn't got hair on his chest, you must leave the floor.' My partner undid a button of her dress to show me her respectable underwear. Then, without waiting for my assistance, she undid two buttons of my open-necked shirt and inspected my sun-burned, but smooth chest. 'Well, I suppose you're too young for it,' she said loudly.

Horribly embarrassed, I led her from the floor.

I devoted much of the voyage to sitting in a lifeboat, reading. By the time we reached the Bay of Biscay I had devoured everything I could get hold of, including the pamphlets produced by the three main political parties for the recent General Election. I had, of course, been too young to vote, but before we steamed up the Solent to Southampton, I had decided I was a Liberal.

My homecoming was an anticlimax. My family were scattered – my father about to be demobilised and preparing to return to his job, Pen no longer a nurse but looking for a job in repertory, Julia teaching and my mother trying to come to terms with the changed circumstances of peace time. I barely had time to see them all before reporting to RN Barracks in Portsmouth. Most of my friends from Dartmouth days were there – not only older, but a bit wiser and less starry-eyed about a naval career.

Sub-lieutenants' technical courses took place almost entirely in the Portsmouth area and lasted for nearly two years. We worked in groups of about fifteen, moving through the various naval disciplines in succession – gunnery, torpedoes, navigation, signals, anti-submarine, flying, combined operations, radar and several more. Depending upon how you did in the exams, you spent a few months more or less as a sub-lieutenant before promotion to lieutenant.

There was a lighter side to these two years of intensive study-ing – a week's leave at the end of each course, plenty of sport and a party almost any evening you could spare from study for the next group of exams. I worked hard enough to avoid any worry and spent most of my leaves climbing in Scotland.

At one party, I met and fell for a girl who lived among the orchards of Kent, too far from Portsmouth for convenience. I decided I had to get a car. I searched the columns of the evening paper and eventually spotted something I could afford: '1934 Austin 7 in good mechanical order £70 or near offer.' I took a bus out to a northern suburb of Portsmouth and inspected the vehicle, which was sitting at the roadside in front of a row of terraced houses. The description had been honest. The owner was an enthusiast, a motor mechanic who was moving on to something more ambitious. For a twelve-year-old vehicle, it was in very good condition: a little green box on wheels with a black roof and a faithful 7 horsepower engine that never let me down. It was capable of a speed of over forty miles per hour when on a slight downgrade running before the wind. This I discovered later. To begin with I just drove it round the block and immediately wanted it more than any other material possession in the world. I offered £65 and got it. The seller, realising that my driving experience was extremely limited, kindly drove me back to Portsmouth Barracks, giving me careful instructions on the special characteristics of my new purchase.

The following weekend's party was in London. I had even less knowledge of the geography of that city than I had of driving a car. Nevertheless, I bought a map and set out at 8 a.m. on Saturday morning. Keeping well in to the left, it only took me a few miles to become thoroughly accustomed to the little machine. There was a throttle on the steering wheel, linked to the accelerator. This was a bonus, because my knees came up high on either side of the steering wheel and to prevent cramp it was essential to be able to move my legs. I found that by setting the hand throttle at a suitable angle, provided I kept my eyes on the road, and one hand on the steering wheel, I could do anything I liked with my legs. I stopped for lunch in a pub somewhere near Guildford. By mid-afternoon I was in the outskirts of London. Then my troubles began. I found that driving and map reading at the same time in a strange city was beyond me, so parked the car and took the London Underground. I cannot even remember the party, but I managed to find the car again and arrived back in Portsmouth at 5 a.m. on Monday with enough time for a shower, shave and breakfast before the first morning lecture. I counted myself a driver.

Scottish Mountains

My experience on Arran, where I was introduced to rock climbing by a member of the Alpine Club – Dr Carroll, the doctor on board my father's ship – had conceived in me a love of the hills and climbing. I spent most of my week-long leaves, between courses, in the Western Highlands, mostly with Richard Brooke (a contemporary at Dartmouth) as my companion. He was already an accomplished climber and later became a member of the Alpine Club, a member of Dr Fuchs' Antarctic Expedition, a recipient of the Polar Medal and an applicant for Colonel Hunt's expedition to Everest. I feel sure that if Hunt or Hillary had known him better, he would have been chosen. His skill and toughness were outstanding and his perseverance Herculean.

In the winter of 1945, after spending Christmas with our families, Richard and I went climbing in the Ben Nevis area. We arrived by bus in Fort William just after midnight, with no money for a hotel. There was no youth hostel nearby, so we decided to look for a shed. The night was cold and wet and it was two hours before we found a shelter. It had a stone floor and my sleeping bag provided no insulation. By 4.30 a.m. I was convinced that anything was better than lying wide awake, chilled to the marrow. I got up, shivering, and with some pangs of conscience shook Richard, who was peacefully snoring.

'I don't know about you,' I said, 'but I'd rather go on in the dark than try to sleep here.' He agreed and we rolled up our sleeping bags, shouldered our heavy rucksacks and set off through a thick, damp mist. We were heading for the Scottish Mountaineering Club hut, situated below the north-east face of the mountain. Once on the move, I warmed up and two hours later my vest was saturated with sweat. Dawn had not broken but it had become light. We were still enveloped in a blanket of cloud, which limited visibility to about fifty yards. To our left there was a burn in spate, rushing down to join the river Lochy in the glen now a thousand feet below us. Beneath a waterfall we found a pool the colour of dark ale. Richard threw down his rucksack. 'Come on, let's have a dip!'

The pool was deep and ice-cold. The first shock nearly stopped my heart beating, but I emerged tingling and able to wolf down stale corned beef sandwiches and chocolate before setting off again. There is something peculiarly energising about Highland rivers and my wife and I still bathe in them from time to time.

At 10 a.m. we broke through into bright sunshine. Around us billowed a sea of white cloud from which countless snowy islands projected – mountain tops, scattered to the limitless horizon. Looking up, we could just pick out the hut we were aiming for, below the black buttresses of Nevis which were crowned with snow cornices.

We spent four days at the hut, using every hour of daylight for climbing. The weather was brilliant with ground temperatures rising above zero in the middle of the day and palpable heat in direct sunshine. We traversed Carn Mor Dearg, Aonach Mor and Aonach Beg. We climbed South Castle Gully, tackling the severe fifty-feet rock pitch by the left wall, then ascended hard snow to the summit. We crossed the top of the mountain and descended to the hut again by way of the arête and Carn Mor Dearg.

For the final two days, we were joined by two climbers from Glasgow University. When in the narrowest part of No. 2 gully, where sheer walls of rock tower on either side and the floor was steep ice, we heard the roar of an avalanche in a neighbouring corrie. Richard was leading and suddenly gave a yell. A few jagged lumps of ice as big as footballs, and a mass of fragments, came crashing down. A small piece struck Richard on the head and a larger piece hit my right shoulder. I was dislodged from the ice step and slipped eight feet before managing to dig in my ice-axe. We then negotiated a steep wall of solid ice near the top, only to find a dangerous overhanging cornice barring our way to the summit. There was no possible route up either of the gully's ice-encrusted walls. The only solution was for Richard to force a passage through the cornice without, if possible, starting an avalanche. As I was bringing up the rear of the party of four and would be in the path of any dislodged snow, I had a special interest in his success.

It took Richard half an hour to turn the left edge of the cornice, one of the coldest and most unpleasant thirty minutes I have spent in my life. The previous day we had sunbathed near the summit while eating our lunch! When eventually the two students disappeared above the cornice, a muffled message – a compromise between a shout which could have set off an avalanche and a whisper I could not have heard – informed me that it was no longer safe to ascend by the same route. Two large cracks had appeared across the lip of the cornice. Held from above, I had to traverse the gully beneath the overhang and climb up its right-hand extremity. As we were descending by a safer route, we heard another avalanche. It sounded as if it came from the gully we had just vacated. Two of the new climbs we had made were recorded by the Scottish Mountaineering Club.

Our next week's leave was not until May 1946. We decided to go to Skye and found the island baking in a record drought. No rain had fallen for nearly five weeks. This time we came equipped with a light tent, a small primus, tinned provisions and a couple of tubes of midge repellent. We found a beautiful camping spot on an open grassy knoll surrounded by birches and rowans in the deep ravine of a burn which descends from Corrie Banachdich into Glen Brittle. This glen fringes the western flank of the Cuillins and faces across the sea to the islands of Rhum and Canna.

Over the years I have had numerous encounters with the highland midge, but this was the first time I was really at war with them. Cooking on the primus was easier outside the tent, but halfway through the evening we had to take the stove inside, where the fumes helped to keep the midges at bay. At night, nothing deterred them. We would fill the tent with paraffin fumes and cheap tobacco smoke, smother our faces, necks and arms with midge repellent, seal every entrance and wriggle into our sleeping bags. Still the midge battalions found their way in and within half an hour the roof of the tent would be black with them. Our nights were spent alternately slapping, scratching, swearing and smearing on more repellent – with very little sleeping. One particularly warm, still night, which followed a day of unusual heat, we had to shift camp at midnight on to the high ground above the ravine, where a faint breeze made offensive operations a little more difficult for the enemy.

From a climbing point of view, the week was a great success. Early on we climbed the Cioch, the nipple of rock which juts from a cliffside on Sron Na Ciche. We traversed the Cuillin ridge, surmounting the peaks of Sgumain, Sgurr Alasdair and Sgurr Thearlaich, and crossed the Thearlaich Dhu gap. We had perfect weather for four days, apart from one surprising squall when we were on the ridge. It brought a few minutes of hail and sleet and compelled us to crouch on all fours with our backs to the blast.

On the last full day we traversed the Cuillin Ridge again, taking in every peak over 3,000 feet. We ascended the Window Buttress of Sgurr Dearg, scaled the Inaccessible Pinnacle, mounting the west side and climbing down the east ridge. We climbed Mhic Coinnich, descending to the gap by Collies Ledge, Sgurr Thearlaich again and the Dhu Ridge from Loch Coruisk, regaining Glen Brittle via Corrie a' Ghrunnda. There, sweating and dusty after our scramble down rock, rubble and scree, we bathed in a lochan which was icy cold in spite of scorching heat in the saucer-shaped corrie.

That sweltering afternoon preceded a superb sunset. We sat on a heather knoll above the camp, smoking to keep the midges at bay, and watched the sun disappear behind Barra. When we woke in the morning, on the last day of the month, the mountains looked sinister under a black canopy of cloud. We passed a lazy day walking on the hills west of Glen Brittle, watching the Cuillin continuously changing colour and the clouds tumbling over peaks which were visible one moment and gone the next. That evening it started to rain and did not stop until we reached the mainland twenty hours later. We were soaked through when we boarded the train for London at Mallaig. Our suntans did not camouflage our midge-ravaged complexions and one old gentleman sharing our compartment moved elsewhere at the first opportunity. Perhaps he thought we had a communicable disease – or perhaps we just smelled!

I next visited Skye to climb three years later. By then I had gained some experience in the Alps. Before crossing to the island, Richard Brooke and I spent three days at Dundonnell in Ross-shire, climbing all the peaks of the An-Teallach group, and found a new route up the gully which connects Loch Toll an Lochan with the peak of Sgurr Fiona.

On that peak I enjoyed one of the great moments of my life. A bright interlude in the prevailing rain and cloud gave us a glimpse of Slioch, Storr Rock in Skye and the Butt of Lewis. As we sat eating our sandwiches a golden eagle, which I had previously spotted from beside the lochan, soared beneath us on full wingspan, not ten yards away. To look down on such a magnificent creature in full flight, from above, was breathtaking.

Once on Skye, we hired a boat in Elgol to go to the head of Loch Scavaig. The boat was owned by three brothers – Ronald, Donald and Dugald MacDonald – only one of whom admitted to speaking any English. They had the west highlander's usual disregard for the clock and we left Elgol an hour and a half after the promised time. We only just had time to find a cave for the night on the north shore of Loch Coruisk before darkness fell. It was a good-sized cave and this time we were not bothered by midges.

Again, we were lucky with the weather. In the course of a week we managed to climb all the peaks we had not previously tackled, as well as repeating a few of the more interesting climbs. In one day we climbed ten peaks and towards evening I saw that extraordinary phenomenon, a Brocken Spectre – a fearful human shadow, vastly magnified by reflection off moisture particles in sunshine saturated with mist. Two Glasgow University students had joined us. We found a new route up Sgurr Coire an Lochan which we described for the Scottish Mountaineering Club Journal. It became known as the Shelf Route.

I had to rejoin my ship before the others needed to leave and we parted on the top of Sgurr na Gillean in conditions of worsening visibility. Carrying my heavy rucksack, I started down the easy tourist path which would eventually lead me to Sligachan, where I was due to catch the Armadale bus the following day. The route was clearly marked, with a series of small cairns and by the easily discernible scratches of the hobnailed boots of countless climbers. I became careless and let my thoughts wander. It suddenly dawned on me that the rocks under my feet were no longer scratched. Visibility was now less than twenty yards and there was no cairn in sight.

I made a very bad decision. Instead of retracing my steps, by which method I would have struck the tourist route, I decided to go on down. I knew that Sligachan meant 'the meeting of the waters'. Presumably by following the first burn I came to I would arrive there. This was a fair assumption, but it overlooked the fact that water often takes the steepest route. The moment arrived when I was compelled to turn and face the rock and climb down a waterfall. My framed rucksack was my undoing. Its base caught on a projecting rock, just as I was poised on one foot, feeling with the other for a lower foothold.

The next thing I remember was sitting by a rock pool with my head in my hands, soaked to the skin, with blood everywhere. I had fallen about thirty feet. There was a severe pain in my right hip, but otherwise I seemed to be in one piece. Below the pool, the slope seemed much less steep, so I picked myself up and began to walk. The pain in my hip subsided to a dull ache and I decided it was only bruised. It seemed I had been incredibly lucky.

The climb down is a blur in my memory but I do recall a moment of huge relief when at last I dropped out of the canopy of cloud and saw the distant white speck that was the Sligachan Hotel. It took me nearly two hours to cover the two miles of heather and bog. At last I walked through the front door and into the hotel lounge. The prosperous fishermen smoking their pipes and middle-aged ladies at their knitting looked up at me aghast, as though I were some kind of apparition. Catching sight of myself in a mirror, I realised why. My whole face was caked in blood. The pain in my hip had served as an effective counter-irritant to the pain in my head. A hot bath was an agonising necessity. The doctor who saw me that evening diagnosed a broken nose and thumb and slight concussion. He straightened my nose with a skilful jerk, put four stitches in the gash over my cheekbone and bound up my thumb. Had I broken a leg, or worse, I would not have been missed for at least forty-eight hours. I have never forgotten that lesson and always ensure that I leave word where I am going and when I should be expected back.

On a train journey to the west coast to climb in the Ben Nevis area, I experienced one of those strange coincidences which cannot be explained in terms of reason. I shared the compartment with three passengers who were chatting together. I was dressed in nondescript clothes and my unlabelled rucksack was on the rack above me. I was happy looking at the West Highland landscape passing by. At a small station, two of the passengers got out, leaving just one middle-aged woman. For a while there was silence apart from the rhythmic rumble of the wheels, then she spoke.

'Excuse me, but is your name Davidson?'

'Yes,' I confirmed with surprise, 'James Davidson.'

'Then you must be the son of Robert Davidson. Wasn't he captured with the Royal Scots at Singapore?' I was completely mystified.

'I'm sorry, but my father is Alastair Davidson and he was in the Royal Navy.'

'But you're the spitting image of Robert. That's astonishing. He must be a relative.'

For the rest of the journey we tried to find an explanation for the extraordinary likeness which had enabled her to pluck my name out of the air. It seemed that the Robert Davidson she knew had family in Aberdeen. Perhaps we shared some common ancestor, resulting in a family likeness, generations later.

Vanguard

The Second Sea Lord's office at the Admiralty was responsible for making officers' appointments. When I opened the official envelope containing the news of my first appointment after completing technical courses and read 'to HMS *Eastbourne*', I was hugely disappointed. She was a minesweeper engaged in clearing up the leftover bits of minefields at the entrances to ports on the east coast of England. No mountaineering. No rugby. No athletics. Probably very few parties. When I joined the ship at Harwich, it was raining.

The captain greeted me with the words, 'God knows why you've been sent here. There's nothing for you to do and the ship is going into the reserve fleet in a few weeks' time.'

A day or so after I joined, I was sent by rail up to South Shields to act as a watch keeper on board another minesweeper which was about to sail down to Harwich and was short of officers. As we came down the east coast in a November gale, I came to the conclusion I had somehow got myself on to the Second Sea Lord's blacklist.

In Harwich a second buff envelope awaited me.

'The Lord Commissioners of the Admiralty hereby appoint you Sub-Lieutenant of *Vanguard* and direct you to repair on board that ship at Portsmouth on 25 November 1946. Your appointment is to take effect from that date.'

The brand new battleship was in the final stages of fitting out for the royal cruise to South Africa. As senior Sub-Lieutenant I would be in charge of a gunroom of some thirty midshipmen and non-executive sub-lieutenants. It was a formidable prospect for a nineteen-year-old.

I wrote a series of letters home on the outward leg of the royal cruise:

1 February 1947 – Portsmouth

After the departure of Queen Mary and the rest of the royal aunts, uncles and in-laws, all officers were lined up in the wardroom and then, in order of seniority, we filed into the royal apartments ... Their Majesties and the two Princesses were standing in line inside the central lobby of their quarters. We shook hands with each of them in turn. We had been told to bow our heads and not to look at their faces at the same time, but the tall among us found this impossible. They are genuinely a very small family, but a charming-looking one. The Queen and the Princesses have lovely complexions and very blue eyes. If anything, their photographs do not do them justice. Sorry, Mother, but I did not notice what they were wearing and it was all over in a flash. I'll do better next time.

7 February 1947 – at sea

On Wednesday I was suddenly told that four members of the gunroom, preferably four who could dance reels, as well as straight ballroom stuff, were invited to an informal dance on the quarterdeck.

The royal family are doing a lot of entertaining. About twelve officers are invited each evening. Six senior ones dine with them before going to some entertainment, usually a film. The other six join the party after dinner. There are only a few of us who dance reels, so Charles Paterson, myself and two midshipmen – Bell and Mackay – put on our best uniforms and at 9.30 p.m. were waiting outside the royal quarters. Part of the deck had been specially lit and curtained off. We were briefed by the equerries and told not to hesitate to ask either the Queen or the Princesses to dance.

...The Queen was wearing a white dress of crêpish material with mauve sequins dotted about, Princess Elizabeth a powder blue dress on very simple lines and Princess Margaret a pink net dress with a full skirt. The king wore uniform like us. There was a short, awkward pause, then His Majesty looked round and said, 'Damn hot out here.' Then, looking at me and one of the midshipmen, he added, 'Come and let's roll up one of the side screens.' He accompanied us as we went to the ship's side and rolled up one of the canvas curtains to let in the night air. He watched critically as we secured the stops with reef knots.

Later I had a long chat with him about the new scholarship scheme of entry into Dartmouth. I believe people get a wrong impression from the King's Christmas broadcasts. He sounds so diffident on the wireless. To me he seemed extremely shrewd and charming with just a touch of impatience in his manner.

I danced with the Queen and both Princesses. Princess Elizabeth was nice, very much at ease and natural. I discussed piping with Princess Margaret because I danced with her directly after an interval when three Royal Marine pipers played. She, too, is easy to talk with and full of life, but I felt that a faux pas would have been less easily forgiven than by the others. The eightsome reel was the highlight for the four of us from gunroom as none of the wardroom officers present knew how to do it.

Yesterday, there was another surprise for us. I had invited some members of the royal household for drinks in the gunroom at 6.15 p.m. Half an hour beforehand, we heard that the Princesses would like to come down, too … The party lasted an hour and a quarter. Please tell my sisters that the Princesses only drank lemonade.

At present we are ploughing along at seventeen knots through a calm sea. The carrier *Implacable*, the cruisers *Diadem* and *Cleopatra*, and the destroyer *St Kitts* are still in company. Tomorrow *Nigeria*, flagship of the Atlantic station, relieves them and they return to England.

10 February 1947 – at sea

The concert on Friday was a great success. You may have heard the excerpt from it broadcast by the BBC … The gunroom sketch, which I wrote and produced, went without a hitch and particularly appealed to the King … I heard that direct from two equerries.

On Saturday evening the royal family came down to the gunroom again for drinks … The King was quite at home talking about gunroom subjects and the Queen liked our cocktail so much that she had two or three glasses.

15 February 1947 – at sea

The day after I closed my last letter, the Princesses, with their lady-in-waiting and the two equerries, all came down to tea in the gunroom … A special menu had been laid on but our guests ate very frugally. After tea we started playing tombola – for chocolate rather than money ... They stayed until 7.30 p.m. so they must have enjoyed themselves. I believe Princess Elizabeth would have left earlier, but she could not catch Princess Margaret's eye. Eventually she had to say to her younger sister, 'I think we had better go now, or we shall be late for dinner and the King will be angry.'

18 February

On Monday we started preparing for entering harbour at day-break. The hills behind Cape Town were clearly in sight through a pink haze, with Table Mountain very prominent. This haze, with a flawless sky even at dawn, was the forerunner of the hottest day Cape Town has yet had this summer ... Soon we could distinguish the buildings of the city as the haze began to disperse. Across Signal Hill was the word 'Welcome' in huge letters formed by over a thousand schoolchildren. They must have breakfasted early to climb up there in time ... We could see the welcoming crowds waiting and cheers became faintly audible. The cheers did not cease for two hours. At the harbour entrance we had to pass through a narrow gap between two moles. Had the gap been any narrower, I think the crowds would have leaped it and surged on board and mobbed the royal family ... As our first mooring line reached the jetty from the ship, we ran up our dressing lines and within seconds the ship was dressed overall with fluttering bunting. This brought a pause in the cheering and a gasp from the crowd. The Governor General, his wife and Field-Marshal Jan Smuts were seen mounting the gangway to greet the royal family. Soon they went ashore again and His Majesty appeared at the top of the gangway wearing a full white tropical dress uniform and, followed by his family, walked ashore. The tumult of cheering died down as the band struck up the national anthem, followed by that of South Africa.

After the King had inspected the guard, a column of Daimlers drew up. Their Majesties entered the first one, an open car, and the Princesses and the rest of the royal household followed in other cars at intervals. Many among the crowd were so moved that they were weeping. Others fainted in the heat. We could hear the cheers fading as the procession drew away.

South Africa

In the following months we were caught up in a whirlwind of social activities interspersed with a share of naval duty, some sport and a little relaxation. In the first few days I attended a garden party given by the Governor General and Mrs Van Zyl at West Brook, their beautiful white house outside the city. I was one of more than 5,000 guests, with the ladies in long summery dresses with wide-brimmed hats resembling anything from a small rock garden to an inverted soup plate or an ostrich's rump.

I had a rather grim spell of watch-keeping when a southeaster, the 'Cape Doctor', blew hard all night and clouds of dust swept the quarterdeck throughout the morning watch. My nose, throat and ears were choked with sand and I wore goggles to keep it out of my eyes.

The dock was almost in the centre of the city and despite the wind, thousands of sightseers moved slowly past the ship in cars or on foot. Dozens of organised parties were shown round the ship and the Officer of the Watch was often asked for his autograph.

One day when I was inspecting the fo'c's'le mess decks, I came across six sailors gently slipping tinned herrings in tomato sauce down the beak of a seedy-looking penguin. It was rocking rhythmically on its heels, staring with glazed eyes at a nude photograph of Phyllis Dixie. It looked unwell so I suggested they should take it to the Sick Bay. I pointed out that the mess decks were already crowded. I believe they found a corner for it in one of the cold storage rooms and eventually released it onto a beach.

Some of us were invited to play tennis at Newlands, a luxurious sport and country club beneath the shoulder of Table Mountain. Afterwards we were taken for a drive over the Kloof Ned along one of the most beautiful coastal drives in the world with the green and brown hills changing shape with each twist, brilliant blue sea fringed with white surf and sand, little Dutch-gabled farmhouses in their vineyards and then a glimpse of the Hottentot Holland Mountains across False Bay, flat and clear like stage scenery. The road itself was blasted out of precipitous cliffs. The drive finished with the opportunity to bathe at Christian Beach, where we saw only white bathers.

I called on the South African Mountaineering Club, hoping to arrange an expedition in the Groot Swart Berg, but there was not enough time. One member kindly offered to take me up Table Mountain by a route more exciting than the cable railway. We met at 8.30 a.m. The mountain was, as nearly always at that time of the day, shrouded in mist and a fine rain kept us cool on the first approach to the Western Buttress. I was wearing climbing boots but was lightly dressed and carrying only four sandwiches, an apple and a camera. Mr Charlton had brought a huge rucksack containing sandwiches, tea, billycans, torches and all the other accessories of a major expedition, as well as a huge amount of bananas. This we had to carry turn and turn about. Before roping up below the buttress, we distributed the contents of the rucksack more evenly by eating most of the bananas and some of the sandwiches. The climb was relatively easy with sound rock and adequate hand and foot holds. I was told that on parts of the buttress there is severe exposure with sheer drops of up to 2,000 feet, but the shroud of mist hid these from us.

We saw many exotic flowers, three buck, a small black poisonous snake and lots of lizards, including a yellow-and-black-striped creature the size of a small crocodile. We reached the top – a wilderness of jumbled rock and scrub, cleft with gullies and with very few trees – early in the afternoon and soon afterwards the sun came through. In three or four minutes, the cloud rolled clear of the plateau, disclosing superb views in every direction. *Vanguard* dwarfed her immediate surroundings but was herself a mere speck in the panorama of ocean, city, mountains and flats. We built a fire, made tea and finished the food. On our way down the easier route on the western face of the Buttress, the wind suddenly veered from north-east to south-west causing the 'tablecloth' to form again almost immediately. We did not come out into sun again for a further 1,000 feet.

A few days later *Vanguard* left Duncan Dock and steamed

westward round the Cape to Simonstown, the naval base on False Bay. Our deep draught meant we had to anchor in Saldana Bay, a lonely spot reminiscent of Scapa Flow, except that the sun was hot and the water teemed with sharks. While at Simonstown we joined in a regatta, in which our gunroom rowing crew came second in the finals, and an athletics match against the South African Naval Forces in which *Vanguard* won all the track events very easily and all the field events except the javelin. I played my part by winning the half-mile and quarter-mile. Charles Paterson and I had trained by going for a long run through the bush. We saw little but arid, undulating scrub and the occasional squalid farm steading. We were disappointed to see no wildlife except for a few snakes. Nevertheless at one point we bounded at top speed because we had lost the small track we were following and feared for our bare legs.

The rugby match against the South African Naval Forces turned out to be the dirtiest I have ever played in. The wing three-quarter outside me had successfully tackled his opposite number, who had tried to beat him with a side step. A penalty was awarded against us, apparently because our man had prevented his opponent from getting up with the ball. We retreated, but as we waited for the penalty to be taken the disgruntled South African wing three-quarter walked slowly towards his opposite number and crashed his forehead right into our man's mouth. He was knocked unconscious. The referee blew shrilly for half time and the offender was sent from the field. We won by eleven points to three, but the South Africans were bad losers and refused to shake hands at the end of the match. We were glad to hear later that the offender had been banned from playing organised sport for the remainder of his service in the SANF.

Our visits to Mossel Bay, East London and Port Elizabeth were marred by bad weather. A heavy seasonal swell made it impossible to lower and run the ship's boats. From ashore, the difficulties were not apparent, and local dignitaries were annoyed that this great representative of the Royal Navy's fleet could not deliver its personnel to the various social and sporting occasions they had organised. We did eventually manage a formal dance and a rugby match in Port Elizabeth.

On our arrival in Durban we saw – and heard – the famous 'White Lady of Durban,' Perla White. A sturdy lady with a voice of operatic power and music-hall quality, she had 'sung in' and 'sung out' nearly every British warship throughout the war. For these sterling services she had been awarded the MBE. Wearing what appeared to be a white nightie, she struggled for a few minutes against the pipers playing on our quarterdeck, but soon they were all overwhelmed by a deafening chorus of steam whistles and car horns. We were accorded the greatest welcome of the cruise, despite the absence of the royal party.

Then it started to pour. I was Officer of the Watch for the first dog-watch (4–6 p.m.) and spent most of the time at the gangway deluged both literally and with questions from sightseers: Did I know if Able Seaman Smith was in the ship? Did I know a chief petty officer called John with red hair? Could they look over the royal cabin? Was it true we had Captain Hardy's snuff box on board and when was it last used? This last was from a newspaper reporter.

On Easter Day, when I was again Officer of the Watch, the ship was open to the public for the afternoon. A queue developed stretching for half a mile and in two-and-a-half hours we had over 11,000 visitors on board.

Just before we left, the quarterdeck was transformed one evening for a dance for Durban's leading citizens and one local newspaper let itself go beneath the headline 'Ball on Battleship'.

Like a fairy-tale palace with moonlit turrets and battlements with an underlining grimness, HMS *Vanguard* was floodlit last night into a beauty that drew crowds who stood on the dockside and gazed. The quarterdeck made a magnificent dance floor with the Royal Marine band to provide irresistible rhythm … A fascinating feature of the decorations was a spurting fountain placed under the grim 16-inch guns. It seemed a strange crystal fire, where the light caught the jet of water and a bank of shaded pink dahlias and blue hydrangeas formed a lovely rockery effect. In the centre of the quarterdeck was a centrepiece of two large brass ship's lanterns and two ship's bells around which the dancers circled.

Marks would have to be deducted from this flowery description because the journalist failed to mention that there were real goldfish in the pool under the fountain and a bar at each corner of the deck!

The Royal Navy was very good at this sort of thing and nobody organises a children's party better. We gave four during the tour and all were equally successful, although apartheid meant that the South Africans only let white children attend. Cowboys and helmeted divers greeted the young arrivals and got them interested before the children realised their parents had left the ship. Pirates' caves glowed with red-hot braziers where the children could get themselves branded with red ink. An aerial torpedo took them from bridge to fo'c's'le. There were slides, roundabouts and swings, a cinema showing Donald Duck and, of course, unlimited quantities of jelly and ice cream.

Some of us were invited to Princess Elizabeth's twenty-first birthday party at Government House. After watching a fabulous firework display, Charles Paterson and I walked to Government House, passing an endless queue of cars. Once inside we waited in another queue on a covered walkway leading to the porch where the Governor-General was receiving the guests. Each male guest was issued with a red or blue ribbon. We could only dance alternate dances because of the modest size of the ballroom. Princess Elizabeth was presented with a magnificent diamond necklace from the people of Cape Town, then the dancing began. Although the Princesses only danced with important Cape Towners, they gave us friendly smiles as they swung past. The assembly of dresses was breathtaking – mostly white and pastels. When the ball ended at 2 a.m., there were no girls to be seen home. They all left in large cars under close escort, so Charles and I walked back through the city streets to the ship.

At one point in the course of that evening, I found myself talking to a Mrs Moore. She asked me how old I was and if I had been at Dartmouth. I told her I had. 'Then you must have known my son Peter, although he'd be a year or two older than you. He was a very good boxer,' she said proudly.

'Yes. I remember him,' I said. I refrained from telling her that it was Peter Moore I had beaten in the final of the lightweight category in the college championships before being rewarded with a penny by P T Harrison.

I am left with many vivid memories of our time in South Africa, but also with the unpleasant flavour of its then political system. I was Officer of the Watch one evening when an ordinary seaman was brought on board by two huge South African policemen. He was a lad from Liverpool, about two years younger than myself, and had been roughly handled. He had lost his cap and was indignant and bewildered. I asked what had happened. In stilted English the police sergeant told me that the sailor had been consorting with a coloured girl and that if he had been any white man other than a sailor from *Vanguard* he would have been imprisoned to await trial. Reluctantly, I thanked the two South Africans and said I would take the necessary action. Once they had left I asked the young sailor for his story.

'I was just walking with this girl along the street,' he said.

'But you've all been warned that consorting with coloured people is against South African law. This isn't Liverpool, you know.'

'I didn't know she were coloured. She weren't no darker than a lot of girls at home. I just thought she were sunburnt.' I nodded and dismissed him.

South Africa was a land of stark contrast between the beauty of the landscape – which we were given many opportunities to visit and enjoy – and the harshness of the political system. It was obvious even then that no system where the majority of people have virtually no civil or political rights can survive indefinitely. The writing was on the wall in 1947. Twelve years later South Africa left the Commonwealth and became a republic. The royal visit may have postponed this action by a year or two but it was inevitable.

Vanguard's Return

In the final hours before departure from South Africa, tons of baggage, hundreds of presents and enough flowers to transform Buckingham Palace into a botanical garden, all arrived on board. There was a spate of last-minute visitors bearing tales and explanations about sailors who had lost their shoes, their health or their hearts.

We played a final game of rugby against the Olympics Club whose team included three former Springboks, one of whom was the legendary fly-half Benny Osler who had captained the South African side in their 1931–2 tour of the UK when they won all four internationals. Our fly-half was injured and I was moved from the centre to take his place. I could not lay a hand on Benny Osler when he got the ball. I was considerably faster than him but his side step and swerve made him untouchable. Fortunately for us three times out of four he kicked for touch. We lost but were not disgraced.

As *Vanguard* began to move away from the jetty, the crowds poured through the police cordons to the water's edge and began to sing, led by a choir and a military band, 'Land of Hope and Glory', 'Will Ye no Come Back Again' and other songs calculated to bring a lump to the throat. Even from outside the harbour basin we could still see the crowds and faintly hear the shouting. Once through the harbour entrance, there was a big swell running and the ship began to roll quite heavily. Some of us not on duty stayed on deck to watch until Cape Town dropped below the horizon. The tablecloth had magically rolled off the mountain and the city basked in evening sunshine.

Within the first few days of the homeward voyage, I was invited with other officers to dine with the royal family. The navigator's wife was among the party. She was South African and had been allowed to take passage to England in the ship at the Queen's special request. On arrival at the royal apartments we were shown a seating plan and I saw that I was to be seated between Princess Margaret and one of the equerries. We knew that on such occasions members of the royal family talk for the first half of the meal to their right-hand neighbours and for the second, to their left, so the equerry took charge of me. The food was excellent but included nothing that had to be chewed and nothing elaborate – clear soup, sole, minced chicken in aspic, a sundae of meringue and coffee ice cream, a cream cheese savoury, fruit and coffee. There was champagne and a choice of other wines. I wondered if the royal family knew what badly prepared food was like, but decided that the King must have had plenty at Dartmouth, and perhaps Princess Elizabeth had in the ATS... I recalled that when serving in *Whimbrel* in the Pacific, we had an American communications officer who complained constantly about the food, which was execrable by US Navy standards: corned beef, dehydrated potatoes, tinned fruit and vegetables, lime juice and anti-malaria tablets were the staples.

When it was time, Princess Margaret turned and started talking to me. She was lively, witty and self-assured, but again I felt she was the last member of the royal family with whom to take any liberties – the only one I could imagine saying, 'Off with his head.' We talked mainly about South Africa, but also about Scotland.

Afterwards, when the ladies withdrew, the King became the hub of conversation while the port was passed; then we all moved into the King's large day-cabin. The Queen was suffering from a bad cold and the family retired at about 10.30 p.m. The whole time I had felt as if I was sitting watching a film.

About a week later, the royal family accepted my invitation to dine in the gunroom. There was a lot to do by way of preparation. We moved the tables end to end and fitted an extra leaf to increase the seating. We had to borrow the best wardroom glasses and cutlery because ours were a bit battered. By the time everything was cleaned and the tables set the gunroom looked, appropriately, fit for a king, but we heard halfway through the day that he would not be able to come! He was unwell and had been confined to bed by the Queen. It would have been the first time in history that a reigning monarch had been dined in the gunroom of a warship, but it was still a unique occasion despite his absence. The usual formality was dispensed with and conversation went on to right and left and across the table. The Queen remarked on the happy atmosphere she always noticed when the gunroom officers were together. We were a very happy crowd. She also talked about Scotland.

There is a tradition in the Royal Navy that the monarch's health is drunk seated – except when there is a Royal Marine band present. This dates from the days when the deckhead in a warship was too low to allow a man of more than 5'6" to stand up straight. We drank the King's health standing because of the Royal Marine string trio, which had been playing in the background. As we sat down, there was a slightly awkward pause until Her Majesty said sweetly, 'I'm sure the King feels much better after that.' Princess Margaret remarked that it remained one of her ambitions to 'drink Daddy's health sitting down'.

The royal party visited St Helena by launch and we also anchored off Ascension Island. What seemed like half the population came out in launches to pay their respects to the King. A couple of nights later I had the middle watch on one of the most beautiful starlit nights I ever remember – flat calm and cloudless. *Nigeria*, keeping station on our port beam, was a black silhouette in the path of the moon.

We passed the Canary Islands one day at dawn. Gran Canaria lay on our port beam, floodlit by a startling sunrise. In the forenoon, the ship stopped while the Queen and the Princesses crossed to *Triumph*, which was accompanying us, to make an inspection. The Queen flew her personal standard in *Triumph*, the first time a queen had ever done so in one of HM's ships at sea.

About ten days into the voyage, the Princesses came down to tea in the gunroom again and we played party games including Drunken Coachmen. The final loser, one of the midshipmen, had to sing Rule Britannia unaccompanied by way of forfeit. We were in the middle of being organised into a Russian choir by the Princesses when members of the royal household began to arrive unheralded and tea turned into cocktails.

We had one more session of Scottish reels with the royal family before arriving back in Britain. The King was now in good health and great form again, laughing, joking and teasing Frank Gillard, the BBC correspondent. The Queen and her two daughters were happy and informal. It was almost like a small party in a private home. Music was provided by three Royal Marine fiddlers, and some of the royal household's Scottish maids joined in.

We started with the eightsome. I was the Queen's partner. At first we were all a little cold, since weather conditions had changed. But soon most of us were sweating – even the Queen's brow was a little moist. The next two dances were less energetic but more primitive – the hokey-cokey and the conga. It was funny watching Midshipman Mackay in the conga, behind Her Majesty. He was clearly in a quandary about placing his hands on the royal hips. I was facing a similar but lesser quandary behind Princess Margaret, but for the sake of the dance we overcame our scruples.

During a break for champagne and sandwiches at about midnight, I talked with the Queen and the Royal Marines' Director of Music. He asked if he might play the Eriskay Love Lilt as a final inspection tune when the royal family left the ship. The Queen answered, 'I shall cry if you do, but then I shall cry anyway; I feel so sad that we shall be leaving the ship in two days' time.' When I asked whether they were taking a break before carrying on with normal duties she replied wistfully, 'No, we will sink straight back into the same old rut, I suppose.'

We had a strange visitor one unusually calm day in the Bay of Biscay. Although the nearest land was over 150 miles away, a golden plover appeared out of the blue and touched down on the fo'c's'le. Later it chose the quarterdeck for another siesta. It allowed people to approach to within a few yards. It was obviously exhausted, and possibly sick, but just after sunset it took off and was not seen again.

The entrance of *Vanguard* into Portsmouth Harbour was greeted so fervently that the reception in Cape Town paled by comparison. The King and Queen had presented the gunroom with a signed photograph of themselves and their daughters, a silver loving cup and – most welcome – the radiogram from the royal apartments.

Though most of us were glad that a unique period of hectic

living, publicity and basking in reflected glory was nearly over, I really felt quite moved as they turned and waved goodbye to the ship.

A few days later, the ship sailed round to Plymouth and leave was given to each watch. I had arranged to go climbing in the Alps with Dr Carroll. It was essential to get as fit as possible in the two weeks before we were due to go. The rugby season was over so I entered the Plymouth Command Athletic Championships and then found myself representing the Navy for the second year running in the quarter-mile and half-mile in the Inter-Services Championships. The track events were all relays, not individual competitions. We were outclassed by the RAF, whose team included three Olympic athletes: Macdonald Bailey, Donald Finlay and the enormous Jamaican, Arthur Wint. In the 4 x 880 yards relay, I took over the baton for the final 880, twenty yards behind the long-limbed Wint and five yards behind the army runner. Wint never exerted himself but finished nearly thirty yards ahead of me. I closed the gap on the army runner, but still finished last. However, I arrived in Switzerland feeling physically on top of the world.

Matterhorn and Eiger

I met up with Dr Carroll and Willi Steuri in Spitz. Willi, a member of a well-known Grindelwald family of hoteliers, was one of Switzerland's leading mountain guides and a professional skier. I realised later how extraordinarily lucky I was to make my first Alpine ascents in the company of a man whose mountaineering skills were enhanced by his cheerful temperament, influence and local knowledge. He was so much in demand that had he not been an old friend of Dr Carroll's there would have been little hope of engaging his services. On arrival at Zermatt, however, Dr Carroll found a message requiring his immediate return to England. It was a severe blow, but it was arranged that I should climb alone with Willi until joined by two of the Doctor's friends a few days later.

After Dr Carroll had left, Willie and I spent the forenoon making purchases for the first expedition and sitting in the sun inspecting the famous profiles of the Matterhorn, Monte Rosa and other peaks flanking the Nikolaithal. After lunch we started on the four-hour trudge up to the comfortable hostel which lies at 9,000 feet – some 3,000 feet above Zermatt on the eastern ridge of the Matterhorn. The hostel was very crowded and Willi's prestige began to be useful. He quickly commandeered a stove, places at a table and bunks for us both.

We turned in early, then rose in the dark at 3 a.m. Breakfast was coffee, bread and jam, and we were the first away. The valley and lower stretches of glacier were hidden by a layer of cumulus cloud, but all the peaks were stark and clear in brilliant moonlight. When the sun came up over Monte Rosa with a green flash, after first tingeing the snow tops a rich salmon pink, we were already above the snow line at over 11,000 feet. I found the route up the Matterhorn strenuous but relatively straightforward. There were one or two exciting pitches with tremendous exposure, but technically the rock climbing was less difficult than in Skye.

By 9 a.m. we were on the peak, where we ate our second breakfast, half in Italy and half in Switzerland. Elated to be on top of one of the world's most famous smaller mountains, I was just a shade disappointed that it had been so easy. We had been too engrossed in the physical challenge and the astonishing panorama of surrounding peaks to talk. Willi had watched me carefully but had not criticised. Now I had proved my fitness, I felt able to ask him a few questions. He led a life that sounded immensely satisfying to me. The family hotel business in Grindelwald gave him a secure financial background. In the spring he hunted the chamois, in the summer and autumn he was a mountain guide and in the winter a ski instructor. It was in the last capacity that he had met and courted his wife – the daughter of a Scottish baronet. I have met few men more likeable. I was surprised to find that this was, in fact, the first time he had climbed the Matterhorn because he came from the Bernese Oberland.

The descent was tiring. I was conscious of the jar and shock on my legs as I fought tiredness and the law of gravity. Just before reaching the Hornli Hut, we had to cross a *couloir* – a narrow vertical gully between two rock buttresses. Ice melting in the sunlight at the top had released stones which hurtled down at speeds of nearly 200 mph. The unfortunate guide of a small party ahead of us lay prostrate on the far side. He had been struck by a stone and was in a bad way with a gash on his head, broken ribs and blood coming from his mouth. Willi and two other guides who came up improvised a stretcher from their ice-axes and spare clothing, then carried their comrade down to the hut where he was given first aid. Willi stayed to help carry him down to Zermatt and I continued down on my own.

On the night of 9 August, we were at the Trift Hostel, with the intention of setting out early in the morning to climb the Obergabelhorn. At about midnight all hell broke loose. If you have been in a gale at sea, a typhoon, a raging blizzard or a thunderstorm amid mountain peaks, then you feel you have seen the wrath of God. I sat at my window for an hour or more, fascinated and not a little frightened, watching the lightning stabbing the snow crests and ridges which were at one moment in darkness, then as clear as day, then eerie beneath the moon which appeared and disappeared between torn black clouds. The timbers of the hostel trembled with every deafening clap of thunder. Our start was delayed until after 4.30 a.m.

There was a dreary tramp along the ridge of a moraine before we reached the bottom of the Gabelhorn glacier, which was carpeted with new snow and deeply crevassed. We crossed it then ascended the 12,700-feet Wellenkupper by a steep but fairly easy snow route. We traversed the ridge between this mountain and the Obergabelhorn (13,320 feet) by alternate snow and rock. Thick cloud enveloped us and Willi decided we should retrace our steps and walk straight down to Zermatt, where we met up with the first of Dr Carroll's friends.

The following morning we caught the Alpine diesel bus and to the accompaniment of its melodious three-note horn, sped up a tortuous road through breathtaking scenery to Saasgrund where the last member of our party met us. After sorting out gear and buying some provisions we set out for the Wissmies Hut, 4,000 feet above. This was a very basic, high altitude hut. Willi did the cooking and we slept in none-too-clean blankets on a shelf, rather like sausage rolls in a bakery. We were on the move again by 3.30 a.m. Unfortunately as the day went on I began to feel an uneasiness in my stomach, later followed by sickness and other unpleasant effects, compelling me to drop behind the rest of the party from time to time. I had to expend extra energy to catch up again and this, together with the loss of the carbohydrates and fat I had consumed at breakfast, meant I was exhausted and miserable by the time we reached the summit of the Fletschhorn. The rest of the morning was a horrible ordeal and I took little interest in the route down.

An afternoon's sleep back at the hut made me fit enough to enjoy a supper of soup and boiled eggs and the following day we got down to Saarsgrund by 7 a.m. and travelled to Grindelwald. We spent a delightful evening in Willi's family's hotel. The following day we were to start out on an ascent of the Grosser Schreckhorn by the South Ridge and the Eiger by the Mittillegi Ridge.

We reached the Strahlegg Hut in time for an early supper. We were on our way by lantern-light before 3 a.m. For over an hour

we trudged up a tedious slope of scree, then roped up to sur-
mount a steep ice slope in which Willi had to cut steps. We
crossed the Schreckfirn, winding our way between crevasses and
across snow and ice bridges until the bottom of the South Ridge
of the Schreckhorn was reached. We started the long ascent up
the rock ridge. This was exciting to climb – very steep, in places
severely exposed, but with sound rock and reassuring hand and
foot holds throughout. It is one of the longest and finest rock
climbs in the Alps. We had only to follow Willi Steuri.

It is difficult to explain the fascination of such a climb to anybody who does not feel the powerful attraction of mountains. For
me it was the exhilaration of pure air and stupendous scenery, the
physical sensation of hand and boot on rock or snow or ice, the
satisfaction of achievement spiced with danger and sometimes
just the quiet, the isolation, the sense of being in a place that has
been gained – not just arrived at.

We reached the sharply defined 13,250-feet peak at 9 a.m. and
settled to enjoy the sun, a snack and a magnificent panorama
which embraced distant Mont Blanc, the Matterhorn and Monte
Rosa as well as the nearer Finsteraarhorn and Wetterhorn. We
traversed the exposed eastern ridge before descending by the
couloir – a mess of shale, scree and flaky rock. The final obstacle
was a tricky rock pitch which had to be abseiled in order to reach
the Schreckfirn.

The sun had widened the crevasses and eroded the snow
bridges across them and some proved quite alarming, but we
finally got back to the hut in time for a late tea. To our annoyance,
it had been virtually taken over by a score of male and female
members of an English Holiday Friendship Union on a walking
tour. They took up most of the available space, monopolised the
cooking facilities to the detriment of the mountaineering parties
and took part in tuneless community singing in the living room
with no thought for those who would be getting up hours before
them in the morning. I hoped their ears burned as much as mine
did at the caustic remarks made in French.

We rose at 4 a.m. to a chorus of English snores and set out on
the six-hour trek across the Lower Grindelwald Glacier and the
glacier which runs the length of the Eiger's southern flank. We

spent over two hours finding our way through this network of crevasses, some gaping and bottomless, some just deep blue gashes, but nearly all too wide to be crossed. As we mounted the steep rock slabs on the far side, we saw several edelweiss, the emblem of the Alps and rarely found except well away from tourist routes. There was only a small snowfield and some 400 feet of steep rock to be surmounted before we reached the crest of the Mittillegi Ridge. By noon we arrived at the small hut perched above a 4,000-feet precipice, the notorious North Wall of the Eiger. Below, looking almost as though you could pitch a stone into the main street, lay the seemingly Lilliputian village of Grindelwald.

The hut was designed for eighteen climbers. It had only two rooms – one for cooking, eating, chatting and drinking wine, the other for sleeping. There was a pervasive smell of food and woodsmoke. The mattresses were filled with straw and the blankets were of a doubtful grey colour. Snow had to be collected for water for coffee or to wash or shave with. The loo was spectacularly primitive. You could stare between your toes at the valley 4,000 feet below. I spared a thought not only for the gallant souls who had risked their lives rescuing over-ambitious climbers over the years, but for those who had struggled up the ridge with timber and equipment to build and furnish this hut.

By 10 p.m. thirty climbers had congregated and we realised once more how fortunate we were in our guide. It was due to his personality and influence that we were first with the stove and single table for supper, first to get turned in and after a very cramped and stuffy night – which several of the thirty were obliged to spend outside the hut – first to get away in the morning. Two of us were with Willi on one rope and Dr Carroll's other friend climbed with a colleague of Willi's, Christian Baumann.

The Mittillegi Ridge of the Eiger is limestone and inclined to be flaky. It is certainly neither as sound nor as reassuring as the granite of the Schreckhorn. The outlook to the north was awe-inspiring, and alarming if one chose to look down. The climb was steep rock from beginning to end. Although a few patches of snow were encountered, there was no ice to speak of. On the vertical pitches, a rope on pitons gave some assurance. Visibility was perfect and the sky cloudless. In such conditions the climb is less difficult than some of the routes in Skye, Glen Coe, Nevis, the Lakes and North Wales, well known to British climbers, but it is a great deal longer and severely exposed in some places.

At the top we rested for a short snack and another magnificent view. We descended by an easy, undemanding route to the Jungfraujoch railway. The little station at first seemed to recede instead of getting closer, but eventually we reached it and finally arrived back in Grindelwald at 6 p.m. having left the summit of the Eiger six and a half hours earlier.

After supper we went to a fair where I won a bottle of Bordeaux playing guinea-pig roulette, then we adjourned to a bar where we drank it and a couple more. It was my last evening in Switzerland. It did not occur to me that I would never return to climb in the Alps. Lack of time and lack of funds denied me another opportunity, although I have since climbed many other peaks in Scotland and elsewhere. The following morning I sadly said goodbye to Willi and took the train to Berne.

Twelve hours later I stood in London drizzle, equipped with nothing more than the clothes I wore, two shillings, the return half of a railway ticket to Plymouth and an Air France luggage receipt. I last saw my rucksack and ice-axe on a trolley at Orly Airport going in the opposite direction in the company of hundreds of expensive-looking suitcases.

Persian Gulf

The great Nafud desert of central Arabia passed beneath us, the sun struggling over a thick wall of haze under a pale cloudless sky; miles and miles of dun-coloured sand with nothing to break the dreariness and monotony but an occasional swell or dip, an oasis of seemingly stunted bushes, a track, or tiny cubes of black – Bedouin tents. Hour after hour we flew across this desolation. Our destination was Bahrein Island, where a small naval base was maintained for the three Royal Navy frigates comprising the Persian Gulf Division and other visiting warships. I was on my way to join one of them – *Wren*.

I had found living in a huge warship moored to a jetty totally demoralising. Half of *Vanguard*'s ship's company had left her. I was given permission to go to the Admiralty to find out what my future might hold. I was told my appointment was only one or two weeks away. The choices were limited: to do a short gunnery course and then go as a gunnery officer in a fleet destroyer; to become first lieutenant of a motor torpedo boat based in Portsmouth; or to become a watch-keeping officer in a frigate in the Persian Gulf. The last was the only division in the Navy with an unlimited fuel allowance and a real job to do: safeguarding our oil supplies and helping to preserve law and order in a volatile part of the world where in 1947 there was an active trade in slaves and drugs. I asked to be sent to the Persian Gulf.

The BOAC flying boat maintained a great circle course roughly along the twenty-ninth parallel. We had already stopped at Aix-en-Provence overnight – where I enjoyed the local cabaret at the expense of the Navy – then for an hour in Sicily for lunch, and for the night in the Nile delta, where I had nearly been arrested for violating Egyptian independence by wearing my uniform. Nobody had warned me not to!

On reaching the brilliant blue waters of the Gulf, the pilot turned on to a south-easterly course following the coast.

Occasionally we spotted an oil derrick or a fertile green patch of date palms. Bahrein itself is a low-lying island part of which, in the north and west, is highly cultivated. At the northern tip is Manama, the ancient capital and port. The rest was then desert, sloping so gradually into the sea that there was no navigable passage around the southern end of the island. The Navy and the British Political Resident and his staff were based at Jufair, a mile or two east of Manama.

As the flying boat circled above Jufair I caught my first sight of HMS *Wren* at anchor. Her hull was painted white, awnings were spread and she was fitted with wooden decks above the living spaces as some measure of protection against the scorching sun. She was the same class of frigate as *Whimbrel*, in which I had served in the Pacific.

The Persian Gulf can claim to be the hottest sea in the world. The highest temperature recorded on board during my twenty-one months in *Wren* was 127°F in the shade at Basra in July, but this was by no means a record. Higher temperatures were recorded ashore and in summer we never ventured up the notorious Elphinstone Inlet, a fjord enclosed by great walls of rock in the Musandam Peninsula.

Temperature readings on a dry-bulb thermometer are no measure of human discomfort. There was no air conditioning in *Wren* for my first six months in her. We suffered most at Bahrein, where on one occasion we had humidity of nearly one hundred per cent. In those conditions nature's plan to cool the body by evaporation of sweat is stymied. The moisture-laden atmosphere can hold no more, so the sweat drips and trickles, soaking clothes and leaving puddles wherever the skin touches a non-absorbent surface. Few of the crew did not suffer from prickly heat or skin eruptions of some sort.

As the newly joined Sub-Lieutenant, though I only had three months to wait for my second stripe, I was allocated an odd package of jobs. In addition to watch-keeping duties I was in charge of the confidential books, boats, education and sport. I was also gunnery control officer and divisional officer of two divisions: a seamen division and a Somali division.

I became very fond of the Somalis, but because I could not

speak their language I had to rely on the Tindal – a petty officer. He was thin as a scarecrow with a crop of white wool above his seamed black face, but he was not as old as he looked. He had served on and off in the Navy for over a quarter of a century and he earned several times the basic rate. He received an additional allowance when employed as an interpreter during certain official visits. In practice, basic pay represented a very small proportion of the Somalis' total earnings. Under the system of canteen messing, they would draw the barest minimum of food from naval sources, recovering the value from the ship's office at the end of the month in the form of mess savings. In the meantime they subsisted on rice and ghee bought at local markets. They were masters of bartering. Good shoes, for example, were cheap in Manama and at a premium in Basra. A Somali rating might land at Basra with his kitbag containing his total savings converted into shoes and return on board with his capital converted into Swiss watches, which could then be sold for cash in Bushire in Iran. The Somalis always seemed to know where we were going next. Provided no illicit merchandise was brought on board, the Navy did not intervene in matters of customs duty.

When I had been in the ship a few months, I heard that the Tindal's wife had died. Thinking he might want an opportunity to visit his home and settle his affairs, I arranged for him to have some leave. On his return I broached the subject with him, saying how sorry I was for his loss.

'That's all right, sah,' he said, grinning broadly. 'She die soon enough. I have her young sister and two camel instead.'

He had paid a large sum of money for the older sister – by no means his first wife. Because she had died before a specified date, he received her younger sister and two camels by way of compensation. The father had apparently sold his daughter with a two-year guarantee.

In 1947 Kuwait was an ancient and primitive city state grouped round a bazaar and enclosed by mud walls except on the seaward side where it sloped to the water's edge. On the foreshore were famous yards for building ocean-going dhows. The putrid stink of the sharks' oil, used to dress the timber before it was shaped into keels, ribs and planks, pervaded the seaward quarter of the town. When there was an offshore breeze, it could be smelled well out to sea. Everything was yellow-brown sand or mud – the square city walls, houses and bazaars, roads and the inhospitable country well beyond the city. Eighteen months before my first visit there, a British-American company had struck oil. The ruling sheikh was on his way to becoming a millionaire but Kuwait showed no signs of developing into the city of fabulous wealth which it later became.

At a cocktail reception on board for British and American residents, one of the other officers let it be known that I was a piper, albeit a poor one. The following evening I found myself playing in somebody's courtyard at the request of a man from Skye. At the first painful groans, a group of Arab children, who had gathered out of curiosity, dispersed with fearful shrieks, but once I had got going properly they returned one by one and listened with flattering attention.

Bagpipe music seems to have a peculiar appeal for the Arab. I noticed this on several occasions. I once played in Iraq after a football match between the ship and a local team. In a matter of moments I was surrounded by children who would not let me stop playing. Eventually I was followed all the way back to the ship like the Pied Piper, a crowd clapping and chanting in time to 'Scotland the Brave'. Many years later I was at a reception in Edinburgh Castle and was touched to see tears pouring down the face of an immensely austere Arab dignitary as the lone piper played at the end of the evening. I have also seen the Pipe Band of the Arab Legion playing at Murrayfield Highland games. Although they were far below the standard of a Scottish regimental pipe band, they made amends by their splendid turnout, numbers and enthusiasm.

I was invited to dinner at the palace of the Sheikh of Kuwait on the strength of my having been on the royal cruise in *Vanguard*. We gathered at the Political Agent's house for some fortification against the teetotal evening which lay ahead. Although no good Moslem drank alcohol, I found that some remained determinedly ignorant of the fact that Pimm's No. 1 Fruit Cup had an alcoholic base. This was often served by members of the Arab aristocracy who had been to Oxford, Cambridge, Harvard or Yale and who must have known better.

The Sheikh's palace was built of mud and comprised four wings, each with its own courtyard. The principal one was for the Sheikh, his sons and his adviser. The other three were respectively for his womenfolk and children, servants and livestock. The Sheikh met us on the broad stairway leading to the front door. His formal greetings were conveyed through a personal interpreter because he claimed to speak no English.

In deference to us, we dined in western style. After drinking glasses of fruit juice in the reception hall which contained an odd mixture of beautiful carpets, priceless ornaments, cheap furniture and gaudy bric-a-brac, we went into a dinner party which, apart from the temperature, might have been held in a house in Kensington. Conversation was stilted and the subject of the royal cruise never came up.

We returned from Kuwait to Bahrein to pick up the senior representative of the British Foreign Service in the Persian Gulf: the Political Resident – equivalent in rank to Consul-General. Sir Rupert Hay looked exactly like Colonel Blimp. The ignorant might have laughed at his stout figure, florid complexion, white walrus moustache and bald head, but this exterior belied a very high intelligence and a warm and hospitable nature. He was greatly liked and respected by all of us. To the Arabs, whose languages and dialects he spoke fluently, he was King George's personal representative and was treated with all the deference and respect that implied.

One of my most vivid memories of the Persian Gulf concerns Sir Rupert's black Labrador. When we were moored alongside the jetty at Jufair, he would pad down from the Residency, at around four in the afternoon, descend the jetty steps, launch himself into the water and swim slowly out in the direction of the harbour entrance. When he was well out from the jetty, a porpoise would swim in through the harbour entrance, leaping and plunging joyfully. The dog would begin to bark and the porpoise would swim directly towards him, leap over him, turn again and swim beneath him. For ten minutes or more the two would play together, the Labrador barking frantically with excitement, the porpoise twisting, turning, leaping and diving. It appeared to be sheer enjoyment for both animals. There was no sign of anger or aggression. At last, exhausted, the dog would turn and paddle slowly back to the jetty steps. The porpoise, with a final leap, would turn and swim back out to sea. This display happened frequently, presumably triggered by some seasonal factor, or perhaps in response to some message picked up by the dog's sixth sense.

Bahrein to Basra

I rode a camel for the first time in the desert at the south end of Bahrein Island. Sir Rupert Hay was visiting a police outpost, a castellated watchtower with the red and white national flag of Bahrein fluttering over it, and he invited a few of us to accompany him. Grouped round the tower were half a dozen black tents and some camels lying with their feet hobbled. When the time came for them to be saddled, they started a terrible racket, as if their throats were being cut.

The sensation of riding a camel had often been described to me, so the strange rolling motion came as no surprise. We were led until we had gained a little confidence, then I was given sole charge of my mount. The most difficult part of riding a camel is balancing on the single hump as the animal rises from a recumbent to a standing position. A walk or a trot was quite pleasant, but the canter was alarming without stirrups. My camel went beautifully, but I found this 'ship of the desert' difficult to steer. There were two strings, one tied to the halter and the other to a loose flap of flesh on the animal's nose. I found I could only turn to starboard. To go to port, I had to turn 270 ° to starboard. Occasionally the beast let eight inches of loathsome tongue loll out and made a noise like a bronchitic old man clearing his throat into a loudspeaker.

We took a detour on our way back to Jufair through a desert area covered in large mounds. This was the 3,000-year-old burial ground of three tribes, still in use. We explored one of the graves which had been excavated – a maze of dark passages with separate chambers for male and female corpses. North of the burial ground lay palm groves and fields of forage crops. Amid the palms was a beautiful fresh water pool with a little white mosque beside it – the source of the island's limited irrigation scheme. Nearby was an unusual ornamental garden around a small lake stocked with turtles and tropical fish.

Basra is mainly memorable for the notorious Bullring district. *Wren* was berthed six miles from Basra at a jetty leased by the RAF. Taxis were expensive, so our visits to the city were infrequent. It was dirty and had few attractive areas to relieve the squalor. There were numerous restaurants and bars, but most of them were out of bounds because of the risk of food poisoning and other diseases. The red light district posed an unhealthy attraction to airmen and sailors and it was the responsibility of service doctors to decide which establishments were not out of bounds. The RAF doctor and our own ship's doctor, both Scots, decided that I had led too sheltered a life and that my education needed to be broadened, so they took me on an eye-opening and mind-shattering tour of the red light district.

It shocked me deeply. I would not have believed that such squalor existed on this planet or that human beings could be brought to such abysmal depths of misery and depravity. What horrified me most was the sight of young girls, some of them just children, who had been sold into this hell and were doomed to degenerate into the poor harridans squatting in grotesque postures at some of the doorways. I was guiltily aware that it was the greed and inhumanity of men that was responsible for this exploitation of women, that men still bought and sold other human beings and lived on the profits from it, that man's selfish lust provided the market for it.

Part of the reason the Royal Navy still had a presence in the Gulf in the 1940s was to try to stop the slave trade. Arab slave traders bought girls in East Africa and took them by dhow to sell into the red light areas. We sometimes stopped dhows and searched them but never found any slaves.

Paradoxically, the traditional site of the Garden of Eden is just a few miles from Basra at the confluence of the Tigris and Euphrates. We were invited to go duck shooting there by the State Gamekeeper. We went equipped with shotguns and ammunition, dry spare clothing, sandwiches, beer and a bottle of whisky. It was late January and quite cold. Frosts were not infrequent there in winter. The two canoes for the expedition were punted by villagers who considered it one of their duties to keep us clean. At odd moments throughout the day, they would squat down and pull mud off our boots. I had difficulty in restraining one from spitting on a splash of mud on my bare knee. He offered to wipe it off with his already filthy shirt. We followed a narrow water-course for a mile or two inland, where we left the punts among the rushes and set off across the marshy flats.

It was a strange day's shooting. We were hoping for snipe, with the chance of some duck in the evening, but the villagers would grip the arm of the nearest of us and point at anything that flew – marsh tit, pelican, flamingo, heron or stork – a finger quivering with excitement like the nose of a gundog. Pleading eyes would be focused on the twelve-bores. They did not seem to mind what we killed as long as we killed *something*. We resisted, but unfortunately snipe were the rarest birds of all and it was an hour or more before the first was shot. We squelched steadily through the marsh, returning to the canoes by about 4.40 p.m., soaking wet, mud-spattered, eaten alive by mosquitoes, but with several snipe to our credit. After eating the sandwiches and drinking the beer, we set off again in a thick mauve haze to await the evening flight of duck.

A long vigil ensued, seated in a puddle and concealed behind a parapet of rushes. The sun had long disappeared into the haze and it was nearly dark when the first three duck came over, high and fast. They were right above me when I fired. Seconds later, the pellets pattered into the marsh all around. For the following hour, by which time it was completely dark, we blazed away almost without pause. It was impossible to see the duck until they suddenly materialised from the haze directly above us. Neither I nor the other three – one of whom was a very good shot – had anything to show for it. I suspect the locals picked up anything that came down. Nevertheless, it had been an exciting hour. I have never seen so much game in such a short space of time. The trudge back to the canoes through the mud and the chilly voyage down the backwater to the main river where our launch was waiting was the least pleasant part of the day, but by the time we had paid the two villagers, changed out of our filthy clothes and settled in the snug cabin with four fingers of whisky in hand, our circulation and spirits were fully restored.

After a year in the Gulf, I began to feel restless and trapped. I realised that although I enjoyed seeing strange places, I really preferred mountains and forests to seas and harbours. I was not sure I wanted to spend my whole working life in the Navy. Without telling anyone, I applied to do a BSc course in general science and forestry or agriculture at Aberdeen University. To my delight I was accepted and I asked my Captain to write to the Admiralty to ask if I could leave the Navy to take up the place. The reply was that I would have to serve ten years from the age of eighteen. I was only twenty-one. I was angry, depressed and bitter. As a thirteen-year-old entrant into Dartmouth, I had never signed a contract. This anomaly has since been changed and young entrants no longer commit themselves unwittingly to long periods of service.

The Captain advised me to make the best of my situation, to try to enjoy myself and not to carry a chip on my shoulder. It was good advice and I made a personal resolution to perform every task which confronted me to the best of my ability. At least nobody would be able to say I was shirking.

Ships of the Royal Navy in the Persian Gulf worked tropical routine. At sea or in harbour, the basic work of cleaning and polishing started at 4 a.m. and by 8 a.m. it had been completed. The forenoon was given over to training and armament exercises. By noon, the heat was intense and in the afternoon everybody who was not on watch or performing some essential task was off duty. In harbour, there was shore leave. At sea, most men slept but I was not then very good at sleeping in the afternoon. These days it is difficult to stop me! I borrowed a set of Linguaphone records from one of the political officers in the Residency at Bahrein and began to brush up the Russian I had started to learn at Dartmouth. My fellow officers thought I was going off my head, but it helped to pass the time.

Our most popular port of call was Abadan. It was then the biggest oil refinery in the world, the thriving centre of the Anglo-Iranian oil company. Later, of course, it was nationalised by the Iranians. The heavy, sickly odour of the refinery could be smelled long before the buildings and jungle of silver and black steel chimneys, cracking towers and pipelines came into view. The place looked like the inside of a chemical laboratory magnified a thousand times. It produced annually over twenty million tons of crude oil and although the invested capital and staff were mainly British, the Iranian treasury derived a vast, steady income from the industry.

The oil company provided everything conceivable for their employees and we were encouraged to make use of the facilities when visiting the port. There were restaurants, clubs, cinemas, tennis courts, playing fields, swimming pools, a sailing club, a golf course, even a polo ground complete with stables, a model piggery and a dairy where a tuberculin-tested herd of Ayrshire cattle was maintained on concentrates in an air-conditioned byre because there was no grazing available.

Most of the European employees lived in a garden suburb of air-conditioned flats and bungalows. Those of middle- and upper-management status occupied a row of fine houses, each with its own shady garden, with flowers and lawns coaxed from imported soil, sloping to the river's edge. Downstream of this residential area were the oiling berths – numerous jetties with pipelines conveying refined oil and its by-products into a vast farm of silver storage tanks.

When there, I met an eighteen-year-old music student from Glasgow called Joan. She spent all her holidays in Abadan where her father was a senior engineer. When we were both in Abadan at the same time, I spent all my shore leave with her and her family. She was pretty – small with fair hair and slightly myopic blue eyes. She was a very good swimmer and an expert diver both from the springboard and the high board. She also sang beautifully to her own accompaniment. Even when she was in Glasgow studying, I sometimes stayed with her parents. They were exceedingly kind to me and I think they expected us to get married. Between our brief but idyllic spells together, Joan and I corresponded copiously. She was a great letter writer, but I think this correspondence built up expectations that could never be realised. I even bought her a ring, though I stopped short of putting it on her finger. It was not until I returned to the UK in 1949 and met her in London that I realised I was not in love and felt too uncertain of my future to get married. I was too immature to maintain a friendship after the break-up but I sometimes wonder about her and hope she found real happiness.

We visited Khorramshahr, the main base for the Iranian Navy, on more than one occasion. We would be entertained by the Iranian officers to vodka and fresh lime juice – fifty–fifty – with cubes of tender grilled gazelle steak served on palm needles. The demand for gazelle steak was met by dispatching officers armed with rifles into the arid surrounding country. When a herd of gazelles was sighted, the technique was to drive among them in a jeep and adjust the speed of the vehicle to that of the fleeing herd while a sharp shooter stood up in the rear seat and fired from the shoulder.

We also visited Bandar Shapur, the southern terminus of a 1,200-mile railway line to the Soviet frontier. It had served as an important supply line during the Second World War, conveying vital materials from Britain and the USA to the southern sector of the Russian Front. The port consisted of two wooden jetties with a few warehouses, offices and bleak dwellings at their landward end. In 1948 the population comprised the Iranian army garrison, railway officials and a few representatives of shipping firms and the Anglo-Iranian oil company. Our visits there were certainly more a duty than a pleasure, though a kind Armenian merchant once gave an unusual party for us. All the important local men and their wives were asked. There was vodka and lime juice, and a buffet supper of strange salads, cold curries and a delicious chicken stew. Best of all was a dish of sour cream cheese and spinach. After supper there was dancing to a radiogram on a huge Kashan carpet, which must have been worth several thousand pounds. One of the ladies present was a princess and a former concubine of the late Shah of Iran. I did not admire his taste.

On the tiny island of Bumusa dwelt one Englishman and his wife, the sole representatives of a British company that was mining red oxide. *Wren* visited the island to make sure all was well in February 1948. As soon as we anchored, a number of small craft surrounded us, loaded with fish and other merchandise. I was preparing the motorboat for lowering to take a small party inshore. As we swung the boat out on her davits, there were shrieks of terror from below. Without exception the occupants of all the craft within a radius of twenty yards plunged into the water, fully clothed. They had never seen a mechanical davit before and evidently thought the boat was going to drop on top of them from twenty feet.

Bandar Abbas had a fabulous bazaar. It offered a fine selection of carpets from the traditional weaving regions – Khashans, Kermans, Hamadans and many others. The opinion of an expert was necessary to make the best use of limited finances, but it was scarcely possible not to get a bargain. Unfortunately there were two major obstacles to my making a fortune: lack of capital and lack of space. I bought a carpet and had it rolled and sewn up in canvas. It occupied half my cabin for the rest of my time in the Gulf and I eventually gave it to Pen, my elder sister, as a wedding present.

Abu Dhabi, Ceylon and Malta

Abu Dhabi was probably the most primitive of all the places we visited with Sir Rupert Hay on board. The Sheikh was rowed out to the ship in a ceremonial galley by a dozen of his subjects who sat on the gunwhales with their backs outboard, manipulating oars shaped like square root signs. The oar blades moved laterally instead of fore and aft but were just as effective as those we are accustomed to. As they rowed the oarsmen chanted a rhythmic chorus, while one of them whined a falsetto solo against this undertone. In the stern the Sheikh himself reclined on a carpet surrounded by his male relatives – and by a powerful smell which became formidable as they bumped alongside. It was the reek of the shark oil coating the galley's timbers. He mounted the accommodation ladder with slow dignity and was accompanied forward to the Captain's cabin.

Formalities over, his relatives sprang from their craft towards the ladder and in a matter of seconds were scattered all over the upper deck. In feature and physique they were far from impressive and many of them suffered from minor deformities. Those whose daggers could be unsheathed, or whose rifles had bolts that opened, set about collecting any grease they could find on the guardrails or the muzzles of our 4" guns and transferring it to their own barrels, bolts and blades. One warrior squatted nonchalantly at the bottom of the accommodation ladder to open his bowels.

A crowd stood round the Quartermaster and excitedly took turns at examining the shore through his binoculars. As the Sheikh reappeared with the Captain, they made a concerted rush for their boats, like children for their desks on the entry of the teacher.

The Sheikh gave a *khuzi* in honour of Sir Rupert Hay during this visit – a traditional Arab feast, with a sheep roasted whole as the main course. Some of us accompanied him. We landed over the beach and were carried through the surf in sedan chairs. The Sheikh's flat-roofed residence was larger and more elaborate than the dwellings of his subjects, but no palace. We were met at the entrance by our host and conducted to an inner chamber through a series of small rooms, all of bare plaster. We sat on the ground in a circle with the Sheikh and half a dozen of his closest male relatives and retainers. Coffee was poured from a brass vessel decorated and shaped like Aladdin's lamp. The guests were served in rotation, beginning with Sir Rupert Hay and ending with myself as the lowliest European present. There were three small brass cups between fifteen of us. A servant squirted about a tablespoonful of liquid from the narrow spout into one of the cups and handed it to a guest. The coffee was warm, strong and unsweetened but highly spiced with eucalyptus. The recipient was expected to drain the cup in one gulp, after which the servant immediately refilled it. It was customary to drink a second cup. To take a third was considered very polite, a fourth slightly greedy. But the cup would be filled again and again until the guest rocked it rapidly from side to side after drinking, indicating a sufficiency. It was then offered on to his neighbour.

The next step in the pre-prandial ceremony was the washing of hands. A servant brought round a large bowl of rosewater, splashing it profusely over the guests' hands and clothes. As visitors from the occident, we were offered a small tablet of well-advertised English soap and a towel. Lastly a crucible containing incense was carried round. Following Sir Rupert's example, we wafted the smoke into our faces with both hands. At last we were ushered into another room for the feast.

On a tablecloth spread on the carpet a number of dishes were set out. In the middle, on a mountain of rice, reclined a roasted sheep, complete except for its feet and fleece. It was covered with a black, trembling blanket of flies. On little dishes around this centrepiece were small roast chickens interspersed with delicacies that variously resembled fishcakes, spaghetti, gravel, meat rissoles and flour. I sampled the last three, which proved to be bread-crumbs, herbal cakes and ground rice.

We had been advised to sit on our left hands because their use for conveying food to the mouth is the worst possible breach of manners. Furthermore, we had to ensure that neither the heels nor the soles of our feet were visible to other diners. Within these restrictions, eating was not easy, although the western habit of talking during meals is discouraged so that maximum concentration is possible. The flies and an unpleasant smell – which I did not discover until later came from something I had trodden in – spoiled my appetite. I hope my neighbours realised that I was not personally the source of the evil aroma.

I managed to pluck a few mouthfuls from the sheep's shoulder with my right hand and split a chicken with a fellow officer. We each grabbed a wing and a leg and pulled it simultaneously like a cracker. The rice was the best part of the meal – perfectly cooked and mixed with roasted nuts and raisins. We followed our host's example, plunging a hand well into the mound of rice, grasping a handful and, after compressing it, stuffing the lump into our mouths. Meanwhile, Sir Rupert, as guest of honour, munched the sheep's eye and swallowed it with the air of somebody tasting a fine wine. Our captain was given the other eye, but treated it more like a dose of cascara.

The Arab host is obliged to continue to eat until his guest of honour announces that he is replete, and it is rude for anyone else to stop eating before this. I was just thinking that one more herbal cake might be disastrous when the Political Resident decided that honour was satisfied. We rose and adjourned to the anteroom where the ceremony of the rosewater, coffee and incense was repeated. On its conclusion, Sir Rupert thanked the Sheikh formally in Arabic and we took our departure.

Soon after that visit to Abu Dhabi, *Wren* went to Ceylon (now Sri Lanka) for a short refit and to have her bottom scraped – essential from time to time in tropical waters. All the ship's company were given ten days' local leave at the services rest camp at Diyatalawa in the central highlands. We were free to sleep, walk, swim or play golf or tennis. The only drawback was the presence of countless leeches in the lush grass. It was a mistake to stand still for more than a few seconds. Their speed and penetrative powers amazed me. If one attached itself to you, the only remedy was to hold a lighted match or cigarette against the repulsive creature to induce it to withdraw its head and drop to the ground. If pulled off, the head was left behind and the wound could become dangerously septic.

I played one game of rugby at Diyatalawa. Nobody stayed prostrate on the ground for more than a second or two as we had seen the speed with which the leeches looped along the ground. This resulted in a game of fast movement and few interruptions. Perhaps leeches could be introduced to improve the standard of the game in some British clubs and to reduce the number of penalties! My first attempt to climb one of the nearer mountains was defeated by these creatures. My legs were covered with them and I ran out of matches, so I had to turn back.

I took a fascinating bus journey, with a wall of rock on one side and a vertical drop on the other for much of the way, to reach Nuwara Eliya from where I had decided to climb Pedrotallagalla. At 8,395 feet, it is the highest point in Sri Lanka. We drove between great hills covered with a dense tropical jungle, thinning to cypress forest near the tops. In the valleys were villages of white plaster cottages and bungalows roofed with red tiles. Above them rose brilliant green cultivated terraces. Being early spring, the rice was half-grown and had not begun to ripen. Tea plantations occupied some of the higher slopes. As we reached Nuwara Eliya, we ran into cloud which prevented me from getting any view when I reached the top of the mountain after a five-mile climb. It was a disappointing outcome. We drove back to Diyatalawa that evening through heavy rain.

When *Wren* returned to the Persian Gulf, it was the season of the south-west monsoon. We wallowed across the Arabian Sea in a huge swell to visit the island of Masira, taking with us two officers of the RAF regiment who commanded the Arab levies there. The island is over forty miles long, sandy, with a spinal rock outcrop running most of its length. When we anchored off the sandy spit at the west end, some of the inhabitants made a special journey in their primitive boats to have a look at us. Our Somali Tindal spoke to them and told me we were the first white men they had ever seen.

In 1948 there was a phenomenal population of turtles there. Some of our sailors went ashore to capture a few. They made good eating, with flesh like rump steak between the veal and beef stage. Their eggs are also delicious. They are soft-skinned and spherical, about the size of a bantam's egg. They have a faintly nutty or cheesy flavour and are particularly good scrambled or as an omelette. We saw countless turtles in the water, one of which must have measured four feet by three. It was floating lazily five yards from the ship's side as we came to anchor.

In the spring of 1949 the ship went to Malta for a full refit – a visit which resulted in a major change of direction in my life. Malta was still the base of the British Mediterranean fleet – a sizeable force comprising aircraft carriers, cruisers, destroyers and many smaller ships. The island then had naval dockyards with all the facilities of a long-established naval port, having been in British occupation for nearly 150 years. I had spent several months there as a toddler in the late 1920s when my father was based there. My main memory is of an encounter with a two-foot cube of ice which was delivered by a man with a sack on his back. Curious, I tried sitting on it and was amazed by the feeling through my rompers!

Very shortly after our arrival in *Wren*, I read an Admiralty Fleet Order from which I learned that preliminary interpretership examinations in a number of languages – including Russian – were about to be held in the Naval Education Centre. With my captain's permission, I entered my name and for the next three or four weeks, while the ship was in dock, I spent many off-duty hours going through my Russian notebooks and vocabulary.

I still found time to take exercise and remember with satis-faction a rugby match when the Royal Navy (Mediterranean and Middle East) surprised everybody by beating the equivalent and reputedly much stronger army team by one try to nothing. Both teams had already beaten the RAF. The try was particularly gratifying because it was against the run of the play. For the whole of the game we defended desperately. I was playing centre three-quarter and do not recall any game when I have had to do more tackling. Then, suddenly, there was the ball bouncing about in front of me. I grabbed it. There was only one man to beat. I drew him, passed, and my wing three-quarter had a clear run of thirty yards to the line. There was laughter on the touchline when I ran beside him shouting, 'On your left, on your left,' hoping that he would pass back to me and I could score the try.

Two days later, I sat the preliminary interpretership exam. Weeks passed and we were back in the Gulf before I learned by signal that I had just scraped through. This qualified me for a long course which sounded too good to be true – a year at Cambridge and six months in Paris. I could hardly wait, but I still had four summer months to pass in that salty cauldron between Arabia and Iran.

By Whaler Across the Persian Gulf

After being accepted for the Russian course, I felt much more cheerful. There were still long hours of watch-keeping on the bridge at sea when little happened to disturb the smooth progress of the ship through the glassy calm of Gulf waters, and times when it was too hot to do anything, but I had an idea which I thought would break the monotony – at least for a day or two. I asked the captain if I could take one of the ship's boats under sail across the Gulf. He agreed, provided I could raise a volunteer crew and put in a written report. The purpose was to find out what it was like living in an open boat in an extremely hot climate.

The ship's whaler was a twenty-seven-foot open boat equipped with oars and three sails: a mainsail, foresail and mizzen. A Petty Officer Telegraphist, a Leading Seaman and three junior ratings volunteered for the crew. We worked out carefully the stores and equipment which we would require: two gallon casks of water, food for three days, medical supplies, a small quantity of rum and brandy, Lanchester revolvers and ammunition, fishing tackle, signalling gear including a walkie-talkie radio set and basic navigational equipment.

We sailed from the island of Jezirat-tunb one cloudless evening. A westerly breeze, sufficient to extend the ensign lashed to the mizzen mast, and a following swell, enabled us to make good progress at the outset. When it became dark, I checked both the compasses by the bearing of the Pole Star. We felt very much alone as *Wren* weighed anchor and disappeared over the horizon bound for Khorfakhan. The moon was in its first quarter, high in the sky. The thermometer gave us a reading of 93.5°F with a sea temperature of 89°F.

The crew was very quiet for the first couple of hours. Perhaps they were regretting trusting themselves to my navigation. We had bread and cheese for supper. At 9.15 p.m. a tanker passed to the south. I called her up with our Aldis lamp and she replied,

'*British Promise* from Abu Dhabi to Abadan. Who are you?' I replied, 'Whaler from *Wren* bound for Khor Kuwei.' The Officer of the Watch may have wondered what we were doing looking for whales in waters more suitable to sharks and sea snakes.

We worked three watches and I gave everyone a turn at the helm. Those not on duty attempted to sleep. One man, who was of less than average height, lay athwart-ships across the water barrels. The rest of us made use of an uncomfortable platform above the thwarts constructed of oars and lifebelts. For some hours we made good progress, running before a light breeze, but shortly after midnight the wind dropped.

By the time the sun, egg-shaped by refraction, peered over the roll of moisture haze which concealed the eastern horizon we were completely becalmed. In the two hours that followed, three tankers passed us, steering west. None of them replied to our signals, although the last (an American vessel) passed so close that her wash set us pitching violently.

We ate our breakfast of fresh lime, baked beans, bread, butter and marmalade in breathless calm and mounting heat. The four-hourly issue of one-and-a-half pints of water per man was made from the extra supply in the rum jars. This water tasted excellent while it lasted, but when we came to draw on the barrels, it was strongly flavoured with tar despite our having vigorously cleaned the barrels before we set sail. We were thankful for a large tin of lime powder we had brought.

For the remainder of the forenoon the boat scarcely moved. The sails hung in lifeless folds. I thought of the captain's parting instructions, 'For God's sake, don't shoot an albatross!' At noon the temperature was 127°F in the sun and 96° in the shade – this was in the bilges, where there was only room for two at a time. We envied the schools of porpoises we encountered. One friendly creature used our keel to scratch its back.

Nobody was able to do justice to the first course of our mid-day meal – corned beef and tinned peas – but the dessert of tinned pears with tinned milk was well received. Salt pills were issued with the water ration. Everyone was sweating continuously – a healthy sign. Only the youngest member of the crew let depression get the better of him. He refused to eat and had to be given extra water. He then lay down on the bottom boards under an awning improvised from a spare sail and slept with his mouth open, breathing noisily. The sea stretched unbroken and oily in every direction to the hazy horizon, which was too indistinct to enable me to make use of the sextant.

Three of us played a desultory game of cards in the early afternoon, but abandoned it in favour of wetting towels in the sea and wringing them out over our heads. The surface had a veneer of sandy scum and numerous yellow water snakes, basking in the heat, drifted by. The youngest sailor woke and repeatedly saw sharks, but only one sighting was confirmed by another member of the crew.

Our luck changed at about 3 p.m. when a light southerly breeze sprang up and increased to about five knots by four o'clock. I altered course two points to compensate for suspected drift and we once again began to make good progress. Just before sunset, I picked out the faint skyline of the mountains on the Musandam Peninsula, some of which reach nearly 7,000 feet. We were now out of the tanker lanes and saw no more ships.

Supper was a much more cheerful meal. Rum or brandy was issued with the water ration. The menu was tinned salmon and beetroot, tomato juice, bread, butter and marmalade. When the Leading Seaman came to light the lamp, it was found that the candles had melted in the midday heat. We recovered the wicks and manufactured replacements with the congealed wax. To our disappointment the wind died away again at midnight. To pass the time and maintain morale, I split the crew into two watches for the night and we each took turns at the oars. The moon set at about 3.30 a.m. but as the sky began to lighten, high land became visible perhaps six miles to the north. I altered course again towards what I took to be the tip of the Musandam Peninsula.

Twenty minutes before sunrise, when I was at the tiller and just as the reliefs for the oarsmen were rousing themselves, a squall from landward suddenly struck the boat. The whaler leaped ahead. The two seamen on the oars simultaneously caught crabs and fell backwards into the bilges. By the time the crew had awoken to the situation, the port gunwale was nearly under water. Somehow the pair in the bottom of the boat disentangled themselves and their oars and scrambled with the rest of us to the weather side. With the whaler close-hauled, two men on the mainsheet, all six of us perched on the starboard gunwhale leaning backwards and only a couple of inches of freeboard to port, we enjoyed half an hour of exhilarating sailing. To crown it all, the sun was rising gloriously beyond the ridge of mountains. The sky changed rapidly from palest aquamarine to lemon, from lemon to pink streaked with ribbons of dark cloud and finally to the dull hazy blue of full daylight.

The island east of the anchorage of Khor Kuwei, our destination, was now plainly visible. I fixed our position four and a half miles south-west of its southern point. When the wind lost its exuberance we settled to our usual breakfast. A quarter of an hour later another powerful gust hit us. The gear in the bottom of the boat lay in tumbled chaos, bespattered with baked beans, tomato and butter. Every time we drew opposite an indentation on the coast, or cleft in the hills, another gusty squall struck us but by 6.30 a.m. the wind backed and resolved itself into a steady ten-knot breeze from the east. We enjoyed an hour and a half of steady progress, running before the wind.

Soon after eight o'clock, we rounded the northern cliffs of Al Chanam Island and, spurning the tide rips, sailed into the Khor in grand style.

To my surprise *Wren* had not yet arrived. Her programme had been slightly amended since we left her. I took the whaler alongside the jetty and made fast. Soon we were surrounded by the friends and relatives of the Arab caretaker who, far from offering us hospitality, tried to purloin our remaining stores and equipment. I produced my revolver and laid it on the thwart beside me.

When *Wren* steamed into the Khor shortly before noon I signalled to her, 'We were about to go and look for you.' Half an hour later we were back on board, disposing of the sweat, grime and growth of forty hours' absence.

I finally left the Gulf in an oil tanker, which sailed from Abadan bound for Plymouth. At first the captain refused to take me. I offered to keep watches as a deck officer throughout the voyage. I offered to sleep on a camp bed in a passageway to avoid inconveniencing anybody. Eventually, with a very ill grace, he relented and allowed me on board. We sailed down the Shat al Arab in appalling heat. Two Lascar stokers died of heat stroke on board even before the ship sailed. Not until we were halfway through the Mediterranean did the captain tell me why he had had refused at first to take me on passage. As a reserve officer during the war he had a few clashes with Royal Navy officers and had vowed never to have anything more to do with them. By the time we reached Plymouth we were on good terms and I had gained some useful experience of watch-keeping on a big merchant ship.

Cambridge, Paris and Norway

Cambridge was a paradise after nine years of naval discipline. In the social league of Cambridge colleges, Downing was not in the top ten but I loved its spaciousness, the clean neoclassical lines of the buildings, the sweeping lawns and the freedom from routine. I had a big, plain room looking across one of the lawns towards a symmetrical building in the same classical style, with church spires beyond it. For the first time in my life I had plenty of space to put my belongings, to work and to entertain friends.

There were nine naval officers on the Russian course – of whom I was the youngest – and half a dozen members of the Foreign Service, all graduates. My closest friend was Ted Sladen, a Lieutenant Commander Fleet Air Arm pilot.

Enthusiastic as most freshmen, I joined half a dozen clubs – rugby, athletics, piping, the Caledonian Reel and Strathspey Club, the Liberal Society and the Slavonic Club. Also like most freshmen, under pressure of work, I dropped them one by one, although I was in the college athletics team and took part in the inter-college competition, which we won.

Our schedule was hard. We were expected to sit the first part of the Modern Languages tripos in Russian in one year instead of the usual two. Although we started by attending every lecture in Russian language, history and literature, by the end of the first term I had dropped all but the essential three or four and was mostly reading and studying in my own room. Professor Elizavita Hill, Head of the Slavonic Faculty, attached more importance to vocabulary than to grammar. Every week we were expected to learn at least forty new words. There were essays to be written, Pushkin, Tolstoy, Chekhov and Dostoyevsky to be read, Russian history to be studied and special classes in Russian naval terminology which had been organised for us.

Alison, the daughter of friends of my parents, was reading French and German at the same time and we soon began to spend a lot of time together – for a meal, to play tennis, to see some foreign-language film. Sometimes she spent hours in my room reading her texts while I studied Russian. The rules were strict and all female guests had to be clear of the college by 10 p.m. The rules of Girton, where Alison had rooms, were even stricter, but we somehow found ways of avoiding the normal entry or exit gates. When the summer came we went punting on the Cam, lay reading in the long grass and partnered one another at three May Balls. At one, the annual ball of the Strathspey and Reel Club, I introduced my sister Julia to Ian Cumming, a Scot at Magdelene College studying engineering. Two years later they were married. Alison and I talked of marriage, too, and even became unofficially engaged. Superficially we had much in common, but there was no firm basis for a lifetime relationship. I was still very uncertain about my future. After graduating, she went to Germany and eventually to the USA. We never met again.

In Paris I lived with a Georgian family of princesses recommended to me by a fellow student at Cambridge. The Dadianis lived in Rue Constant Coquelin, a cul-de-sac off the Boulevard des Invalides. Eka Dadiani, who was dark, serious and aquiline of feature, was the head of the household. She was in her forties and worked on the permanent staff of the Paris Motor Show. Russik, a younger sister in her thirties, was tall, blonde, slim and elegant, with an infectious smile. I never found out where she worked. She was continually courted by a succession of impressive suitors. Otar and Tamara were the children of another sister who had died. Born and bred in Paris, they had French citizenship and Otar, who was in his final year at school, was aiming at the French Foreign Service. Tamara was about fourteen, very intelligent and self-possessed. Eka and Russik had another older sister who had opted to stay in her native country and a brother, who appeared from time to time. He spoke eleven languages fluently and had been a colonel in the Free French Forces during the war, serving on the staff of General Leclerc.

Altogether, they were an impressive family, vibrant with intelligence and vitality. The only problem from my point of view was that they did not speak Russian very much. Among themselves they spoke French; the sisters occasionally spoke Georgian to one another, though they did try to remember to change to Russian with me. However, I soon decided that the attractions of living with them far outweighed the lack of Russian conversation. I arranged to take lessons elsewhere – twice a week with the charming Madame Bibikova, and twice a week with a man who was a fanatical member of an émigré group dedicated to over-throwing the Soviet government. He had served in the Tsarist Navy and was therefore an excellent source of nautical terminology. Towards the end of every lesson he would produce his maps and point out vast areas of the Soviet Union which he claimed were controlled by dissident groups.

With Madame Bibikova I developed a system which did more to improve my Russian than anything else I did in Paris or at Cambridge. She would read aloud from the Russian classics (Pushkin, Tolstoy, Chekhov) or from a technical English piece I gave her, and I would write down a translation in English or Russian as appropriate. After half an hour of this, we would go through what I had written and correct it. I would note all the words I had not known and spend an hour learning vocabulary each night.

On the strength of my membership of London Scottish Rugby Football Club, I was able to join Stade Française. They did not have room for me in the three-quarter line, but gave me a spot as flanker. I found the French team's desire to win at any cost, regardless of the rules, difficult to understand. On one occasion, after the opposing scrum-half had scored a try, I was publicly reprimanded by my captain for not tripping him up as he came round the scrum.

That season, Scotland played France in Paris. In the evening I went with a group of my fellow countrymen to a nightspot on the Left Bank. There was a floor show, mostly pretty girls, but in the middle of the act, a large and swarthy man appeared in the centre of the floor wearing a parody of a kilt reaching just below his crotch, a feather duster for a sporran, black silk stockings rolled down to just above his knees and a white satin blouse with lots of ruffles. He started to perform a burlesque of a Highland Fling. We watched in silence for a few minutes, but suddenly I could endure it no longer. I got to my feet, walked slowly to where he was performing, and tipped my full glass of red wine over his head. I waited to see what would happen. Wine was dripping from his chin and ears, all over the blouse and on to the floor. He took a deep breath and a stream of what I took to be foul language was directed at me. I had no repertoire of French swearwords. The best I could muster was, *'Vous êtes un sale poulet jaune,'* which I hoped meant he was a dirty yellow chicken. I turned my back on him and returned to our table, knowing my friends would warn me if he came at me from behind. Instead he disappeared back to his dressing room. We danced with some of the girls, still wearing their show costumes, and invited four of them back to our table. It seemed that the buffoon was a bully, greatly disliked by staff and artistes alike. The waiter even brought us a bottle of wine, on the house.

I saw one small incident which seemed to me to typify the attitude of many Parisians. Travelling on a very overcrowded tram, strap-hanging with my left hand and holding a case full of books in the other, I watched as a young woman got on, carrying a child on one arm and a full shopping bag in the other hand. No one offered her a seat. The tram rattled on with the young woman struggling to keep her balance. From time to time the baby's foot brushed the ear of a young man sitting reading a newspaper. First he glared, then made some ill-natured remark. Surely, I thought, he will give up his seat. Instead, without any change in his bad-tempered expression, he folded his newspaper, placed it across his knees, and took the child from its mother and sat it, held at arms' length, on the newspaper. I was astonished by this solution but both the adults involved seemed to be satisfied by it.

During my stay in Paris, Julia came to work as an au pair with a wealthy family some miles out of the city. It was not a success. The family exploited her and she rarely had any spare time. She cut short her time with them, but before she left we organised a party to ski in Val D'Isère. The party grew until there were about eighteen of us, all friends of my two sisters or myself. At this time Pen was coming to terms with the death of her husband, whom she had married while I was in the Persian Gulf. Heartbroken, she had stayed on in South Africa for nearly two years. She loved the country but hated its political system. Late in 1950 she returned home and this was the first time I had seen her since early in 1947.

It was an exhilarating holiday; the weather and the skiing were both superb. Our large party, evenly balanced between the sexes, made its own entertainment. There was some pairing off, but the atmosphere was more like that of a large family and nobody was left out. I remember particularly one day when a friend and I took the chairlift for a walk and found ourselves invited into an open-air family wedding party.

I returned to Paris revitalised for three final weeks of intensive study before the Civil Service Commissioners' interpreter examinations, which took place in London in May. I was awarded a second-class certificate, a clear recognition that while I could read, write and understand the language reasonably well, to a native Russian speaker I would be recognisable as a foreigner. Almost immediately, I was called to the Admiralty, where I was informed that I would be going as Assistant Naval Attaché to the British Embassy in Moscow in the summer of 1952. My excitement at this news was qualified by the knowledge that I would be spending the intervening year as a Boys' Training Officer in a squadron of frigates based at Rosyth to 'make sure I had not forgotten my skills as a naval officer'.

The frigate I joined carried out eight-week sea-training courses for Boy Seamen. We sailed up the east coast of Scotland, through the Pentland Firth and down through the Minches, all the time carrying out seamanship, signalling and 'damage control' exercises whatever the weather. I have a lasting memory of lecturing to groups of sickly white faces as the ship rolled its way through the notorious Pentland Firth. From time to time a boy would bolt to the leeward guardrails to puke over the ship's side.

Although the frigate fulfilled her function efficiently, the wardroom was the unhappiest I ever experienced. The Captain lived a life aloof from the wardroom, where the key figure was the First Lieutenant, a man who possessed all the qualities I dislike most. He was crude, self-centred, ruthless, less than honest – and only moderately competent. His defects of character were magnified because he was in the last stages of the 'promotion zone' – the six years between being promoted Lieutenant-

Commander and knowing he had no chance of going any further. I found myself the object of professional jealousy. Although I was only a junior lieutenant, my track record was good and somewhat unusual. Following the royal cruise to South Africa and a private investiture at Buckingham Palace, I wore the ribbon of the MVO on my uniform. This was like a red rag to a bull. He bellowed at me through a megaphone from the bridge. He reprimanded me in front of junior ratings. When I was picked for a Royal Navy rugby trial, he would not give me leave to play. He spoke openly in a sexual way about a girl he was involved with, the daughter of a prominent landowning family. She was a nice girl, much younger than him – and very wealthy. He speculated about how much she was worth and once suggested to me sarcastically that I might like to 'take her over'. I was the only Scot among the officers and I had to listen to his continuous flow of criticism of Scotland and the Scots – the climate, the accents, the customs and, of course, the kilt.

On one occasion we were taking part in NATO exercises in the company of a number of other small ships of the NATO Navies. I was Officer of the Watch and we were using a new American signal book, with which we were unfamiliar. When a certain signal was received by R/T – which would have to be executed within minutes – we had difficulty in interpreting the American jargon. The First Lieutenant and I disagreed on the correct interpretation. There was little time to spare. The Petty Officer Yeoman of Signals agreed with my interpretation and when the order was received, I acted accordingly. When the First Lieutenant realised that I had been right, he gave me a furious look and hissed, 'Get back to your croft, Davidson,' before stumping off the bridge.

In the spring of 1952, our ship was detached from normal duties to take the Prime Minister, Clement Attlee, on an official visit to Norway. On the first evening at sea, the captain brought Mr Attlee down to the wardroom. He seemed to me to be very amiable and relaxed, and interested in the ship itself.

Among those present was a Paymaster Lieutenant with very right-wing views on hanging, immigration, strikes and taxation. Ignoring the conventions of hospitality he questioned Mr Attlee aggressively in a way that would never be permitted by the Speaker in the House of Commons. The Prime Minister parried the questions adroitly and with good humour, refusing to get involved in argument. By convention, politics were not discussed in an officers' mess. After Mr Attlee had retired (with dignity) I asked the paymaster lieutenant whether he would have followed the same line of questioning if Mr Attlee had been a naval Captain during the war rather than a Colonel. A dirty look was his only reply. The Prime Minister did not visit the wardroom again.

During Mr Attlee's official business in Oslo, the ship cruised up the west coast of Norway. While we were anchored off one village, the Captain lightheartedly suggested that I might like to entertain the villagers by playing my bagpipes on a rock which projected some ten feet above water, about 200 yards from the shore. I agreed and was deposited there by the ship's motorboat. As I played, a small crowd collected on the beach. They even clapped when I paused for breath between groups of tunes. I was not a good piper, but distance and atmosphere lent merit to my performance. After an hour I became tired and cold and my audience began to drift away. I waved in the direction of the ship and somebody waved back. I could see the boat secured to the boom, but there was no sign of the crew manning her to come and collect me. The arrangement had been that they would come for me when I stopped playing. Nearly three hours passed before the boat drew alongside. 'Why the hell didn't you come sooner?' I asked the coxswain. 'First Lieutenant's orders, sir,' said the Leading Seaman, looking embarrassed. For once I felt justified in saying what I thought of the First Lieutenant in front of the boat's crew. I got the impression that they agreed with me.

Official notice of my appointment as Assistant Naval Attaché in Moscow reached me in April. The ship was alongside a jetty at Rosyth, disembarking a draft of boy seamen who had just completed their initial sea training. They were not the only ones who left that frigate without regret.

*James's grandparents with family, Nairn, 1908;
his father in Naval Cadet's uniform*

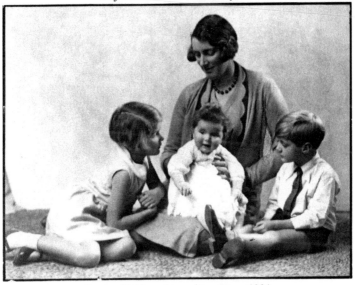

James with his mother and two sisters, 1931

September 1940 - newly selected Naval Cadet
Photograph courtesy of Gilbert Bowley

*Inspection of Royal Naval College,
Dartmouth by King Haakon of Norway, 1941*

Battleship HMS *Anson in the North Atlantic, May 1944*

Climbing in Skye, 1946

The Royal Family on HMS Vanguard, 1947, with the gunroom officers (Sub-Lieutenants and Midshipmen). James seated next to HRH Princess Elizabeth - the future Queen

At the Mittillegi Hut en route to the peak of the Eiger, 1947

HMS *Wren at Muscat, 1948*

The Kremlin, Moscow, from the roof of the British Embassy, 1952

The British Ambassador, Sir William Hayter, with his diplomatic staff, presents his credentials to the Soviet Ministry of Foreign Affairs, 1953 (James fourth from left)

*HMS St Kitts off the coast of Southern France –
Navigating Officer Lieutenant J D G Davidson, 1954–55*

The farm of Tillychetly with Bennachie in the background

Adoption of Parliamentary Candidate, 1966.
From left to right, James's mother, sister and father

Tillychetly after a heavy snowfall

JAMES DAVIDSON
For
West Aberdeenshire

Election leaflet, 1966

Sandy, Ros and Polly on a caravan holiday, 1967

Press cutting from the Aberdeen Evening Express, 1969 - closure of Inverurie Railway Works. Photograph courtesy of the Evening Express

James (left). Visit to House of Commons by Afghani delegation, 1967

Wedding day picture of James and Janet, 1973

Chief Executive of the Royal Highland and Agricultural
Society of Scotland, 1970–1992

H M the Queen visits the Royal Highland Show - James (far right) jokes with the Lady-in-Waiting

Grampian Television 1977 report – Presenter of Country Focus, *James with Rob Riach, tractorman at Tillychetly*

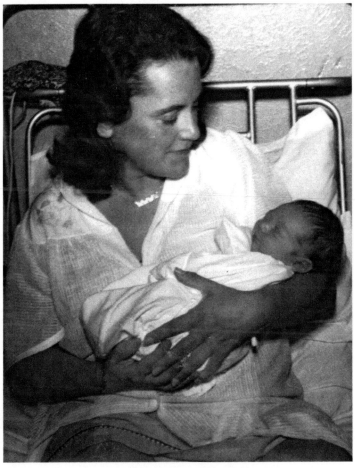

Janet with newborn Calum, 1978

*Stuart Jeffray, David Sole, Lorna Smith, a volunteer university student,
and James (right) - the parachute team which raised over £10,000 for the
Flower of Scotland Campaign, 1993*

Earthwatch project - river otters of Chile - 2001

James in his seventies with Sheila

James conducting a Canadian group on a walking tour, 2003

Lochindorb Treasure Hunt with younger grandson, Max, 2006
(granddaughter Didi looking into the boat!)

Trustees celebrate a reprieve for the Wildcat Centre, 2006

James in his eighties with Cymbal

By Ship to Leningrad

On 2 May 1952, I boarded the SS *Beloostrov* in London docks. The Cold War was at its coldest. Soviet propaganda against Britain, America and the West was nonstop and uncompromising. I knew that westerners in Russia were followed everywhere; travel there was very restricted and KGB agents tried to frame foreigners whenever possible.

SS *Beloostrov* plied regularly between London and Leningrad, calling at Helsinki and Stockholm, and was well known to generations of diplomats. My cabin on the upper deck was small but comfortable with a well-sprung bunk and a basin with hot water. It was scrupulously clean, freshly painted, and furnished in mahogany.

Supper was served when we were still in the Thames Estuary. It consisted of borshch, veal, spaghetti and a salad, then a strange fruit salad of prunes and orange with a strong flavour of tar. The Russians call this *kompot* and I got used to it over the ensuing two years. *Kompot* or ice cream were the usual desserts at Russian meals. The menu in the ship's restaurant rarely changed, but the décor did – sometimes for reasons beyond our understanding. For instance, at this first meal, a huge portrait of Stalin covered one bulkhead. By the time of our second meal, it had disappeared.

Breakfast the next morning consisted of boiled eggs, slices of ham, sausage, salami and bread with butter and caviar. The butter was unsalted and almost white, the caviar the cheaper red variety derived from salmon not sturgeon.

We crossed the North Sea in a flat calm and reached the end of the Kiel Canal about twelve hours after leaving London. It took the ship nearly nine hours to get through the canal, but it was a pleasant way to spend a day. Nearly all of the eighty-three passengers stayed on deck enjoying the hot sunshine and the placid German countryside. Along the whole fifty-five miles of the canal we saw rich pastureland, well wooded and dotted with red-roofed farmhouses, vivid against the bright spring green of the trees and fields. Soon after entering the Baltic, the sky became overcast and the Swedish and Finnish girls in their swimsuits quit the boat deck.

Among the other passengers were Sid Harper and his family. A Flight-Lieutenant, he was going out as second Assistant Air Attaché. I became Uncle James to four-year-old John Harper and retained this honorary rank for the next two years. The Harpers were a delightfully normal family who did much to maintain the balance in an embassy where personnel varied from the brilliant academic with feet that never touched the ground to the security guard whose mind never rose above his navel, and from the diplomat's wife whose sole ambition was to socialise with other wives of more senior diplomatic rank, to the typist who would have been happier in the office of a local branch of Woolworths. Sid Harper and I had plenty of opportunities to practise our Russian on the *Beloostrov*, including a long argument with the ship's purser about having to pay cash for our excess baggage, which practically cleaned both of us out of sterling.

John Harper found the Russian children on board – who were mostly pale, fair-haired, quiet little people – somewhat mystifying because they did not understand him and would not play with him. When two Russian boys older than himself laughed at him, he attacked them with a wooden hammer from his building set and had to be pulled away. I was approached by one or two of the Russian passengers who were mostly diplomats returning home. I felt I had to be wary about what I said to them.

As we reached the entrance to Stockholm Fjord at about 7 a.m. on 6 May, a queue of impassive Russians formed at a table in the smoking room. We had to wait while the Swedish passport official took them through the slow progress of being granted temporary visas. British, Commonwealth and Finnish subjects had no need of visas.

I went with two or three others to look round the centre of Stockholm. I was surprised at how very different the city looked from Oslo and its clean white buildings. Stockholm was red and grey and dun-coloured. In anticipation of months of Russian food, we treated ourselves to a meal in the Operakellaren –

smorgasbord followed by beautiful steaks, schnapps and pilsner.

We were only alongside for an hour at Helsinki, with no opportunity to go ashore, but I was very impressed by the beautiful natural harbour. It is entered by a narrow cleft between two rocky fortified islands. Within there is a great expanse of water, enhanced by two inhabited islands.

I was up at dawn the following day to miss nothing as we entered Leningrad harbour: the ships at anchor, the Sudomekh ship-building yards, the docks and jetties. We had seen the shining gold dome of the St Isaac Cathedral from miles out to sea, but the approaches to the city were not inspiring. Leningrad, now again St Petersburg, was like a woman who had once been beautiful, but whose health had been broken by some addiction. The fine outline and bone were still there, but the closer one looked, the more dilapidated and unkempt were the exterior details – buildings discoloured, with plaster falling off shoddy brickwork. Away from the centre, the roads were full of potholes and flanked by ramshackle wooden houses.

I was met on the dock by Captain Roy Talbot and the man I was replacing, Lieutenant Commander Mark Alford. I had carried on a long correspondence with the latter, who had sent me pages and pages of advice and instruction on what was required and how it should be done. He was small, exuberant and sociable, a nonstop and extremely well-informed conversationalist overflowing with self-confidence, but he was also fantastically untidy and unmethodical. I had a week in which to take over from him. By the end of it I was in a state of confusion coupled with mental and physical fatigue. Captain Talbot, the Naval Attaché, was a deceptively simple man with a sublime sense of humour, which he deployed with supreme skill. It ranged from quoting purple passages culled from cheap novels to mimicry and to the shrewdest irony. He could also act. I never saw him lose his temper, but when he pretended to, the victim was prostrated. Despite this gift, he could be serious and was always humane. I could not have asked for a better superior. His wife was sophisticated and elegant, with a quiet humour of her own. The pair of them were immensely hospitable to me and to many younger members of the British and other western embassies. With kindly perception, they appreciated the pressures we were under, caught in the crosscurrents of a highly artificial social life and the pervasive hostility of the host country.

After a quick tour around the centre of the city I was taken to the Astoria Hotel, the only permitted Intourist accommodation in the city, a place redolent of early Victorian luxury. The dining room was a vast hall with an orchestra playing at one end and a small dance floor in the centre.

During my short tour of Leningrad I had noticed women doing heavy manual labour everywhere. It was not unusual to see them digging holes in the road or swinging great hammers with a male overseer looking on. At least half the men were in uniform of one sort or another, though the material was of poor quality. The women who were not breaking up concrete were adequately dressed, though extremely drab. The Russians did not seem to be the cheerful people portrayed in the Soviet films I had seen. Their faces tended to be gloomier than those of commuters on the London Underground on a Monday morning.

The train left Leningrad at midnight. We travelled in 'soft' compartments, rather like old-fashioned first class on a British train, with twin berths. I woke early in the morning and for some hours watched the landscape go by – for mile upon mile a monotonous vista of birch scrub occasionally relieved by more distant glimpses of pine forests beyond the unenclosed fields, and sometimes a wooden farmstead or tumbledown village.

The outskirts of Moscow were depressing, though no more so than the fringes of many western cities. The ramshackle wooden houses looked uncared for; the few skyscrapers and imposing buildings seemed out of place. Typical was an area of waste ground dotted with dilapidated wooden houses and dreary, badly finished blocks of tenements, in the midst of which loomed an enormous statue of a pair of well-developed young workers, striving towards a glorious future.

Stalin's Moscow

The British Embassy was, and as far as I know still is, the palatial pre-revolutionary mansion of a business tycoon, facing north across the Moskva River towards the high red walls and variegated onion-shaped cupolas of the Kremlin. By standing on the Embassy roof I was able to take a photograph of the Union Jack fluttering over the Kremlin. Except for the Ambassador's living quarters, the whole building was used for offices. Its dark woodwork, thick carpets, high ceilings, public school accents and occasional colourful uniforms combined to produce an atmosphere that was at the same time impressive and old-fashioned.

The Naval Attaché's office was at the rear, on the ground floor, overlooking the garden and tennis court. We never spoke indoors on confidential matters, though some of the diplomats were careless in this respect. We suspected that even the Embassy garden was vulnerable to microphones and powerful directional receivers.

In my early days in Moscow, I lived in a dacha in Perlovka forest, originally built for Metro Vickers' employees when they were constructing the Moscow underground railway. I shared the middle floor of the three-storey building with Squadron Leader Peter Knapton, the senior Assistant Air Attaché. It made a pleasant flat, with two bedrooms, bathroom, kitchen, sitting room and dining room. Two of the Embassy typists lived on the lower floor, while the third floor was unoccupied.

I found life at the dacha positively luxurious. We had a Russian cook and a maid, allocated by Burobin, the Soviet staff agency. The food was excellently cooked. Unlimited meat, butter, eggs, cream and cheese could be bought on the open market – at a price. The official exchange rate was then eleven roubles to the pound, but the British government gave us forty roubles to the pound to enable us to shop locally. The Americans bought almost everything at their PX store and therefore seldom met or talked with ordinary Russians.

The only place where ordinary workers could afford to buy goods was in a state shop, where they first had to wait in long queues to purchase vouchers, then join another queue to exchange them for goods at a subsidised price. A housewife seeking a scarce commodity had to get there on the day when it reached the shop and then hope that it would not be sold out before she reached the head of the queue. There was no competition between shops because they were all state-owned. They simply had the equivalent of butcher, baker or general store, with an identity number, written large outside. The privileged, such as Communist Party officials, officers, ballet dancers or foreign diplomats, could shop in the open markets where there were unlimited quantities of certain goods at very high prices. It took seventy or eighty roubles to equal the purchasing power of a pound at home.

Except within the Embassy, the dacha, or the homes of other western diplomats, there was no respite from the intense suspicion, the unrelenting anti-western propaganda and the sickening, all-pervading glorification of Stalin and Lenin. Newspapers, hoardings and banners proclaimed their names; songs and speeches blared nonstop from the public address systems in every shop, station and public place. On the Moskva Canal, where the Volga enters the Moscow Sea, there were vast granite statues of Lenin and Stalin on either bank. They stood in traditional fashion, one hand raised in paternal benediction – or they could have been slinging mud at each other across the water.

I talked to Russians whenever I could – to taxi drivers, people in trains, men building houses in Perlovka, a woman lifting potatoes, two students practising the use of theodolites. Aloysha, my Russian chauffeur, gave me unstructured lessons in colloquial Russian on my way to and from the Embassy. The Navy provided me with a Ford Pilot car and it took us half an hour to drive into the Embassy each morning. The authorities put every sort of obstacle in the way of foreigners driving themselves.

I developed a reasonable relationship with Aloysha and Pasha, our maid. My impression was that the younger the person, the greater the barrier caused by fear and suspicion of foreigners. They had spent a greater proportion of their lives under the regime. At the time of my arrival in Moscow, the cinemas were showing an American Tarzan film. It was hugely popular and children went around splitting the air with the Tarzan cry. Pasha told me, 'All the girls in Moscow dream about Tarzan.' All trace of its American origins had been removed and the film was dubbed in Russian.

Lunching with friends at their apartment, we were given duck as the main course. I asked their cook, an old woman who must have seen many changes in her time, where it came from. She replied that it was an Estonian duck. I wondered why ducks were imported from Estonia when there were plenty round Moscow. Her ironic reply echoed the all-pervasive propaganda. 'I suppose because the ducks near Moscow are all peaceful, free ducks.'

Some things about Moscow surprised me. The trains were terribly slow, rarely travelling at more than thirty miles per hour but they were always on time. Waiters, taxi drivers, barbers and porters all expected tips, or accepted them willingly, although they were a breach of the Communist code. Ice cream was on sale everywhere, even in midwinter. It was good, cheap and consumed in vast quantities by adults and children alike.

There was no doubt that the standard of living had begun to rise rapidly. A lot of domestic construction was going on, but there was still far to go to equal the western standard of living. The city was alive with police and MVD (Ministerstvo Vnutrennix Dyel – Ministry of Internal Affairs) troops. There was no unemployment because thousands were employed where hundreds would have sufficed, yet I saw more beggars and drunks in my first two weeks in Moscow than I would have seen in two years in a city at home.

We were only allowed to visit a few places in the vicinity of Moscow: Zagorsk, with its cathedral converted into a museum, containing priceless mediaeval treasures; Yasnaya Polyana, Tolstoy's home; and Klin, the village where Tchaikovsky lived for a large part of his life. I went to Klin with Peter Knapton, an Australian girl and Barbara, the only member of the American Embassy staff younger than myself. She was tall, glamorous and blonde. She came from California and had an arts degree and a perfect figure – but a very limited vocabulary which was dominated by the word 'fabulous'.

Tchaikovsky's house was small, but the guided tour took two hours. The guide was well informed, but spoke so fast that I could barely understand him myself, let alone translate for Barbara, who spoke no Russian. On the way there we had been in a small church where a Russian Orthodox service was in progress – a rare event then. It was the church where Tchaikovsky had hoped to be buried and so it was allowed to remain open. Barbara thought the scene was 'fabulous.' I found it repellent. There were dim lights, glittering icons, guttering candles, priests with stringy hair and grey matted beards wearing tawdry vestments, the smell of incense mixed with soap and sweat, incantations in Old Slavonic and occasional squawks from babies clasped in the arms of their mothers.

On our way home, we stopped for a late picnic lunch. This was against the rules – we were supposed to go direct to the permitted destination and directly home again. This time, however, our 'tail' did not appear from the silver birch scrub holding a bunch of dandelions as he had done once before. Instead, a crowd of gypsies gathered round us, demanding food and wine. They told all our fortunes – the fortunes they thought we would want to hear.

I had a strange encounter on a visit to Tolstoy's home. There were no toilet facilities in the house, so I had recourse to the garden. I found a very large shrub, something like a rhododen-dron, which had a dark interior as big as a black house in the Hebrides. I was about to undo my fly buttons when I noticed I was not alone. Lying on the ground in another part of the extensive bush was an old man smoking a pipe. Although he was wearing tattered old garments and his face was dirty, he looked contented. It was too late to retreat and being caught more or less literally with my pants down I turned to him and asked *'Mozhno?'* (May I?) In a voice heavy with sarcastic resignation he replied, 'Of course! Everything in this country is free.'

One of the highlights of my early weeks in the city was a visit to the Bolshoi to see the ballet. Ulanova was dancing. She was nearly forty years old, small, pale and ethereal. She was certainly the slenderest Russian woman I had seen – a total contrast to the hefty women on the streets and building sites. The Russian public worshipped her. She took up to ten curtain calls after each act. The ballet was *The Fountain of Bakhchisarai*. The music by Asfiev was not exciting but the settings were superb, Ulanova like gossamer and the male dancers more athletic than any western dancers I had seen. I had taken Barbara with me and she thought it was all 'fabulous'. I know that we were privileged to see one of the greatest ballerinas of all time. Not long before this visit to the Bolshoi the Russian wife of an American journalist had been snatched from the steps of the theatre. Her husband was out of the country and she had been accompanied by two Australians, but her companions were too astonished to react. She was never seen again. Marriage between Soviet citizens and foreigners was not encouraged.

My relationship with Barbara reached stalemate. She wanted us to get married. I knew it would not work out because our minds were on different wavelengths. In July 1953 I went to an American party to which Barbara was not invited, as she did not have diplomatic status. With the usual Manhattan in hand, I was chatting to the US Assistant Military Attaché and his wife, the Jaegers. Across the room, in the bright evening sunlight by a window, I saw a girl talking animatedly to some people I did not know. Even at that distance she shone with vivacity and intelligence. Mrs Jaeger followed my gaze and took pity on me. 'That's Grace Kennan,' she said, 'the Ambassador's daughter. I'll introduce you.'

For the next hour or more we talked together. There was an immediate and mutual empathy. I ceased to be aware of anyone else, falling completely under the spell of her beauty and personality. Eventually I realised that I was the only guest left in the room. 'I'd better go,' I said. 'I hope we'll meet again soon.' She nodded in agreement. I thanked the hosts and their wives, who smiled at me with kindly amusement, and then I left.

My mind was in turmoil. Somebody might have told Grace about Barbara. I could not extricate myself from that relationship without hurting Barbara, but Grace would be expecting me to contact her. I did not know what to do. We were both at the same parties on one or two occasions, but without an opportunity to talk together alone. I saw her and her beautiful Norwegian mother playing tennis outside my office. I could not leave my work to go and talk to her. Just before Grace was due to return to the States, I got up the courage to invite her to a small dinner party at the dacha with an American couple and Peter and his Australian fiancée. Again, I could not find an opportunity to talk to her on my own. Peter contrived to leave to take his fiancée home, and to get the American couple out of the room for a few minutes. Lamely, hurriedly, I tried to explain, but she did not seem to understand. 'You are a fool,' she said sadly as the others called for her to go. I consoled myself with the thought that she was due back in Moscow again in the summer. This would give me time to sort things out with Barbara. I would not make the same mistakes again.

Two months later, the American Ambassador was on his way back to the United States. He gave a critical – too critical – interview in Berlin, condemning the Russians for their intransigence, and was declared *persona non grata*. I never saw Grace again and was left wondering if I had imagined that she reciprocated my feelings and if I had missed a unique chance of happiness. I immersed myself in work again.

In the November of that year I was asked by our Ambassador if I would play 'The Flowers of the Forest' on the pipes at the Remembrance Day service, following the two minutes' silence. I practised all day Saturday until I had the three parts of the lament note-perfect. The room was packed. I felt extremely nervous and the two minutes seemed like two hours. To my relief, when the moment came, the chanter and all three drones came simultaneously into tune and I started to play. Whether it was the inspiration of the occasion, my recent emotional turmoil, or just the long afternoon of practice, for the first and only time in my life my fingering and timing were up to a standard which gave me personal satisfaction.

Captain Talbot claimed that there had not been a dry eye in the house. That was certainly an exaggeration, but it did inspire a group of younger members of embassies' staff to start weekly Scottish dancing evenings and I was appointed instructor. Mostly we danced to records, but once in the course of each evening I would play the pipes for an eightsome reel. It was all sweat and gym shoes, but I believe these evenings served a valuable purpose: they appealed to a broad mixture of nationalities and grades. An Indian Counsellor would dance with an Australian typist, the Canadian Military Attaché with a Third Secretary from the British Embassy. We could see the Russian militiamen standing outside in the snow under the streetlight, smiling as they watched.

Arctic Assignments

In the autumn of 1952, I accompanied Captain and Mrs Talbot to Leningrad. They were to travel on from there to Helsinki for a short visit. For me, it was an opportunity to have a look at the Soviet warships being built in the Sudomekh yard in a sensitive area of the city. Captain Talbot and my predecessor had always been stopped before they could get near the yard, but this time we worked out a careful plan.

As the train steamed into the outskirts of Leningrad, Captain Talbot ordered tea for his wife and himself. When it arrived, he tasted it then turned angrily to the Konduktarshka.

'This tea poisoned,' he protested in pidgin Russian. Nobody could create a scene better. The Konduktarshka, a respectable middle-aged woman, looked aghast but vehemently denied the possibility. Captain Talbot worked himself up into a rage. 'Get the Kommandant immediately!' Every long-distance train carried an officer wearing the uniform of the Soviet State Railways but with the insignia of a full colonel. White-faced, the Konduktarshka hurried to find her superior. By now, Captain Talbot was fuming, waving his arms in all directions and shouting 'poison!' at the top of his voice. By the time the train slowed down for entry into the station, there were at least five uniformed officials in the compartment. I moved out into the corridor and waited, looking out of the window, until two men in dark blue overcoats and cloth caps, our 'tails,' emerged from the compartment next door to see what was going on. Very soon they, too, were enjoying Roy Talbot's consummate performance. Mrs Talbot was keeping an admirably straight face. I slipped up the corridor and into the lavatory, where I put on my Russian overcoat and fur hat. Before the train had even stopped I was out of the carriage and on to the platform, walking towards the barrier in approved Russian fashion, head down, looking at my boots.

I had found out in advance where the taxi rank was. I got into the first taxi and asked to be taken to the Mining Institute. The driver did not query my accent and we chatted amiably during the drive. Once there, I got out and walked to the edge of the quay, as if to get a breath of fresh air. The Sudomekh yards were immediately across the River Neva. I could see the stage of construction of every ship on the stocks. By good luck there were few people about and those who were took no notice of me. I had fully ten minutes to observe and inwardly note what I could see before turning away to walk back into the centre of the city.

I had carefully studied the town plan so that I knew my way to the hotel where we were to be staying and I was not stopped until I was within a quarter of a mile of it. I was accosted angrily by two uniformed MVD officers who wanted to know where I had been. I told them I had been taking a walk to look at their beautiful city and was on my way back to the hotel. They did not search me because of my diplomatic status, although others broke this rule whenever it suited them. They had to let me go. Our plan had been a great success. No doubt my tail and the bewildered Konduktarshka were severely reprimanded for their negligence. For the remainder of my time in the Soviet Union I was followed more assiduously than ever.

I made three trips to Murmansk to inspect two old four-funnelled destroyers, originally American, which had been transferred to the Royal Navy for transatlantic escort duties in 1942, in exchange for island bases, then loaned to the Soviet Navy for convoy escort duty. Now the Royal Navy wanted them back for their substantial scrap value. On the first trip Captain Talbot and I decided the ships were capable of being towed, provided weather conditions were reasonable. A naval shipwright was flown out from London and I accompanied him to inspect the ships below the water line. He confirmed that they were seaworthy.

My third journey was to meet a Royal Naval ocean-going tug, which had finally been given permission to enter the Kola Inlet and tow the vessels back to the Inverkeithing breaking yards on the Firth of Forth. I was accompanied by Lieutenant Kostyukov, allegedly an officer of the Soviet Navy. He was a small man with a sallow, pockmarked complexion and a nervous manner. He spoke good English but he knew nothing about ships or the sea. I suspected that he was an officer of the MVD dressed in a naval uniform. The first time we had to cross a narrow gangplank from the jetty to the upper deck of one of the rusty destroyers, my suspicions were confirmed. He was rooted to the spot, quite unable to step on to the gangplank. Two Soviet sailors, seeing his predicament, grabbed him and hauled him across. His face was the colour of beeswax and his forehead sweating in a temperature well below zero.

Lieutenant Kostyukov was not good at holding his drink. At one point on the long train journey from Leningrad to Murmansk, he left me to go to the restaurant car. I settled back to enjoy an hour or so of peaceful reading. Then I heard the sound of broken, tuneless singing. The door was flung back and the Lieutenant appeared, grinning broadly in my direction, though his eyes were unfocused. He fell forward into the compartment, on to one of the seats, gasping, '*Ya ugibshi!*' Literally this meant, 'I am having been perished' or, I supposed, 'I've had it!'

I was faced with a dilemma. If I were found manhandling him into his bunk, I might be accused of anything. If I left him where he was, he was in danger of suffocating. I compromised by ringing for the sleeping berth attendant to help me get off his jacket and heave him into his bunk, where he slept like a log for the next six or seven hours.

The railway timetables, which ensured that trains never arrived late, also meant long stops at quiet rural stations where it was possible to buy fresh produce from peasants' stalls. At one station on the east side of Lake Ladoga I saw a long train of cattle trucks halted. Sentries with the sky-blue epaulettes of security troops and armed with rifles stood at intervals of about twenty yards along the whole length of the train. In the trucks, through openings with sliding covers at head height, pale faces could be seen pressed against metal bars. Here and there, a white hand was thrust out between them. The locomotive was pointing north, like our own, but there appeared to be a branch line off to the north-east. I reckoned the unhappy passengers were heading for the salt mines near Arkhangelsk.

I spent one convivial evening in Murmansk in the Arktika

Hotel, a Soviet provincial *gostinitsa*, typical except for the large moth-eaten stuffed polar bear in the foyer. The pre-Revolution furniture was heavy and sombre, the curtains of dark, well-worn velvet. The food was poor, except for fresh fish, and the plumbing archaic, but the best quality vodka was freely available.

After the evening meal, I sat with Lieutenant Kostyukov and a group of young naval officers. We drank several toasts in vodka the Russian way – emptying our glasses *do dna* – to the bottom and in one gulp. Later on someone produced a balalaika and sang some folk songs. By this time I was being called James by all except my escort. 'Sing us a song of Robert Burns, James, sing us a Scottish song.' I did my best and they applauded my efforts generously. The goodwill was almost palpable. When out of reach of authority, Soviet citizens could be excellent company. I found Russians naturally friendly, sentimental, generous and musical. Sober and under pressure, they could also be fearful, suspicious and fiercely nationalistic.

It was on my final return journey from Murmansk that I came closest to making a genuine Russian friend. Kostyukov had disappeared. In the restaurant car I was seated opposite a young artillery officer of about my own age. He asked me what country I came from. I told him I was British and that I had been inspecting some destroyers on loan to the Soviet Navy. Later I told him I worked at the Embassy and that I was a Scot. We found we had much in common. We drank wine, discussed our lives and our families and played a game of chess. He beat me easily. He told me he was part of the Moscow garrison. As we neared Moscow, he suggested that we should meet again. He wanted me to meet his fiancée and suggested I bring a girl along. I knew that Jill Shepherd, a Second Secretary, would be glad to make up a foursome. We agreed on a time and place five days hence and shook hands, parting on the best of terms. Two days later the telephone rang in my office. A frightened voice spoke rapidly. 'James, this is Andrei. I cannot talk. We cannot meet on Friday evening. You will understand.' The line went dead.

Russian Jungle

One autumn Sunday, at about 5 p.m. Peter and I set out through the woods behind the dacha in the forest of Perlovka to walk off the after-effects of food and wine. Some friends had been to lunch. We had walked for about an hour, in a broad arc, when we heard voices ahead. We came upon some soldiers playing volleyball in a clearing, with a few tents beyond. Rather than turning back into the arms of our inescapable 'tails' we kept going, past the camp and up a road through the trees towards a rise, beyond which we estimated the dacha lay, about three kilometres away. As we reached the ridge three soldiers appeared beyond it. 'You are in a forbidden zone,' a sergeant announced officiously.

I replied that the area was not marked on the map of forbidden zones the Embassy had been given showing such areas. The sergeant, a round-faced peasant wearing a baggy, unpressed infantry uniform, did not reply but pointed his kalashnikov at me and with his other hand gestured towards a gap in the trees. We had no choice but to go where he pointed. After about ten minutes we arrived at a military encampment enclosed by a high barbed wire fence. Two further infantrymen were on guard at a wooden shelter, open on three sides at the gate. We were told to wait there. The two sentries pointed their weapons at us, glaring as if we were dangerous animals.

We waited. At intervals, cars arrived and were ushered through. We waited for more than four hours. It had been a warm day but by 11 p.m. we were chilled and covered in mosquito bites. We slapped ourselves to make life difficult for the mosquitoes and to keep the circulation going. Attempts to speak to the sentries were ignored. Their attention to duty was admirable. This was probably the most exciting thing that had happened to either of them since they had been conscripted.

We tried shouting to a soldier inside the fence, asking him to bring an officer. One of our guards continuously told us we were, among other things, 'unacceptable people'. Eventually a captain of infantry emerged and told us we were being held for being in a forbidden area and that he was waiting for 'the command'. About an hour later, a colonel arrived by car and went into a wooden hut some fifty metres inside the perimeter fence. Not long after, the sergeant ordered us to be escorted there. The hut was only about six metres square and full of soldiers and tobacco smoke. There were three officers, of whom the colonel was the senior. He asked us the same questions we had already answered: Who were we? Where had we come from? Why were we there? Why had we entered a forbidden zone?

Peter produced his diplomatic card but they were unimpressed. I did not have mine with me. We were taken outside again, where we stamped around in the cold and semi-darkness for a further hour. Peter was more patient or more diplomatic than I was and I shouted again that we wanted to see an officer. When the captain of infantry appeared again, I made a show of righteous indignation. He soothingly explained that they were awaiting the arrival of a representative from the military liaison section – our usual (indeed our only) official contact in the city. At last a car arrived carrying a colonel I recognised. We were taken to a smaller hut containing seven officers. For more than half an hour, with the gun trained on us, they tried to persuade us to sign a document – an *akt* – stating that we had knowingly entered a forbidden zone. We refused point blank. Their persistence was ominous. I demanded to be allowed to telephone the British Embassy.

'There is no telephone to Moscow.'

'Then how did you contact the liaison section?'

My question was ignored.

We were then told that a soldier had reported seeing me with a camera. This was completely untrue. I had nothing in my pocket but a handkerchief, but I was thoroughly searched. Peter avoided this indignity because he had his card with him.

An NCO appeared at the door and nodded. Promptly, a colonel offered to show us a sign, which he said we had passed, indicating that this was a forbidden zone. The ruse was transparent and I pointed out that they had had several hours to put one up. We would still not sign the *akt*.

At last, at about 3 a.m., they decided to let us go. A major, a corporal and two privates were assigned to escort us back to the dacha on foot. As soon as we were out of sight of the camp, the Major abruptly said goodnight and disappeared among the trees. For ten minutes or so we continued along the path with our silent escort of three. Then there was the sound of a revving engine behind us, a cracking of branches, and an army vehicle like a jeep burst into view. All five of us stopped, astonished. The major was unceremoniously pushed out of the back.

'Go all the way to their dacha with them,' one of the colonels ordered from the front passenger seat.

I commented to the major, 'This has probably been as inconvenient for you as it has for us,' but he would not answer.

The following day, the Embassy made an official complaint to the Foreign Ministry, but there was no reply.

On another Sunday afternoon I set out to sample a few of the many forms of Moscow transport. I travelled on the Moscow Metro, originally designed by Metro Vickers engineers, from the centre to a station at the western side of the city, returning by river bus down the Moskva and sailing between the red walls of the Kremlin and the British Embassy. There were thousands of Muscovites bathing in the turgid water or lying on the banks in the sun. East of the Kremlin, I landed to look at an old monastery, then took the tram back to the centre. From there I went by taxi to the Yaroslavsky Station and thence by suburban electric train to Perlovka. Watching the frantic efforts of my blue-capped tail to keep me under surveillance, while he tried to remain invisible, added to the fun of this variety tour.

During my second summer in Russia, I did a lot of travelling by train. I had dismissed Alyosha and Burobin had refused to allocate me another driver. The new Morris Minor I had ordered had not yet been delivered. I was sorry about Alyosha but I had no choice. We were expected to supply our Russian staff with clothing from the UK. Some of the Embassy diplomats ordered suits from London tailors, partly to prove a point about English quality, but I could not afford to do that. I had therefore ordered a good navy serge uniform (without badges) from Naval Stores in Portsmouth. Alyosha was not just disappointed, he was furious.

When I handed it to him at the front door of the Embassy, he screamed at me, swore and flung the suit across the hall at the Chief Security Guard, a fellow Scot from Glasgow. Alyosha was by race a Tartar. I picked up the suit, turned to him and said, 'You're fired.' Never have I seen a man's temper subside more quickly.

'You cannot sack me,' he said.

'I just have,' I answered, and told him I would be making a written report to Burobin. It was a pity because we had got on well and he had taught me a lot of colloquial Russian which I could not have learned from textbooks or Russian émigrés.

When at last the Morris Minor arrived, it caused a sensation. The beetle-shaped body was the latest in sophisticated stream-lining and made the nearest Russian equivalent, the Moskvich, look like a motorised perambulator. The Russians always wanted to look under the bonnet. The reaction was invariably the same: a look of envy, a shake of the head and a muttered *'nichivo osobyennovo'* – 'nothing special'. At traffic lights, every car would gun its engine to prove it was faster and more powerful, but only the big Zim and Zis, modelled respectively on American and German limousines, actually were.

I drove on an international licence but was harassed continually. Time and time again I was stopped and made to produce the licence. The militiamen pretended not to know what it was. Once they tried to frame me for bumping into a pedestrian. He literally jumped in front of the Morris as I was rounding a sharp corner very slowly. He made a great show of rolling about on the pavement. He must have been a stooge – or a professional footballer in the making. He was in no way injured.

The brilliant Tom Brimelow, who later became the senior professional diplomat at the Foreign Office, was the only member of the Embassy staff to hold a Russian driving licence. The test was unbelievably difficult, especially for foreigners. It involved not only a stringent test of driving skills, but also an examination on one of the handbooks for the Zis, Zim, Pobeda or Moskvich. Tom Brimelow learned the Pobeda handbook off by heart. They grilled him for hours, and in answer to every question, he quoted the appropriate section of the handbook verbatim. Eventually they had to pass him.

Although I now had the Morris Minor, and Burobin had agreed to allocate me a driver again, I often took taxis because the drivers were an independent breed and often willing to talk. One of them made a really strong impression on me. I waved her down to go to a party at the Swedish Embassy. I knew at once I was in for an interesting journey. She talked fast, without a break, giving a highly unconventional commentary on life in Moscow and the world in general. She made jokes, few of which I could follow and laughed without restraint after each one, looking back to see if I had got the point.

It was the time of evening when the senior members of the Politburo were leaving the Kremlin and returning to their dachas. Our route took us along the Arbat, the street taken by many of them. Every twenty yards there were militiamen standing at attention, posted to keep watch over the official route. A half-hearted attempt was made to turn us back, but my taxi driver took no notice.

As we passed each soldier, she slowed down and shouted through the open window, 'You stupid dummy. Never done a day's work in your life! You stuffed parrot. You silly kid dressed up as a soldier!' The militiamen stood at attention, looking angry and embarrassed, but unable to move. Between each one, she speeded up, hooting with laughter.

'Do you do this often?' I asked her.

'From time to time,' she replied. 'When I want to let off a bit of steam.'

When we reached the Swedish Embassy, I got out and paid her.

'Thank you, young man,' she said. 'Have a good time!'

'I already have.'

Death of Stalin

Moscow in the spring of 1953 was a city of oppressive gloom. The skies and the snow were grey, the temperature around -12°C. At 2 a.m. on Wednesday, 4 March, Moscow Radio broadcast a bulletin on the state of health of Comrade J V Stalin – the first news to the world that another of the small handful of outstanding twentieth-century figures was poised for the high jump into history.

His illness was announced as 'a misfortune which has overtaken our Party and our people.' This left little doubt that his final collapse and death were imminent. It was difficult to guess what the people were thinking. Their behaviour did not yet appear to be abnormal, although their leader's condition must have been the main topic of conversation. The view among our Russian servants was that at this stage Molotov was favourite for the succession with Malenkov a close second.

According to the official announcement on 6 March, the actual death occurred at 9.50 p.m. on Thursday, 5 March. Stalin's body was to lie in state at the Hall of Columns. That morning scores of lorries appeared in Red Square, packed with MVD troops. Buildings were hung with red and black flags. Already the numbers of red-tabbed militiamen seemed to have doubled. Apart from the Metro, transport in the city centre soon ground to a complete standstill. Roads were blocked by parking lorries end to end across them.

Earlier that year, Peter and I had at last been allocated a flat inside the city, in a modern block on the Sadovaya – the broad twelve-lane road which went right round Moscow at a radius of approximately two miles from the Kremlin. When we went for a stroll at lunchtime, we saw a marching column of militia stretching as far as the eye could see. Some were in civilian clothes but it was obvious from their bearing and physique that they were plain-clothes police, presumably intended to mingle with the crowds. By using our diplomatic cards, we were able to get through several roadblocks to Sverdlov Square with the House of the Unions just beyond. At this final barrier, the crowd was almost out of control. Small groups would break through only to be herded back by the guards. Throughout this period none of the troops or police used to control the crowds were armed. Armed troops were held in reserve, but kept well out of sight. The decision to deprive them of their arms – presumably Beria's – was a wise one. Although some people showed signs of resentment at their exclusion from the Hall of Columns where Stalin's body was on display – and sometimes from their own houses in barricaded streets – the crowds were in general remarkably patient and good-tempered.

At 2 p.m. on 6 March, it was announced that the Hall of Columns would be open to the public from 4 p.m. Enormous crowds began to build up and an interminable queue formed on the Sadovaya. A member of the Australian Embassy followed the queue back for five kilometres without finding the end. Only a trickle of officials was allowed to enter the Hall of Columns. I got caught in a huge crowd on the Sretenka and was stuck for nearly an hour. The crowd surged back and forth without any apparent purpose, packed so tightly that it was impossible to raise an arm. Militiamen were lifting people who had proved their right of entry over the lorry barricades. The condensation of breath above the heads of the crowd was as thick as smoke and at times reduced visibility to a yard or two. The US Naval Attaché watched as a crowd rushed a barrier on Sverdlov Square. Having left his office at about noon he was unable to get back for ten hours. Our Russian servants reported that many injuries were caused by the horses of the mounted police and that the hospitals were full.

The hours for viewing the illustrious corpse were restricted and only officials had any hope of being admitted. This was the subject of bitter comment among servants of the diplomatic colony, who resented the fact that foreigners were accorded a privilege they themselves were denied. Captain Talbot's cook stood in the queue without moving for three hours before giving it up as a bad job. Our cook, a keen young Komsomolka, waited all night and caught a bad cold but only moved forward a few hundred yards. The troops and militia controlling the queues and barriers did nothing to inform the patiently expectant crowds, probably working on the basis that the best way to preserve their docility was to keep hopes of eventual admission high.

During the day, several announcements were published about the future government, and it was clear that the general effect of the changes would be to centralise the reins of control still more firmly in the hands of the new Chairman of the Council of Ministers, Malenkov, with Beria now controlling internal and external security, standing at his left shoulder to crack the whip.

On the Saturday, I set off at 11 a.m. for the Hall of Columns, armed with my diplomatic card. With its aid and by announcing confidently that members of the diplomatic corps had the right of direct entry, I negotiated seven barriers without incident. However, in Pushkinskaya Ulitsa, no more than 200 yards from the entrance to the Dom Soyuzov, a determined militiaman refused to let me through. By enlisting the help of a senior officer with a friendly face, I got myself included in a transport workers' delegation. Strangely, they did not object.

The broad staircase was lined with solemn-faced MVD troopers. Somewhere in the distance a muffled orchestra was playing mournful music. Within the Hall the air was sickly with scent. The candelabra and light brackets were covered with black gauze like dirty cobwebs. Young soldiers of the MVD, their tunics ill-fitting and their boots unpolished, stood on either side of the queue at intervals of a yard. Stalin's body lay on a bed of greenery and artificial flowers. In the corner of the room the orchestra, ensconced in an embrasure somewhere at ceiling level, changed to another morbid dirge. We had an unobstructed view of the coffin. To give praise where it is due, the embalmers had done a creditable job, but it was hard to believe that this benign, inoffensive-looking little corpse had been the earthly vehicle of such an iniquitous vitality. Few people appeared to be deeply affected, although one or two women wiped away a furtive tear. The men just looked curious. I left with the impression of having seen a cheap Hollywood film set – garish, tawdry and lacking in dignity or restraint.

When I got to Captain Talbot's residence at 1.20 p.m. to

report, I found that arrangements had been made in the interim for the whole of the diplomatic corps to pass through the Hall of Columns that afternoon. My second visit was very different. The Corps Diplomatique, assembled at a distance from the Dom Soyuzov, presented an aspect of odd compromise between civic dignity and common sense, the temperature being several degrees below freezing. The sun shone from a watery sky, catching the sheen of top hats, the glimmer of sable, mink and lesser furs, the glitter of gold braid. It glinted with impartiality on the red, white, black, yellow and brown faces of the world's representatives in Moscow. A small boy in the crowd was heard to comment, 'Look, a real toff', when he saw one of the senior British diplomats in his top hat. It was half an hour before the British, modestly walking near the end of the line, entered the building. We mounted a red carpet to an anteroom cluttered with photographic and lighting equipment. The cameras were focused, not on the bier, but on the line of visitors. Round each vast wreath of artificial flowers, gold lettering on a scarlet sash left no doubt as to the donor. Only a small proportion of the wreaths had found a place inside the Hall, the others being disposed around the exterior of the building, the museum opposite and in Red Square. A large wreath of real flowers cost twice as much as artificial ones – about 6,000 roubles. None of this floral display had been there when I passed through with the transport workers' delegation earlier in the day.

On Sunday evening, 8 March, invitations to the funeral were delivered to the Embassy. The Ambassador was to follow the cortège and the Service Attachés were to be present on the tribune beside the mausoleum on Red Square during the ceremony. The tickets were delivered at three o'clock in the morning. We were to be on Red Square by nine o'clock.

The day was fittingly overcast, and the temperature -6°C. We walked from the Sadovaya down Gorki Street where the armoured patrol cars and artillery about to take part in the parade were drawn up in readiness. The volume of troops and militia deployed had still further increased. A conservative estimate put the figure at a quarter of a million.

It was a bitterly cold wait until 10.30 a.m. when a military band took up the strains of Chopin's funeral march and the cortège appeared at the end of the square. The gun carriage bearing the coffin was preceded by ranks of representatives of the autonomous republics which made up the Soviet Union, all carrying wreaths, and marshals and generals, one of whom carried Stalin's medals on a scarlet satin cushion.

Then came the coffin on a khaki artillery gun carriage minus barrel, drawn by four small black horses with harnesses that needed a polish. The coffin was closed and swathed in scarlet bunting, but a transparent plastic blister at one end enabled onlookers to see the face of the corpse. Behind the coffin walked members of Stalin's family and the expected dignitaries – Malenkov, Beria, Molotov, Voroshilov, Khruschev, Bulganin, Kaganovich and Mikoyan among others. Finally there came the heads of delegations from foreign governments and a double rank of armed security troops.

The coffin was placed on a pedestal draped in black and red at the mausoleum, forty yards from where we stood. The Soviet leaders mounted to the upper tribune of the mausoleum itself. There followed an hour of infinitely tedious speeches from Malenkov, Beria and Molotov. Malenkov's voice was his only redeeming feature, Beria sounded as mean as he looked, while Molotov spoke with a slightly senile tremor.

At 11.55 the leaders left the tribune and the coffin was carried into the mausoleum. A thirty-gun salute was fired, the national anthem was played and throughout the country every available hooter and whistle sounded. Five minutes' silence followed.

At about this time, the Talbots' cook, Zina, was sitting in the kitchen with Mrs Talbot, quietly sobbing. 'Our little father is dead. Who will care for us now? Russia is lost. Who are these men? We don't know them. Why can't we have someone we know to look after us? Why can't we be like the English? They know what is going to happen. When their King died, his place was taken by a beautiful young Queen they all know and love. Why can't we have Stalin's son? He is a good man.'

'Yes, that would be good,' said Nadya, the maid; but Ina, an extremely anti-Soviet Finn, snapped, 'You must be mad – such things don't happen in communist states.'

'Oh, yes, they do!' replied Zina indignantly. 'First we had

Marx, then Engels, then Lenin and then Stalin. Who will look after us now? Who will guide us?'

On conclusion of the gun salute, the Red Flag above the Kremlin was hauled down. The band struck up a march and the parade of troops and vehicles crossed the square. As the last squadron of armoured personnel carriers roared through, the fly-past commenced – a single IL28 escorted by four MIG15s was followed at a height of about 2,000 feet by successive flights of IL28s – sixty-three in all. Sixty-three MIG15s followed, also in flights of three.

Now I had my third opportunity to see Stalin lying in state, this time beside the sarcophagus containing the embalmed and floodlit remains of Lenin. We were able to pass within a foot or two of the body and thus able to appreciate fully the extent to which the great man had been idealised in Soviet photography and art. Perhaps a small table by the door, loaded with bottles of mineral water and fruit cordial, was for the revival of disillusioned comrades.

A few weeks after Stalin's funeral, I took Jill Shepherd to dinner in the Kievsky Restaurant, at that time probably the best of several ethnic restaurants in Moscow. At a table near us three senior Soviet Air Force officers were eating and drinking. One of them, dressed in the uniform of a full colonel, had clearly had too much to drink and was talking loudly and indiscreetly. He caught sight of Jill and after a few moments of whispered discussion with his companions, rose unsteadily to his feet and came across to our table.

'Good evening,' he said. 'May I join you?'

We were encouraged to talk with Soviet citizens as much as possible. Every conversation added something to our knowledge of the country. The opportunity to talk informally with a senior officer of the Soviet armed forces was not to be missed.

For the next hour or more, Jill and I were treated to an astonishing catalogue of criticisms of the Soviet regime, of the quality of life in Russia and of almost everything that the orthodox Soviet citizen was supposed to hold dear. The colonel made no attempt to speak quietly. The whole restaurant could hear every word he said.

We were aware that the men at his table were getting worried. One came across and tried to persuade their senior officer to rejoin them. He brushed him off, saying he was enjoying himself and would come back when he felt like it. His attitude to Jill and me remained polite and friendly, but he was becoming incoherent and repetitive. Two uniformed NCOs of the militia approached us and deferentially invited the colonel to accompany them but again he refused.

At last, two MVD officers entered the restaurant. Without a word they took position on either side of the drunken officer, grasped him by the elbows and lifted him to his feet. They propelled him to the exit. As he disappeared, he turned and called across the room, 'I have enjoyed myself. I don't regret anything I have said – it is all true!'

A shocked silence followed. The two remaining Air Force officers got to their feet and left. Gradually, table by table, a murmured conversation was resumed. Jill and I were stunned but excited. Was the man an agent provocateur? Had it been some sort of trap? Would anybody believe us when we lodged our reports?

The incident slipped to the back of my mind until many years later when my wife was reading a book by Svetlana Alleluyeva, Stalin's daughter, who was by then living in the United States. In it she recounts how her brother Vasily fought as an MIG pilot during the war, how he received rapid – too rapid – promotion and became commandant of the fighter aircraft squadrons allocated for the defence of Moscow. The premature promotion, responsibilities of senior rank and the limelight reflected from his father drove him to drink. She recounts how, following a drinking bout with foreigners in Moscow, he was removed from his post and placed in a sanatorium for alcoholics.

Everything fell into place; the date, the rank, the circumstances – even the colonel's features.

Georgia and Baku

On the date of the Queen's official birthday in 1952, every member of staff of the Commonwealth embassies received a souvenir from the British Ambassador, Sir Alvery Gascoigne: a glass ashtray with the royal coat of arms painted on it. They were manufactured in communist Czechoslovakia and cost one shilling at Gamages. After that, anything was going to be an anticlimax.

That same month I accompanied Captain Talbot to the port of Odessa on the Black Sea. Despite its maritime climate, the city was a disappointment. It had largely been rebuilt since the war and we were not allowed near the naval installations. We did visit Osipenko, the little town where Chekhov was born. It was not hard to understand why boredom and frustration are the themes running through his three plays which are so important in Russian literature.

Captain Talbot flew back to Moscow, but I returned by rail. I had to change trains in Dnepropetrovsk in the Ukraine. The station was a vast modern edifice in the Soviet style with an interior of polished stone, like a Victorian museum. On one wall hung a huge oil painting of a victory celebration dinner which must have been painted just after the Second World War. Stalin and leaders of the armed forces and post-war Politburo were clearly recognisable. Incongruously, though, a stone pillar had been painted which almost bisected the canvas. I was staring at this strange phenomenon when a small boy came up to me. In Russia children were universally treated with great kindness and affection. I never saw a Russian child being publicly reprimanded or punished. As a result they tended to be friendly and trusting.

'What are you staring at, Uncle?' I was asked. 'Uncle' was a friendly form of greeting to a stranger.

'I'm looking at the big pillar in the middle of this picture.'

He burst into peals of laughter. 'That's where Beria used to be,' he said. I joined in his laughter and soon a small crowd gathered round us, all pointing to the picture and laughing. Beria, the head of Stalin's secret police, who had been eliminated shortly after the death of the dictator, was now being systematically eliminated from public places and from the history books.

The British Embassy subscribed to the *Soviet Encyclopaedia*. The publishers had an excellent system which allowed the volumes to be constantly updated: it was supplied in loose-leaf covers. In the summer of 1953 we received a section: a scientific treatise on the Bering Strait, the hundred-mile-wide channel between the USSR and Alaska. The section was exactly the same length as the section on Beria and the subscriber was instructed to remove that section and insert this instead. No doubt the school history books were similarly amended. The names of streets and institutions were certainly changed.

Tbilisi, the capital of Georgia, was the most attractive city I visited in the USSR. It was also the only one in which I was welcomed into a private home. The city enjoys a climate like Madrid's and is as different from Moscow as Grenoble is from Glasgow. People there were taller and slimmer than the average Russian and they showed unusual frankness and friendliness. I found that our 'tails' were less sophisticated. I had a happy hour in a public park with my shadows popping out from behind bushes, tripping over one another and staring innocently at blank walls in a way which would have done credit to Charlie Chaplin.

Doug Gall, our Naval Clerk, had asked me to get him a *kinzhal* – a Georgian dagger in a decorated scabbard. I spent a whole afternoon in the back streets looking for one worth buying. Nationalism was always a powerful force in Georgia, and in the early 1920s weapons had been proscribed. This meant that most of the old *kinzhals* had their blades cut off. Eventually I found two that pleased me – one with the blade cut off but with a beautifully carved and painted ivory handle and scabbard. This I eventually sold to Doug at cost price. The other, with a handle and scabbard of hard wood bound in silver filigree and other metalwork, was a rarity because, although dated 1916, it had a blade. I still have it.

I had been told that there were still one or two craftsmen making Georgian bagpipes and I began to ask where I could find such a person. Somebody said there might be one on Silver Street and gave me directions to a steep, stone-paved back street, too narrow for any vehicle and overhung by small flower-filled balconies. I had to ask from door to door. Third time lucky – a handsome, middle-aged woman pointed to an archway some thirty yards further up the street. I entered the archway and knocked at an inner door. It was opened by a dark, fierce-looking man of about fifty who asked me, slightly suspiciously, what I wanted.

'I understand you make bagpipes,' I said.

'Yes, from time to time,' he shrugged.

'Ya Shotlandets.' [I am a Scotsman]. 'I play the Scottish bag-pipes and would be interested to see Georgian pipes.'

His fierce features broke into a charming smile. 'Come in, come in!'

The house was spotlessly clean, the plain white walls adorned with a few rugs and brightly coloured tapestries. My host gestured me to sit and disappeared for a few moments. He brought back two sets of pipes. The bags looked more like the skins of small animals than the stomachs of sheep. There were no drones, just mouthpieces, and elaborate chanters which consisted of two separate pipes with finger holes, bound together with brass strips and decorated with coloured stones. The outer ends of the two pipes were united in a cow's horn rimmed with brass, presumably intended to magnify the sound like the loudspeaker on an old-fashioned gramophone.

With his permission, I tried to raise a tune from one set but only succeeded in producing a noise like a sheep in pain. He shook his head and laughed, then took up the other set and began to play. It was a strange sound to my ears, monotonous and lacking the grace notes which are a feature of good Scottish or Irish piping. When he stopped, I asked if either of the sets was for sale. He looked doubtful.

At that moment, a vision appeared in the doorway, carrying a tray with tea in a silver pot and two glasses in silver holders. She placed the tray on the table, then stood with her hands folded at her waist. I stumbled to my feet and stammered, *'Strastye.'* [Hello].

My host's daughter said nothing, but bowed her head slightly while looking straight into my eyes. No sooner had she appeared than she was gone again. I spun out my negotiations with her father for fully half an hour in the hope that she might return. I simply wanted to look at her again. I had never seen any young woman more austerely beautiful – tall and slim with slightly aquiline features, black hair and eyes and silken skin the shade of café au lait. Eventually I concluded a bargain, thanked my host for his hospitality and, with the *kinzhals* and bagpipes tucked under my arms, threaded my way through the back streets to my hotel.

In the summer of 1953 I travelled with Captain and Mrs Talbot down the Volga to Astrakhan – a journey of nearly 2,000 miles, past Gorki, Kazan, the former Tartar capital, and Stalingrad. We were able to go ashore in Gorki and Kazan, which was unbelievably dingy, but only saw Stalingrad by night. The accommodation and food on the riverboat were adequate, though poor by western standards. We had more than twenty-four hours in Astrakhan, a typical little Soviet town devoid of the romance its name suggests, although both the people and the climate were friendly and there were melons and grapes galore in the market. We flew on from there to Baku, then a small oil town with a few pleasant modern buildings. The old Azerbaijani quarter was being knocked down to make way for modern workers' flats. We drove forty kilometres, mostly through oilfields, to a bay where the water was clean and we had a swim in water so salty you could just sit and float.

Throughout our voyage we had used cameras whenever opportunity offered, although we had to be discreet. We did not want our films confiscated. By the time we got to Baku I had some interesting pictures of submarines being built. This confirmed what the Admiralty had long suspected: submarines were being constructed on the Volga, sailed down the river to Stalingrad then, by way of the Tsimlyansk Reservoir and the canal system, to Rostov and through the Sea of Azov into the Black Sea. They could sometimes end up in the Baltic – a fresh- and sea-water journey of over 10,000 miles.

The Talbots flew on to Tbilisi, while I was to fly back to Moscow from Baku. My flight to Moscow was at 8 a.m. the following morning and I had been booked into a hotel for the night – the best I encountered in the Soviet Union. It was situated on the seafront, facing south, and the park on the hill behind it provided a splendid panorama of the city and harbour. My plan was to have an early supper, arrange a call for 6.30 a.m. and go to bed early.

As I settled into my room, stowing away my suitcase, with camera and films locked inside, underneath the bed, there was a knock at my door. I opened it to find a very smartly dressed young woman standing there who explained that she was from Intourist and that, unfortunately, the flight to Moscow was full. To compensate, Intourist had arranged tickets at the local theatre where there was to be a performance – a splendid performance – of Azerbaijani folk music and dancing. She would be accompanying me. She knew I was interested in such things.

This implied a degree of communication with Moscow. As it happened, my flight had been confirmed before we embarked on the riverboat nearly two weeks ago.

'If you don't mind,' I said, 'I do not feel like going to the theatre tonight. I just want to get something to eat and then go to bed early.'

'Then let me accompany you to the restaurant,' she said invitingly. We were both having to think quickly.

'I have some fruit with me,' I said, pointing to a bunch of grapes. 'I think I'll just eat here in my room.' She gave me an angry look and shrugged her shoulders. I shrugged mine in turn and smiled. Temporarily defeated, she turned and walked away down the corridor. I duly ate my grapes and, after locking the door, settled down to read. I was still hungry. I decided that I would take a taxi to the airport in the morning and simply wait there until I could get on a flight to the capital. Then there was another knock at the door.

'Who is it?'

'I have something for you,' said a soft female voice.

I opened the door. Before me there stood a pretty young waitress holding a bottle of champagne.

'With the compliments of the management,' she said, holding the bottle out to me. I put out my hand to take it, but instead of letting go, she held on to it firmly and came into the room. I suspected that the wine was drugged and that the girl was there to make sure I drank it.

'I must open it for you,' said the waitress. She produced a glass from somewhere and put it on the table at the end of the bed, removed the foil and wire, and deftly twisted the cork. This pre-empted any opportunity to check the foil for a needle hole or some other sign that it had been tampered with. It opened with a pop that seemed suspiciously subdued, even for Russian champagne. She filled the glass, the yellowish liquid bubbling reassuringly.

'I'll get another glass,' I said, turning towards the bathroom.

'I do not drink wine,' she replied.

'But I don't want to drink alone.'

She smiled. 'You drink. I sit with you.'

'I am not going to drink unless you do.' She stopped smiling. Stalemate. It was her move and she did not know what to do. She rose to her feet.

'I will leave the wine with you,' she said angrily. 'You can drink it when I have gone.' She left.

I locked the door again, poured the wine down the lavatory and sat down in a hard plush chair to read. I was wide awake and I knew for certain now that they wanted to get in and search my room. Once during the night I heard a faint noise at the door and saw the handle turning very slowly. There was no bolt on the door, and they undoubtedly had master keys. I coughed loudly. The door handle went slowly into reverse, then there was a faint click as a hand let go of it on the other side.

At this stage, I got fully dressed. I found myself wondering what would happen if they kidnapped me and then informed the Embassy that I had asked for political asylum. Nobody who knew me would believe it, but there was such a thing as brainwashing... The night was a very long one.

In the morning I took the suitcase into the bathroom with me while I washed and shaved, then set off down the two flights of stairs with it grasped firmly in one hand. I was ravenous and went straight into the restaurant. I ordered and wolfed down eggs and black bread and butter. I only drank a mouthful or two of coffee in case it had been doctored though, in daylight, that seemed unlikely. Feeling better, I took up my case and marched into the foyer where I asked the receptionist to prepare my bill and order a taxi. Looking nervous, she disappeared into a back office. The Intourist lady appeared looking much less affable and less well turned out than she had the previous evening.

'Where are you going? There is no point in going to the airport. I told you, there is no room on the plane to Moscow.'

'When is the next plane then?'

'This evening, but that is full, too.'

'I do not believe you,' I retorted. 'I shall go to the airport and wait until there is a seat.'

'You would be much more comfortable here in the hotel.'

'I do not feel comfortable in this hotel and I may miss a chance to get a flight if I am not waiting at the airport.'

A look of resignation clouded her face. 'If you insist.'

I sat for at least an hour in the foyer waiting for a taxi. I tried to ring the British Embassy but could not get through. I began to wonder if I would spend the rest of my life in Baku, but at last the Intourist lady reappeared and said that a taxi was waiting. She would come with me to the airport.

'That is not necessary,' I said, but she pretended not to hear me. The driver tried to take my suitcase as if to put it in the boot but I hung on to it. At the airport a porter looking suspiciously like a plain-clothes MVD man was waiting to open the taxi door. As he did so, he also tried to take the suitcase, but I refused to let it go. He scowled and made a gesture of disgust. The Intourist lady was looking less friendly by the minute. I went straight to the desk and asked when the next flight was leaving for Moscow.

'This afternoon, at three o'clock,' the young woman behind the desk replied pleasantly. I handed my ticket across. She looked up and asked me why I had not been on the flight I had booked for. I turned and gestured to the Intourist representative. 'Because she said the flight was full up.'

I then witnessed a situation I had experienced before – the sight of two Soviet officials at cross purposes, each accusing the other of being an idiot. The airport check-in girl won. I was issued with a boarding card and was irrevocably booked on the afternoon flight. The porter made one last attempt to detach me from my suitcase but I hung on to it grimly repeating, 'Hand baggage, hand baggage.' The Intourist lady put a brave face on it and wished me a pleasant journey. Thankfully I went through into the departure lounge. When at last the old Ilyushin headed up the Caspian coast with the snowy peaks of the Caucasus to port, I felt a profound sense of relief. My suitcase was gripped firmly between my feet.

Marriage in Moscow

In January 1954 I married Kit Jamieson, the Canadian girl I had first met at the Scottish country dance evenings. Kit came from the Ottawa Valley in Ontario where her father owned a small tweed mill. Both her parents were of Scots origin. Kit was a graduate of Toronto University, now Secretary to the Canadian Chargé d'Affaires in Moscow, Mr Ford. She was a beautiful girl, slender and fine boned. She was very demure and rather undemonstrative. One or two people asked me if I was quite sure about committing myself to marrying her, but I was.

It was sad to be so far from both our families for such an occasion, but there was a certain glamour about getting married in Moscow. The wedding took place in the Ambassador's study at the British Embassy. Flowers had been flown in from Helsinki a few days before by the Embassy chaplain and kept wrapped in wet moss in the basement. One of the Embassy wives played on a small organ in the corner of the room. After the ceremony, we went back to the Canadian Embassy for a reception from which I was eventually carried shoulder high by friends.

We spent the first two days of our honeymoon in Vienna, then went on to the snows of Kitzbühel where we stayed in Schloss Lebenburg, a castle converted into a hotel run by the Austrian aristocrat who owned the estate. We were told that he had got rid of his first wife by throwing her out of a racing car at high speed. He was, however, an expert hotelier. We had access to the ski slopes and superb views over frost-bound forests and snowy peaks. I have an atmospheric photograph taken from the window of our room very early in the morning, with the surrounding peaks, snowy caps stark against the dawn sky, projecting above a frosty haze which encircled the Schloss and blanketed the village of Kitzbühel.

It is difficult for me to express the depth of my feelings for Kit at that time. If some fortuneteller had told us what lay in the future for both of us, I for one would not have believed them.

Back in Russia, we moved into a small flat on the top floor of the dacha at Perlovka. The Reverend Isherwood, who had conducted our wedding service, had a parish which included all the British Embassies behind the Iron Curtain and his parishioners included all the English-speaking Protestants and agnostics who went to church. When Peter and I were sharing a flat on the Sadovaya, Mr Isherwood used the spare bedroom during his visits to Moscow. The thing I remember best about him was the case of the washing machine. For some reason, the Israeli Embassy had broken off diplomatic relations with the Soviet Union and a dispersal sale was held of all their equipment, including a Bendix washing machine. Peter and I had been feeling guilty at seeing our young Russian maid doing our household washing by hand. We decided to lighten her load and put in a successful bid. It seemed, however, that Natasha thought it would be a betrayal of her native land to use a capitalist washing machine, so the Bendix was sitting unused when the Rev Isherwood came to stay.

There is, of course, no commandment 'Thou shalt not covet thy neighbour's washing machine', so covet it he did. He played on our feelings, telling us time and time again how desperately he needed a washing machine, what a beautiful machine it was (how much had it cost?), what a pity it was that it was sitting unused when he could make such excellent use of it... We eventually became so riddled with guilt, so worn down by his pleading, that we decided to let him have it at the price we had paid at the sale – about fifteen pounds. When we heard a few weeks later that he had resold it to the Lebanese Embassy for five times that amount, our faith was, to say the least, sorely tested.

Kit was not accredited to Finland as I was so she had to stay behind when I made my periodic visits to Helsinki. On one such visit I heard Sir Edmund Hillary lecture on the ascent of Everest. This achievement had barely been acknowledged in the Soviet Union, although I had culled one short and inaccurate account from a Russian mountaineering journal which I translated and sent to Sir John Hunt. He wrote me a very nice letter of thanks.

In February 1954 I heard that my replacement, Lieutenant Commander James, would be arriving in June. To preserve continuity, the Admiralty arranged for changes of staff to be phased over a period of six months: first Captain Talbot was relieved by Captain Bennett; then our clerk, the eminently dependable Douglas Gall, would be replaced; then Lieutenant Commander James would replace me.

I took an instant dislike to Douglas Gall's replacement. His name was John Vassall. He was ingratiating and obsequious. After Douglas's quiet, straightforward efficiency, I found Vassall's affectations infuriating. Within a fortnight of his arrival I reported to Captain Bennett that I thought Vassall was totally unsuitable for the post of naval clerk and that he should be sent home.

'You're just being intolerant,' the Naval Attaché replied.

I was needled at this. 'With your permission, sir, I would like to write an independent report. I think my views are worth consideration.' He gave me permission and I duly sent a report on Vassall to the Admiralty, stating my view.

When the end of my tour of duty came, Kit and I planned to leave Moscow by the Trans-Siberian railway. Unknown to the Russians, I arranged through the Admiralty for a British ship, engaged in the Far Eastern timber trade, to pick us up in Nakhodka, the commercial port for Vladivostok. We would be the first westerners to leave the Soviet Union via this route. To our surprise, we had no difficulty in obtaining exit visas via the Far East. Our belongings were packed and farewell parties were held, but forty-eight hours before we were due to depart we still had not received our rail tickets. The Soviet authorities explained that as there were no air or sea services out of Nakhodka, there was no point in our travelling there. Twenty-four hours before our departure was due, the British Embassy officially informed the Soviet Ministry of Foreign Affairs that the SS *Stanburn* of the Stanhope Steamship Company was due to arrive at Nakhodka on 12 June to unload a cargo of sugar and embark timber, departing on 15 June for Sasebo in Japan. Passages had been booked on the ship for Kit and myself and for an American friend, Lieutenant John Dugger USN. It was too late for our exit visas to be withdrawn. On the very morning of our departure, to the astonishment of the whole western diplomatic community, our tickets were delivered.

In 1954 the Trans-Siberian trains had three classes of compartment – International, Soft and Hard. John Dugger and I had applied separately but simultaneously for International compartments, which were old-fashioned double-berth compartments with a connecting bathroom. Instead we were allotted three berths in a four-berth Soft compartment. The fourth berth was, of course, taken up by an MVD man, wearing the uniform of the Soviet Railways, who was to shadow us throughout the journey. We protested, but were told that all the International berths were taken. This was untrue. Not only was the International carriage virtually empty, but so were most of the Soft compartments. They remained unoccupied throughout the 9,300-kilometre journey to Ugolnaya, not far from Vladivostok, where we had to change trains for the last 173 kilometres to Nakhodka.

Poor Kit found herself in a compartment six feet by seven with three men for ten days. The manners of the 'railway official' were above reproach. When I suggested he might be more comfortable in his own compartment he replied affably, 'The comrades might not like that,' but he did move out of the compartment for long enough to let Kit change at night and first thing in the morning. Otherwise he never left us. He ate when we did and looked out of the window whenever we did. Our only escape was to take a stroll along the platform at the various halts. He would not converse with us, so we were reduced to getting on with things as if he was not there.

We had carefully noted on a map any sites we particularly wanted to see, correlated with the railway timetable. As we approached them, either John Dugger or I would leave the carriage to use the lavatory where we could look out of the window unhindered while at the same time distracting our watcher who was torn between staying in the carriage or following one of us along the corridor.

The journey was tediously uneventful and we settled into a routine. We ate mostly from tins we had brought with us, supplemented by bread, hard-boiled eggs and the occasional radish bought from peasants at the little stations along the line. Keeping clean was a problem the state railways did not seem to have provided for.

The monotony of the scenery was depressing. The only two sections of the journey with any scenic merit lay east of Irkutsk, where the line passed through a mountainous region and skirted the western end of Lake Baikal, and the last section between Ugolnaya and Nakhodka which had thickly forested hills and steep gradients. The rest of the terrain was a repetition of minor variations on a theme of birch scrub and grass clearings stretching to the horizon.

After nine days we arrived at Ugolnaya late in the evening. No one could tell us exactly when the train for Nakhodka would get in, but we were informed that it would not be until the following morning at the earliest. The station facilities comprised a tiny booking hall, a *restoran* – no more than a counter offering tea and biscuits tasting of wood – and a single very large waiting room. There was no hotel in the village, which had one unpaved street lined with single-storey wooden buildings, so we were reduced to sleeping in the crowded waiting room, which served as a public dormitory. It was equipped with basic iron bedsteads, each with a thin hair mattress covered by a greyish sheet. Kit and I found two adjoining beds and John Dugger got one opposite us. On my other side there was a woman fast asleep, breathing noisily. She was fully clothed in the traditional black dress of the Russian peasant and wearing her felt boots. Her head rested on a black bundle. There were no pillows. We followed her example, resting our heads on our suitcases.

I slept fitfully and the night seemed very long. Early in the morning I was woken by a rooster crowing from underneath my neighbour's bed. This was followed by clucking noises and I saw that she had three or four hens in one basket and the rooster in another. As I watched, I actually saw an egg emerge from one of the hens. The woman's snoring was only marginally less loud than the cock's crow, but at least it was rhythmic and continuous. The dormitory was filled with a cacophony of snores and heavy breathing, not unlike musicians tuning their instruments in some distant orchestra pit. However, so far as I could see, my neighbour was the only one with livestock. Perhaps that was why the two beds next to her had been left empty!

When I looked around in the grey dawn light, I could not see our 'tail' and assumed that he must be comfortably asleep at some police office, secure in the knowledge that there was nothing to see in Ugolnaya and no way of escape. The light also revealed that the sheet on which I lay was not just plain grey, but blotched and speckled with sinister stains and what appeared to be old blood spots. I decided it would be preferable to be outside and walking about, however cold. I whispered to Kit that I was going outside. Once outside I realised how foul the air had been in the dormitory. Soon Kit and John joined me and we must have walked many miles up and down that platform before the train for Nakhodka arrived three hours later.

The port was a frontier town hacked out of the coastal forest and was still under construction. With great relief we found the *Stanburn* already lying alongside one of the few completed jetties. She proved to be a modern diesel-powered freighter of 6,000 tons. Our captain was a Welshman, Evans by name. He looked like a pirate but was warmly hospitable. Kit and I were given the magnificent double state room intended for the owner, a Mr Billmeyer, who was reputed to have got a foothold in the shipping business by trading with both sides during the Spanish civil war. The state room was walled in satinwood veneer with huge mirrors, a private bathroom and a separate day-cabin. The contrast with the waiting room at Ugolnaya could not have been greater. John was allocated a smaller but equally luxurious cabin.

It was pouring with rain when we went on board and continued to rain for the next forty-eight hours. The ship's cargo of unrefined Cuban sugar in sacks could only be unloaded in dry weather. It was three days before we eventually sailed for Sasebo. From there the US Navy flew us to Tokyo. As we approached Yokohama the top 4,000 feet of Fujiyama were projecting impressively above the clouds.

Navigation or Agriculture?

After a short stay in Tokyo we were flown across the Pacific to San Francisco by the US Air Force. Denied any respite, we were obliged to fly direct to Ottawa to be debriefed by the Canadian authorities. Then, after staying with Kit's family for a week or two, we crossed the Atlantic in the old Cunarder *Samaria* and travelled by train to Edinburgh where Kit was introduced to my parents and sisters. Kit was warmly received by them, but she already had reservations about Scotland. My Uncle Duncan had died while I was in Russia. Because his only son had been killed in action in Burma, I inherited the hill farm of Tillychetly which had been in the family since 1773. I had to decide what to do with it. I still had two years to go in the Navy before completing ten years from the age of eighteen, when I could ask to be put on the 'retired list'.

There was a break while I awaited my next appointment, so we took the opportunity to look at the farm. I had been driven past the road end a few times as a child but had never really seen it. It had been let to a Harry McCombie, who had recently died.

The whole farm lies 700–1,000 feet above sea level. Its 275 acres cover the western half of a hill south of the village of Alford. When we first visited it in August 1954 it appeared attractive but poorly maintained. The fences and dykes were dilapidated, the oat crop appeared moderately good, although infested with thistles and weed grasses; there was also some poor-looking barley and what had been a turnip crop, but the steep arable land was mostly under grass. The store cattle grazing it looked good. There were a few stands of Scots Pine up on the hill, but also a lot of broom. Of course I was not looking at it through a farmer's eyes, but through those of a proud new proprietor.

The farmhouse and one of the cottages, both of grey stone with darker slate roofs, crouched into the hillside, their backs to the north-east and the splendid view across the Howe of Alford to

Bennachie. The front windows looked through mature trees and across a haugh in an arable field towards the highest point on the farm. The houses had clearly been built with the cold winter winds out of the north-east in mind, rather than the view. The garden round the farmhouse had run completely wild. Outside the back door there was a pile of empty tin cans, some new, some rusty with age. Kit stayed in the car when I knocked at the door.

It was answered by a dishevelled woman in her middle thirties, wearing a grubby flowered overall. She brushed her hair out of her eyes.

'Fit d'ye want?' she asked. I assumed she was the housekeeper.

'I'm James Davidson, the new owner,' I said. 'My wife and I would like to take a quick look round the house if that's all right?'

'Did y'ask Mrs McCombie?'

'Isn't she here?' I asked. I had assumed that Mrs McCombie, the widow of the late tenant, lived in the farmhouse.

'Mrs McCombie bides in Kemnay.'

'I just want to take a quick look round to see if there are any repairs needing to be done.'

'Och weel,' she sighed. 'There's nae hairm, I suppose.'

We found that the house was ill-kept, but it had possibilities. On the upper floor there were four bedrooms and a bathroom of sorts. On the ground floor there was a big kitchen with a stone-lined milk room, a scullery with two large sinks and three other rooms – one of which was quite large. Four of the rooms were not in use and had Victorian wallpaper peeling off the walls. Meat hooks hung from the bedroom ceilings and there were damp spots to be seen. We commented on the new fireplace and decoration in one room and asked the woman who, it transpired, was the grieve's wife, if it was her living room.

'Na, na,' she replied guilelessly, 'Mrs McCombie keeps this room tae mak siccar she hauds the lease.' This was an interesting admission. It was a condition of the lease that the tenant farmer must occupy the farmhouse.

We returned to Edinburgh with very mixed feelings. The annual rent from the farm was negligible but in order to farm it ourselves, thousands would have to be spent on the property to make it attractive or even viable. Yet I did not want to just let it go. It had been my family's first home when they ceased being farming tenants in 1773.

As a child I had been shown a flat, weathered gravestone in the old kirkyard of Tarland, some nine miles away across the hills to the south-west. It was barely legible then, less so now, though I have twice paid to have it cleaned. In the oblique sunlight of early morning or late evening the lettering could still be read:

> Here lys John Davidson who was born in the beginning of the present century, lived all his lifetime in Tarland and died there on the third of March 1787, going 82 years of age; with two of his children, James and Jean Davidsons, who died in their infancy. This being the burial place of their Family for Several Centurys, where many of them are interred since the first of whom, a Captain, was settled in this country by the Irvine of Drum for a particular favour he had done that Family at Edinburgh, in the time of the Stewarts or Scottish Kings.
>
> Done by the care of Margaret McCombie, the defunct's relict, her eldest son John Davidson of Tillychetly and his Daughter Ann Davidson in Tarland. His second son Charles Davidson died in Jamaica some time ago.
>
> Praise on tombs are vainly spent
> This defunct's character was an ornament.

The captain referred to was Alexander Davidson, who was born about 1610. He was captain of a troop of horse in Montrose's army. The laird of Drum had been incarcerated in the Tolbooth in Edinburgh for his royalist sympathies. In 1645 Captain Davidson was with the Master of Napier and Nathaniel Gordon when they reached the outskirts of Edinburgh. They were met by a deputation from the town council who offered them money and humbly admitted that they had been forced to rebel against their better judgement. The plague had been raging and the Tolbooth was full of suffering royalists who were immediately released – among them the Irvine of Drum.

That was the favour that Captain Alexander Davidson did the Irvine of Drum – releasing him from the Tolbooth into the Edinburgh sunshine.

Alexander and two of his sons were tenants of the Irvine family on the farms of Ruthven and Balnastraid when the Howe of Cromar was raided twenty-one years later by MacDonalds from Glencoe. This followed the murder of Alexander Mac-Donnel of Keppoch in 1663 by the members of the same branch of the MacDonalds, for which crime they were outlawed. A group of them – a hundred or more armed men – took to the hills and lived by raiding far and wide. On 5 October 1666 they plundered the peaceful Howe of Cromar, carrying off livestock and goods to the value of £7,750 14/- Scots. A year later the Lady Irvine, a widow, and her son, brought an action in the High Court against Archibald Campbell, Earl of Argyll, in his capacity as feudal superior of the MacDonalds of Glencoe and were awarded more than £7,000 in compensation. No doubt this was among the scores which Argyll sought to settle when he connived at the massacre in Glencoe in 1692. The Irvines of Drum generously used the money awarded in compensation to reinstate their tenants.

The second John Davidson referred to on the tombstone was born in 1740 and practised in Tarland as a writer, or lawyer. On 29 July 1769 he married Ann Farquharson, a direct descendant of Finlay Mhor, the virtual founder of the Clan Farquharson. Finlay Mhor was killed at the battle of Pinkie in 1547, bearing the Royal standard. Ann's father and brothers had fought and died for Prince Charles Edward Stewart at Culloden. It was John Davidson – my ancestor – who bought Tillychetly from John Badenoch in 1773 and the property of Mill of Kincardine on Deeside in 1795.

Ann bore seven sons and one daughter, of whom only Duncan – our ancestor – and Charles survived to adulthood. Charles died in the Caribbean, where he was practising as a physician, in 1804. Duncan distinguished himself and became Professor of Law at Aberdeen University. The Davidson family lived at Tillychetly until the 1830s, when the farm was let to the McCombies, perhaps related through Margaret McCombie. Now I had been given the responsibility for deciding its future.

My knowledge of farming was nil, but I had heard of a body called the Agricultural Executive Committee, which had been set up during the war. Over the following months, I consulted them and asked for guidance. They inspected the farm and reported that the tenants had not been running it adequately. I must let the farm to new tenants or take it on myself. On the way up from Edinburgh that day in August, Kit demonstrated that she knew even less about farming than I did: seeing some sheep on the hillside she pointed and said, 'Look, Jamie, look. Little woolly pigs!'

Later in the month I received my new appointment from the Admiralty. I was to join the destroyer *St Kitts* as navigating officer and third in command. I was delighted to find that my commanding officer was to be my fellow Scot, David Mellis and the Captain 'D' commanding the Fourth Destroyer Squadron was my former boss in Moscow, Captain Roy Talbot. I was to enjoy my year as navigator of *St Kitts*, but for my Canadian wife it was to be a different story. The ship was based at Plymouth and we started looking for accommodation there. After an intermittent and demoralising search of several weeks, we eventually found a two-roomed furnished basement flat, but in an unattractive part of the city. I had only spent a couple of nights there when we were dispatched to the Mediterranean to take part in joint NATO Fleet exercises. Kit gave up the flat and went back to Edinburgh to stay with my parents.

I was away for two months before summer leave, which I spent in Edinburgh. We then took part in further NATO exercises before three destroyers of the squadron were sent to pay a courtesy call on the Navigation School at Bremen, in then British-occupied West Germany. We would be the first HM ships to visit the city since the war and it would involve a journey of more than fifty miles up the River Weser. I was not amused to see on my Admiralty charts that for much of its length the river was still mined, except for a narrow channel which had been swept.

We arrived off Bremerhaven, in the estuary of the Weser, in thick fog late one evening in early December. The waterway was packed with merchant shipping at anchor, waiting for the fog to disperse before taking pilots on board to proceed upriver. We were due to arrive off the Navigation School in Bremen at 8 a.m. the following morning, but no pilot would take the ships up due to the poor visibility – down to about fifty yards and decreasing. Captain Talbot was faced with a difficult choice: to signal that we would arrive late, thereby risking the ridicule of our German hosts, or to proceed upriver without a pilot. Typically, he chose the latter.

The convoy of three destroyers set off with *Saintes*, Captain Talbot's ship with the Squadron Navigator, leading the way and *St Kitts* in second position. David Mellis wisely insisted that I should navigate as if we were on our own and not play follow my leader, although the sternlights of *Saintes* should be visible, and we would be in instant voice communication by radio telephone.

Thus began the most exacting navigational exercise I had ever been involved in. It was a matter of counting the buoys on the radar screen, matching them with the markings on the chart and constantly transferring bearings and distances from the navigational radar to the chart – all extremely quickly. The ships could not travel slowly for fear of losing steerage way and drifting out of the swept channel.

When we had been underway for about an hour with David Mellis keeping me constantly on my toes by demanding to know exactly where we were, there was an urgent call over the R/T from the leading ship.

'*Saintes* to *St Kitts*, *Saintes* to *St Kitts*. Report your exact position! Report your exact position!'

I was able to reply with precision, something like, 'Bearing 185 ° forty-five yards from buoy Q15.'

'Repeat, repeat.' The voice of the Squadron Navigator was urgent with tension.

'Bearing 135 ° thirty-nine yards from buoy Q15.'

There was complete silence in the bridge plot then the R/T crackled.

'*Saintes* to *St Kitts*. Thank you!' I recognised the relieved voice of Captain Talbot. We drew our own conclusions.

There were two or three more hours of intense concentration before we reached Bremen. The river was still blanketed with thick fog. On orders from Captain 'D' we reduced speed to a few knots, just sufficient to maintain steerage way. The cable party was already on the fo'c's'le and the anchor ready for letting go. In total silence, maintaining distance by radar from the ship ahead, we crept towards the anchor berths we had been allocated by signal from the German authorities before our arrival in the estuary. Simultaneously the anchors from the three ships splashed into the turgid waters of the Weser. When dawn broke the fog had cleared. The officers of the Bremen Navigation School must have been surprised to see the three British destroyers swinging at anchor in their allotted berths.

We played a game of rugby against the Duke of Wellington's regiment which provided the British garrison at Bremen. We were beaten, but I was very impressed with one of their second row forwards, a very large young man by name of Mike Campbell-Lammerton. Over a beer after the match I asked him if he had Scottish connections. He confirmed that he had. Shortly afterwards I wrote to a former Scottish rugby international who had put my name up for membership of London Scottish, suggesting the Scottish Rugby Union should make contact with this huge youngster serving in the army's leading rugby regiment. At the time Scotland was very short of big men and I like to think that it was due to my letter that Mike Campbell-Lammerton was given a Scottish trial the following season. He became a Scottish international of high repute and captained the British Lions in South Africa.

We made some good friends among the staff of the Bremen Navigation School. One of them, a former U-boat officer, was later to invite himself to stay with Kit and myself in Scotland. We received expensive gifts by post in advance of his arrival. He was separated from his family in East Germany and I wondered if he had been put under pressure by the Russians to find out why a former British Assistant Naval Attaché in Moscow was farming in the wilds of the north of Scotland. I believe he returned to Germany convinced that I was not involved in some nefarious form of electronic espionage.

I had only a week in Edinburgh for Christmas that year. Kit was four months pregnant and very depressed. Although my parents did their best to afford us as much privacy as possible, it was not a merry Christmas. I became convinced that Kit was not going to be able to adapt to the life of a naval wife. The possibility of farming Tillychetly began to loom large in my mind.

Mud Student

I decided to apply to be placed on the retired list rather than resigning my commission. That way the Navy could call me back if they needed me. When the time came I was a bit offended at the alacrity with which my request was granted. I somehow felt they should have been reluctant to let me go! What I did not know – and nor did David Mellis, or he would certainly have told me – was that the Admiralty was planning to offer a handsome golden handshake to a large number of officers aged between twenty-five and thirty-five in about eight months' time, as an incentive to leave the service. Their Lordships had decided that there were too many young officers for the number of ships they could afford to keep at sea. I have never quite got over the fact that, had I remained on the active list for another eight months, I would have been offered £6,000 in cash and an index-linked pension of £300 a year for life – soon to be worth thousands of pounds per annum. I reckon that by being placed on the retired list at my own request in June 1955, I inadvertently saved the Admiralty a fortune. Instead, I received a gratuity of £1,000 in recognition of ten years' man's service from the age of eighteen, with a nice letter of thanks from an anonymous civil servant in the Second Sea Lord's office.

St Kitts had been in Londonderry when our son Sandy was born and I did not see him until he was two weeks old. I now had a wife and a child to consider in my decision about the future. We had decided to try working Tillychetly, but I still knew little about farming. I applied to become a 'mud student' – under a scheme open to ex-servicemen – preferably on a mixed farm with livestock and crops somewhere in the north of Scotland. I started a correspondence course on agriculture and read everything I could lay my hands on. I was offered a position with Captain Ian MacPherson on Delny, a large farm on the northern shore of the Cromarty Firth, which carried with it a small cottage comprising two bedrooms, a bathroom and a kitchen-cum-living room. It had been modernised to the extent of having electric light and a coal-burning stove to heat water. I was to be paid a basic working wage, part coming from the farmer and part from the Department of Agriculture and Fisheries for Scotland.

We moved in September, at the beginning of the potato harvest. I realised straight away that Captain MacPherson meant to get value for money from me. I was set to howking tatties on to the tattie dresser. Once the farm squad realised that I was there to learn and eager to do so – and not spying for the boss – they offered me friendship and skilled instruction in the great variety of jobs a farm worker was expected to do. The only thing I was never allowed to do was drive a tractor. The tractor drivers had a closed shop and it was not until I took possession of Tillychetly that I began to learn by trial and error how to use farm machinery.

The farm at Delny produced hundreds and hundreds of tons of potatoes. The King Edwards were dressed and carted straight down to the station. The Kerr's Pinks, apart from a few bags for the farm staff, were kept in long pits at the roadside for sale later in the winter. Nowadays potatoes are mostly stored in purpose-built ventilated potato stores, but at Delny in 1955 the traditional 'pit' was used. First, a well-drained part of the field was chosen and Kenny Ross, the big, powerful leader of the squad, would clear off all the loose soil, leaving a hard surface. The tractors would back their bogies up to this flat area and tip their loads on to it, making a heap sometimes two or three hundred yards long. The heap was kept even and symmetrical so that when covered it would shed water like a roof. Next came bundles of wheat straw, laid side by side to form a thatched roof which allowed the potatoes to breathe while being protected from frost. This work of art was topped by several inches of earth from an open drain round the pit which could withstand snow, rain, flood, frost and wind – and in no way resembled a pit!

The tattie harvest went on for two months. Most of the lifting of potatoes into baskets and thence into the tractor trailer was done by a big team of women and children from the villages and farms round about, reinforced by itinerant groups of tinkers. At the end of November when the potato harvest was nearly complete, a bitter east wind was sweeping sporadic showers of sleet across the field. During one vicious hail shower I was preparing the site for the next cartload of potatoes when I saw a tinker baby, no more than eighteen months old, sitting in an old pram behind a heap of wheat straw. The poor little creature, slumped forward into the harness, was wearing only a grubby vest with the hail lashing its back and neck. At first I thought it was dead, but suddenly it awoke, cried briefly, then went back to sleep again. I thought of covering the child with something, but suspected I would only get abuse from the mother.

After the tattie harvest came the howking, topping and tailing of neeps. On fine, frosty days, there was threshing of oats and barley, spreading of straw in the cattle courts or other work with cattle and sheep.

I would return to the cottage physically exhausted, but had to settle down to a couple of hours at my correspondence course. Sometimes I gave Sandy his bath. We still had the Morris Minor so at weekends we were able to go shopping in Dingwall or Tain, or explore the countryside. We were lucky to meet Doug Budge and his wife Liz, who introduced us to some of the younger members of the farming community. Doug did his best to stop some of the gaps in my farming education which would otherwise have remained unfilled except at the cost of bitter experience. He persuaded Captain MacPherson to let me accompany him to markets. Being from a traditional farming family, originally from Caithness, Doug appreciated the vital importance of buying and selling livestock in the kind of farming I was about to embark upon. There were two significant links between Doug and myself. He had been serving in the Cameron Highlanders in Burma with the same unit as my cousin Duncan when he was killed. We also both played for the Ross Sutherland rugby team.

On the farm, I acquired my most valuable knowledge from the grieve, Bob Watson – a dour Banffshire man, highly skilled in all the arts of arable farming; from the cattleman, John Farquharson, and from the shepherd, Jock Beaton. Once I had proved to Bob Watson that I did not expect any favours, he increasingly gave me jobs where I would learn new skills and gain experience. I found he enjoyed answering questions which showed a respect for his knowledge, and when the time came he gave me excellent advice on the purchase of essential second-hand machinery for my own farm.

From early December until the sowing started, I was put to work with John Farquharson in the cattle courts. There were more than 150 cattle to be fed, provided with bedding and generally attended to. I gained a good general knowledge of what to do and, on one traumatic occasion, what not to do. We were roping stots to dress them for ringworm – lassoing them as they galloped, some more exuberantly than others, round the court. Once caught, we took a half hitch round one of the railings above the feeding troughs to administer the necessary treatment. John Farquharson, despite his forty years of experience, got a loop of rope round his thumb. The beast lunged away, taking the thumb and the tendons from his forearm with it. Horrified, I saw the blood gushing from the raw wound into the straw and dung. I led him out of the court into a passageway, tore the sleeve of his shirt and bound the hand as tightly as I could and put on a tourniquet. I made him sit down while I ran to tell Kit what had happened and ask her to inform his family, the MacPhersons and Bob Watson. Then I drove him to the nearest doctor. The man sat stoically, white-faced, and did not complain once. The doctor performed the essential emergency treatment and then I drove the injured man twenty miles to the hospital in Dingwall. The initial shock had worn off and he was in agony but still he did not complain and even made a joke of it. This was the first, but by no means the last, farm accident I was to see. The others were caused by machinery rather than by livestock, and included the loss of the end of one of my own fingers. Forget woolly lambs, fluffy chicks and funny ducks: farming is one of the most dangerous occupations around.

For the next few weeks John Farquharson's son and I took over the cattle; then, when the spring sowing commenced, I worked with one of the tractormen, filling the combine seed drill with seed and fertilisers and learning to calibrate the machine. When lambing was due to start, I became Jock Beaton's assistant. I look back on that lambing season as one of the great experiences of my life. There were two full flocks on the farm, one of Scotch

Half-Breds and one of North Country Cheviots – nearly 1,000 ewes in all. The lambing continued from the middle of March until early May and demanded our attention from first light to dusk.

Jock Beaton was a man of great intelligence, personality and skill, but he had a weakness. The weakness was concealed in half-bottles under flat stones on the top of drystane dykes at strategic points around the farm. Jock's aunt, known to all as Auntie Beaton, kept house for him. She was a woman of inexhaustible kindness and humour, but of stern religious principles. There was no room for whisky in a house she kept. Nothing but the Bible could be read on a Sunday and Jock, though well looked after, was subject to firm discipline despite being in his late fifties.

Jock was the son and grandson of shepherds from the west coast of Ross-shire. In his youth he had entered the police force. He reached the rank of sergeant when still in his early twenties and had been tipped as a future chief constable. A fine figure of a man, he had the brains and the presence to fulfil the role well. However, over a period of months he was put on duty at Hamilton's Auction Mart in Dingwall. He had many friends in the farming world and his friends liked to stand him a dram. He began to take too many drams and so ruined his career prospects.

When Auntie Beaton died, Jock married a girl from the Black Isle more that thirty years younger than himself. Before doing so, he paid me the compliment of asking my advice. Was it acceptable, she being so much younger than him? I gave him the only answer I could in the circumstances. 'If you think you're going to make each other happy, why not?' I know they started a family, but not whether they made each other happy.

Jock came to Tillychetly once or twice to see us and helped me dress a ram for the Keith Show. By then he was shepherd of a commercial flock of Cheviots with no great reputation. The last I heard of him was a court report in the *Press & Journal*: he was accused of driving under the influence of drink. His defence was that he had been weaving the van from side to side because his employer kept sheep on both sides of the road.

We left Delny before the end of the 1956 harvest to take over Tillychetly at 'separation of crop' – a convenient time for a farm to change hands because the crops are valued independently and paid for by the incoming farmer who then takes responsibility for the harvest. There was much still to be done to make the farmhouse habitable, so we moved into a cottage owned by cousins a few miles away on Deeside.

We only had savings of about £2,000 between us and I knew that was not going to be enough for the work needed on the house, for essential fencing and for basic machinery and livestock. I applied to the Scottish Agricultural Securities Corporation, knowing that under the right conditions they would lend up to two-thirds of the value of a farm. A famous figure in the farming world, James Durno of Uppermill, Tarves, accompanied by his daughter Mary, came to value the farm. He asked many searching questions and walked very rapidly through the fields and buildings. I could see he was not impressed. I am sure that in his wisdom he decided not to saddle me with a loan bigger than I would be able to repay. I was very disappointed that the farm was valued at only £4,800 and I was to be offered a loan of £3,200. I was able to sell some Scots pine from the hill, many of which had in any case been blown down in a gale a couple of years previously, for a further £2,000. This total of £7,200 was a better sum with which to work, but if I had realised that for the next twenty years I would have a bank overdraft, and a bank manager constantly breathing down my neck, I might have had second thoughts about embarking on a farming career. As it was, I could not wait to get started.

All our neighbours were helpful, although their advice was conflicting. Peter Watt, the oldest and wisest of them, looked round the steading and every one of the fields. He took it slowly and in the course of the afternoon he must have shaken his head a thousand times. He saw fences consisting of drooping rusty wire and rotten posts; timber not harvested, much of it lying rotting on the ground, passable crops of oats, but barley which was a complete failure – a sure sign that the acid soil was crying out for lime. Drystane dykes were tumbling down through lack of attention and weeds grew everywhere – dockens, knotgrass and creeping thistle. At the end of the tour he turned to me and said, 'I kent the place was in a bad way, but it's deen, Jim, the place is deen.' I should have been deterred, but I was not. Another neighbour suggested I put a match to the whole place.

Doug Budge and Jock Beaton, not wanting to discourage me, suggested that I first stockproof the fencing and put on livestock. Tests of the ground showed that I would need to spread at least three tons of lime on every acre of arable ground. For the following seven or eight years we struggled to complete the fencing, repair the dykes, hang gates, drain the wet places, kill or cart off the weeds and reduce the acidity of the soil so that fair crops of barley, potatoes, turnips and even wheat could be grown as well as good grass for hay and eventually silage. Slowly, room by room, the farmhouse was made habitable and attractive and I had the two cottages modernised. The steading was repaired and partly converted into a piggery. On the rare days when there was nothing else to do, we carted stones from the fields – hundreds and hundreds of tons of them. We only bothered with those bigger than a turnip.

I managed to borrow another £4,000 from a source few people had heard of – the Revolving Loan Fund. This was a residue of Marshall Aid dispensed by the USA after the war. I was informed that I was literally the last person in the British Isles to receive – and in due time pay back – a loan from this source. It was a godsend. It allowed me to buy half a dozen breeding sows and a hundred cast Blackface ewes. I could not afford cattle of my own. For the first two or three years I auctioned any grazing not needed for the sheep or for making hay, for cattle only, with the object of improving the fertility of the land. We kept some poultry – twenty or thirty Rhode Island Reds – for eggs, and fattened litters of pigs on home grown barley and sent them as baconers to Lawsons of Dyce.

Rosalind, our elder daughter, was born in August of our first year at Tillychetly. She was the most beautiful baby I had ever seen, quite perfect. The matron at the War Memorial Hospital in Torphins generously agreed that this was not just paternal pride. Sandy was thriving in the hill air and dry summer sun. They were a pair to be proud of, but Kit was not happy. Local young farmers and their wives included us in their invitations, so we had some social life, but I was constantly exhausted and Kit never missed a chance to make unfavourable comparisons between the rural highlands of Scotland and the comfortable suburban Canada she was familiar with.

Farming Challenges

In my first year at Tillychetly, lambing the old, cast Blackface ewes on the steep south-facing side of the farm, I achieved a more than respectable lambing percentage of over 140, but I did make one terrible mistake. One old ewe had been struggling for a long time to give birth, or so it seemed to me. I knew not to intervene too early, but at last decided she needed assistance. The large red protuberance at her back end had failed to convert itself into the expected and recognisable shape of a newborn lamb. Having caught her as she tried to get away from me, I was totally mystified by what I found. I could feel the lamb all right, but instead of being enveloped in a thin membrane, it was surrounded by a barrier of flesh. I tried for five minutes to lamb her, but without success. I decided there was something badly wrong and I would have to ring for the vet. It took me ten minutes to get to the farmhouse and another half an hour for the vet and myself to get back to the ewe. He took one look and said, 'She's put her lamb-bed out. Prolapse of the vagina.'

Jimmy Stewart made me hold the ewe up by her hind legs while he cleaned and then replaced the lamb-bed. By the time he got the lamb out – a big single, but dead – I was tired and depressed and the ewe would never be fit for breeding again. I never made the same mistake. The next season, on Jimmy Stewart's advice, I got hold of a neat stainless steel contraption which could be inserted into any ewe showing signs of prolapse. Tied to the wool on each side of the vulva, it apparently gave the animal no discomfort and, in nine cases out of ten, she would lamb naturally without further trouble and without assistance.

This was just one of the many instances of 'learning by experience' which I endured over the next decade, some more painful for me than for the livestock. At the autumn sales I sold the old Blackface ewes with their lambs at foot and got a good price. I went up to Lairg and bought 120 cast North Country

Cheviot ewes off Altnaharra. I also went to the ram sales and bought three North Country Cheviot tups, having first gone to considerable trouble to ensure that they were twins, not singles. My plan was to breed only from twins, thereby improving my lambing percentages.

The morning my newly bought rams were delivered, one of them escaped from the paddock in front of the house and set off up the hill. I set off after him. I had a working dog, but he was only half-trained and nearly uncontrollable until he got tired. The ram was heading for some distant sheep about a mile away on a neighbour's land. Although he had never been on the farm before, he seemed to know where to find all the gaps in the fences and drystane dykes. I knew I would not get a chance to catch him until he became tired so I kept about 200 yards behind him. It was near noon on a sunny autumn day and I began to sweat.

Eventually he came to a fence he could not find a way through. I increased my pace and got within about twenty yards of him. Then began a battle of wits. He knew very well that I was trying to corner him. He was a fine specimen with a strong Roman nose and a compact body with sturdy legs. When I got within five yards of him he stamped a forefoot and tossed his head, then suddenly tried to dash past me. I called on my two decades of rugby experience to fling myself sideways in a desperate tackle. I got him by the hind legs, my face buried in wool, bringing him to the ground with great difficulty. There we both lay, panting and sweating, for fully two minutes. It began to dawn on me that I had no easy way of getting the ram back to the farm. I had no means of leading him and he was too heavy to carry. I took the only course open to me and removed my belt, tied his hind legs together and thankfully rose to my feet. Immediately my trousers fell about my ankles. Months of hard physical work had honed me down. The cool breeze was welcome round my legs, but I hauled my trousers up and, holding them with one hand, set off for the farm. I looked back at the ram. He was still lying as I had left him, breathing even more heavily than myself. He knew he was beaten. It took me an hour to get the ancient Land-Rover, load him on board and ensure there were no further gaps in the fence before I let him loose again in the paddock.

Thereafter the ram and I treated each other with respect. He proved to be a great breeder and sired the best of the ewes which formed my registered flock a few years later. The year after I bought him, I entered him for the Keith Show. Jock Beaton came and helped me dress him for the occasion and by 6 p.m. on the evening before the show he was looking extremely elegant, his back as flat as a board and his fleece as smooth and compact as a sand dune. Jock predicted I would get a second or even a first prize with him, then went home.

By 6 a.m. the next morning, the animal was unrecognisable. He had got himself filthy during the night. I had just an hour to sort things out, so I bathed him in detergent and dried his wool with Kit's new-fangled hairdryer. The result was astonishing. Instead of a nice compact fleece, his angry face and four legs stuck out of a great ball of fluffy white cotton wool. He looked ludicrous and he knew it. In the pens, he was an object of comment by shepherds and flockmasters. Children and women were enchanted. They thought he looked like a fluffy toy. The perplexed judge awarded us a fifth ticket, in a class of six, after asking what had happened.

It took me a couple of years to get Tillychetly registered for Hill Cow Subsidy, although all the land lay between 800 and 1,000 feet. By 1960 I was able to buy my first batch of cows. I started going down to the autumn sales at Hawick and methodically set about purchasing in-calf heifers. I would arrive very early at the sale, go round all the pens and put a mark in my catalogue against every beast I was prepared to bid for. I judged them by appearance, by the reputation of the farms they came off, by the published calving dates – and whether or not they had been vaccinated against brucellosis. Then I would set myself a ceiling price above which I would not bid. After that, it was a matter of always being at the ringside when a heifer I had marked was due to be sold. I had decided to go for the Blue-Grey, the progeny of a Galloway cow and a white Cumberland Shorthorn bull. They had a reputation for good mothering qualities, plenty of milk and extreme hardiness.

Very early in a sale, when bidding was slow, I bought two or three. In the middle of the day, when many of the buyers were having their lunch, the average price dropped considerably and I would buy one or two more. At the very end of the sale the price dropped again as buyers went home, and I was able to leave Hawick with seven or eight in-calf heifers of excellent quality. I pursued this policy for five or six years and over that period built up a good Blue-Grey herd of about forty cows.

Only one heifer I bought proved to be a disaster. She dropped her first calf on a night in November and in the morning it was nowhere to be seen. She had obviously calved, but showed none of the signs of a beast which has lost its calf. We found its body among the tall broom, showing clear signs of having been trodden on. It was the only calf we lost the first year. The following October I was forking silage from a trailer for the cattle on the hill, some of which already had calves at foot. Hendry, my grieve, was driving the tractor. I noticed that the cow which had abandoned her calf the year before was not there. Then we heard a noise coming from among the tall broom. Hendry and I walked towards the sound, which was a combination of squealing and angry bellowing. We emerged into a clearing to see the cow kneeling with her forelegs on her calf, her hindquarters high and her tail lashing. She was battering the calf, which was still shrouded in the afterbirth, with her head. Luckily I had brought the fork with me and I lunged at her to get her away from the calf. She rose, glaring at me, red-eyed, her head down and her tail lashing. I shouted to Hendry to get the tractor and cart while I held her off. Twice she lunged at me, but I jabbed at her and she retreated. It seemed ages before the tractor came crashing through the broom in top gear, the cart rattling and jolting behind it. Hendry leaped from the tractor, picked the calf up and dumped it in the cart. I turned towards the cart myself, keeping the fork directed at the angry cow. She charged the cart, hitting the side board with a sickening thud. Hendry opened the throttle and we crashed downhill with the cow, blood oozing from a cut on her tossing head, trotting behind us, still bellowing. The calf survived, but the cow was sent down the road a week or two later. I could not risk having her in-calf a third time.

The bank manager in Alford was a man who had not been promoted for many years. The branch had only two or three employees. He 'managed' within very narrow limits, carefully defined by his head office. I was allowed no seasonal flexibility; I could not buy when seed or fertilisers were cheap; I could not hold on to my calves or lambs or grain in order to get a higher price. Soon I ran into a cash flow crisis. In frustration I mentioned the problem to my lawyer in Edinburgh.

'Change to another bank,' he said. I was taken aback. This was long before people played one credit card off against another and the bank was a place where you spoke in hushed tones. 'Who's going to take me on, overdraft and all?'

'I'll find you another bank,' he replied. And he did.

I was invited to transfer my account to the British Linen Bank in Aberdeen. It was a rich bank with lots of money in its vaults and a manager who took a cool, humorous and slightly cynical view of life. Provided I explained to him what I was doing, and kept more or less to my predictions, he couldn't care less if I went a thousand or two over my overdraft limit. For the first time in my farming career, I was able to plan more than six months ahead.

One morning in January 1960, I was standing with a neighbouring farmer by the stack of bales in the centre of a field on the north side of the house, looking across the Howe of Alford. There had been a good hay harvest and I had several tons for sale. An inch or two of dry powdery snow had fallen during the night and the top of Bennachie, four miles away to the north-east, was white capped, shading to grey and brown at the foot. It was cold and despite a clear sky there was an icy north-east wind. The farm steading was fifty yards to our left. A spume of white was blowing off the roof. Jimmy Duncan had noticed it too. Simultaneously we realised that it was not snow, but smoke. I had three sows with litters at foot in that wing of the steading. The young piglets were being kept warm by newly purchased patent paraffin heaters – the very latest thing, strongly recommended and advertised.

We set off at a run. When I reached the nearest door in the east wing and flung it open, a thick cloud of smoke belched out. I could hear the crackle of flames, but there was too much smoke to see the fire. I yelled to Jimmy to phone for the fire brigade and began to open the doors of the pigpens. Pigs rushed past me, squealing with excitement. They could see better than I could because they were below the choking pall of smoke. By now, I could see the flames leaping towards the rafters; it would only be a matter of minutes before this wing was engulfed.

The building was shaped like a capital E with the upright facing towards the north. It was the top of the E that was on fire. The icy wind was driving the flames towards the rest of the steading. I opened the doors to let out the baconers – pigs varying in size from 50 to 200 pounds. The east wing was now an inferno, fanned by a relentless wind. The diesel oil tank was at the west end. Luckily the wind was driving the fire away from the farmhouse.

The fire engine arrived from the village two miles away within eight minutes but its pipes were frozen solid. It was forty minutes before the part-time firemen managed to thaw their pipes with blowlamps. By a miracle, the oil tank, set separately on stilts a few yards clear of the steading wall, survived intact, but the rest of the building was reduced to blackened walls of undressed granite. At the height of the blaze I swear I saw a pig fly out of the loft window in the gable, fifteen feet above the ground, but it may have been my imagination. There was no way in normal circumstances a pig could have climbed a ladder into the loft. Eventually we rounded up the surviving pigs unharmed, but half of the litter in the pen where the fire had started were burnt to little cinders.

In the months following that fire, I truly came to appreciate the kindness of most of the farming community and the generosity of my neighbours. Any piece of equipment I had lost was replaced by gift or loan without mention of repayment. I had no need to ask for help; it simply arrived. So much for mean Aberdonians! Careful, yes, but seldom mean.

The pigs became rather wild from being kept in small shelters out on the hill until the steading – which fortunately had been adequately insured – was rebuilt. One day I was chased for a quarter-mile by an angry sow whom I had disturbed when she was farrowing. I eventually escaped by throwing myself over a drystane dyke. According to a book I had on pig husbandry, the pig is 'designed by nature for crashing through the woody undergrowth'. She proved it!

In the summer of 1962 a visitor came unheralded to the farm – a pleasant, middle-aged man wearing a tweed suit, apparently from MI5. He showed me his identification and began to question me about my 1954 report on John Vassall. What had made me suspicious of him? Why had I written that adverse report? I replied that I had found Vassall both inefficient and nauseatingly obsequious. Although unaware of his homosexuality, I had sensed that he was both vulnerable and unreliable and altogether unsuitable for the post of confidential clerk to the Naval Attaché's office. The Naval Attaché had told me I was being intolerant, but he had allowed me to make an independent report. Vassall had later been compromised by the Russians and blackmailed into spying for them. Exposed and found guilty, he was sentenced to eighteen years' imprisonment in 1962.

On 17 February 1963, we suffered the worst snowstorm Scotland had experienced for more than a decade. The farmhouse was at 800 feet above sea level and the north side of the steading was very exposed.

I went up the hill to feed the sheep at about 4 p.m. By the time I had tipped the feed into the troughs and replenished the hakes, a fine powder snow was being blown horizontally from the northeast. On my way down, the snow was coming at me in thick billowing curtains and visibility was down to a few yards. This is known as 'blin' drift' on the hill farms of north-east Scotland. I looked into the newly rebuilt piggery and was met by a wave of warm, pungent air. Through a haze compounded of condensation and dust from the barley meal I could see Hendry pouring whey, which I bought in barrels from a cheese factory, on to the barley meal in the glazed tile troughs. The pigs thrived on this mixture.

'Do you need a hand? It's a hell of a storm and you'd better get home as soon as you can.'

'I'm near finished,' he answered and continued pouring the whey. The piggery resounded with the greedy grunting and sucking sounds of two or three hundred pigs doing what they liked doing best. I crossed the yard to the farmhouse.

By morning the wind had dropped completely. The sun shone on a world of virgin whiteness beneath a sky of faultless blue. The trees were decorated with sparkling powder as for a celebration.

Every sign of contagion was obliterated. The snow had drifted and blocked the road between the back of the farmhouse and the steading to a depth of twenty feet. I got across to the steading and was surprised to find Hendry dozing on some straw bales. Hearing me enter, he sat up bleary-eyed. I saw that his hands were lacerated and caked with blood.

'What have you done to your hands?'

Hendry told me that he had left the steading ten minutes after I had. By then the storm was so wild he could see nothing. He set off home – a journey of 150 yards down the farm road, then fifty yards along the public road. The farm road was already filled to a depth of three feet, so he decided to take a short cut diagonally across the field. In the dark, the tearing wind and the blin' drift, he lost his sense of direction and ended up side-stepping, hand over hand along a barbed wire fence. A long time later, he saw a light and climbed over the fence, tearing his clothes and hands even more. The light was the one he had left on in the piggery.

I wondered why he had not come across to our house.

'Once I got behind a door wild horses couldnae have dragged me out into that storm again!'

Hendry's wife had spent a sleepless night wondering what had happened to him, but with no telephone and with young children to look after, there was nothing she could do. In the same storm, a few miles away, two children died of exposure between the end of a farm road where the school bus had deposited them and their homes less than a mile away. Our tractor-mounted snowplough could make no impression on our own farm road and for two weeks we had to bypass the steading by a track to the north of it. I had to ski down to the village for supplies.

Ill Health and Politics

A few months after Rosalind was born, my mother-in-law came from Canada to stay with us. She noticed that Kit's neck was slightly swollen and I learned for the first time that Kit, when twelve, had had a suspected thyroid condition. The Ottawa Valley where she grew up suffered from a deficiency of iodine in the soil and water. We made an appointment with a specialist and it was agreed that an operation should be performed in the early summer to remove part of her toxic thyroid. Kit was very anxious about the operation but there was little I could do but try to reassure her that many such operations were carried out successfully every year.

In the following two years Kit's behaviour became erratic and she spent more than six months of the twenty between June 1959 and February 1961 in three separate spells in the Royal Cornhill Hospital in Aberdeen. There were times when I thought she was cured and it was during the second of two long spells of comparative good health that Polly was born – another beautiful child who enjoyed a robust constitution and an enviably happy temperament. There was a slow but continuous change of Kit's personality. By the time she came out of hospital at the end of May 1964, she was a quite different person from the one I had married ten years earlier.

Sandy was at the local primary school but not fulfilling his obvious potential. Under pressure from my parents though knowing that I could not really afford it, I sent him to an expensive boarding school in Edinburgh. It was not a success. Sandy was temperamentally unsuited to the atmosphere of the school and reacted by withdrawing into himself. When, two years later, I sent him to Robert Gordon's College in Aberdeen as a weekly boarder, he discovered science and in the course of one year rose from the lowest class to the highest for his age group. From then on he never looked back and both he and I owe a great debt to the staff of that college for their sympathetic attitude and teaching skills.

Rosalind was consistently at the top of her class but at home she suffered from a lack of maternal support and sympathy. She had a passionate love of animals and we bought her a small riding pony. Polly was a bright and cheerful infant who seemed to suffer least from Kit's fluctuating condition.

During this period, and perhaps in a subconscious attempt to escape from my difficulties at home, I began to get interested in farming politics, particularly as they affected the smaller farmer. I was elected to the North-East Area Executive of the Scottish NFU. When the 1959 General Election was called, I decided to help the Liberal candidate for West Aberdeenshire, only to discover that there was none. As a result of my enquiries, I was invited to a weekend Liberal seminar in Perth. There I met three men who greatly impressed me: Jo Grimond, the charismatic leader of the Parliamentary party; John Bannerman, a man of magnetic charm whose achievements included more than thirty international rugby caps for Scotland and gold medals for singing at the Gaelic mod; and George Mackie, the Chairman of the Scottish Liberals who had an enviable reputation in the farming world and had won the DSO and double DFC as a pathfinder bomber pilot during the war.

All participants were asked to speak on a topic of their choice. I chose Anglo–Soviet relations. Before the end of the seminar, George Mackie asked me if I would consider my name going forward as prospective candidate for East Aberdeenshire, where he thought the sitting member might be reasonably easy to shift. I answered that I would much prefer to consider West Aberdeenshire, where I lived and farmed and had family connections going back 300 years or more.

After doing some research and talking to some Liberals of long standing in the area, I told George that I would like to try first to build up a Liberal organisation in West Aberdeenshire and then, if the prospects appeared good, I would be willing to let my name go forward. Kit treated the whole idea with sceptical condescension. I do not think it ever occurred to her that I might actually win. I had no illusions. I knew that the only way I could succeed where other, possibly better, candidates had previously failed was by forming a better organisation. In 1960 we knew the names of less than twenty Liberals among the 40,000 voters on the electoral roll of West Aberdeenshire.

I continued to work hard on the farm from early in the morning until nightfall. I attended NFU meetings to discuss topical issues and new techniques. We found time to take the children for picnics or to ski locally. Occasionally I would take my gun and shoot something for the pot – a pheasant, grouse, hare or rabbit – on the high ground of the farm or along the margins of the fields. Weekends were often as busy as weekdays, but once a month I met up with three or four dedicated members of the re-established West Aberdeenshire Liberal Association and we dropped canvassing cards in a predetermined area. Starting from scratch, our objective was to form twenty or more branches throughout the whole constituency, which covered a vast area from the suburbs of Aberdeen and the coast north of the city to the foot of the Cairngorms at Braemar and Corgarff, to the headwaters of the rivers Dee and Don, and as far north as Huntly and the borders of Banffshire. About a third of the electorate dwelt in the Aberdeen suburbs of Bridge of Don, Bucksburn, Cults and Milltimber. One third lived in the medium-sized towns of Culter, Inverurie and Huntly and the rest were scattered between twenty or more villages.

Early on a Saturday afternoon half a dozen of us would descend on the chosen area. We would drop a leaflet giving a brief summary of Liberal policy and a reply-paid card through every letterbox, inviting the householder to let us know if he or she was interested in forming a branch. Sometimes there were only one or two replies, but however few were returned, we would publicise and convene an evening meeting two or three weeks later inviting those who had responded. I would speak briefly, answer questions on anything from local organisation to defence and foreign policy, then form a committee. We were thrawn [stubborn]. We would not leave until we had at least found a Secretary. The ideal was to recruit a Chairman, Secretary and three or four committee members to organise social events to raise money and find where the supporters were. Over a period of two years we formed no less than twenty-three branches. At the same time I began to write regular articles for the local papers.

We picked up supporters in strange circumstances. One wild February night there was a knock at the farmhouse door. I opened it to what looked like a polar explorer – a man warmly clad but plastered with snow from hood to boot. He told me that his car had gone off the road into the ditch half a mile away. We gave him a cup of tea while I put on warmer clothes and got my powerful torch. Then I got out the tractor, wrapped the heavy drag chain round the hydraulic power arms and with the benighted traveller standing on the draw bar, drove through eighteen inches of snow to the end of the farm road and down the hill to where his car was cowped with both right hand wheels well into the ditch. Within minutes we had the vehicle back on the road and the engine restarted. He thanked me warmly and insisted on knowing my name.

'Are you the Liberal mannie?' he asked.

'One of them,' I said. 'They're as common as rabbits hereabouts!'

'Well now, you won't regret tonight's work,' he said. And I never did. My friend was a well-respected farmer from the far side of Huntly and his support was invaluable among the farming community in that part of the constituency.

By 1963 I was convinced we had an outside chance of winning the constituency and agreed to have my name put forward. My adoption meeting was held in Alford village hall and the main speaker and proposer was the famous and beloved Johnny Bannerman. The hall was packed. He charmed everybody for twenty minutes, then it was my turn. I knew I did not have his powers of oratory, but I had a very clear idea of what I wanted to see done for Scotland and for the north-east. When the time came for questions from the floor, I found I could handle them. This ability later proved useful during election campaigns, when I learned to recognise the catch question, to parry the aggressive one with a touch of humour and to answer the straightforward one in the way it was asked. Above all I was willing to admit if I did not know the answer and would take a name and address and offer to find out. Johnny Bannerman complimented me on my ability to think on my feet. Coming from a man of his achievements, I regarded this as one of the greatest compliments I had ever received.

The first objective at the General Election in 1964 was to overcome the credibility gap. Time and time again people said, 'We'd like to see you win, but it just can't be done. The Tories are too well entrenched.' When the count took place, I had polled nearly 12,000 votes. The Labour candidate almost lost his deposit and the sitting member, though victorious by over 4,000 votes, was severely shaken.

One issue which polarised opinions in the western extremity of West Aberdeenshire was the policy of the owner of the Candacraig Estate, bought many years later by Billy Connolly. He was planting trees on the low ground by the river, which was ideal for rearing livestock and, at the same time, reclaiming hillsides as pastureland, collecting government grants for both operations simultaneously. As a result of this policy, many tenanted farms in Strathdon were made uneconomic and the foresters faced great difficulty in keeping newly planted young trees above the vigorous growth of grass and weeds on very fertile land which had been grazed for centuries.

I had a duel with the laird both in my newspaper column and in person at the dinner associated with the Lonach Gathering, the long-established Highland Games in Strathdon. I was the guest speaker and the laird of Candacraig was present as a guest. I had decided to be uncontroversial and had prepared what I hoped was a suitably light-hearted after-dinner speech with no political content. As I spoke, the laird began making rude, unnecessary and irrelevant interjections. At least half of those present were his tenantry. Eventually I got riled and turned on him.

'You've had too much to drink. Would you either shut up or go home?'

You could have heard a sporran squeak. I continued my speech where I had left off. Before I reached the end, the laird rose unsteadily to his feet and left the hall. At once there was a palpable relaxation of tension and in due course the evening concluded in good spirits. However, there was an unsavoury sequel to the affair. The laird owned the hall in which the dinner had taken place. He owned the field in which the Lonach Gathering was held. He threatened that unless I was banned from future dinners of the Lonach Society, neither property would be made available to the Society in future. The committee responded by refusing to ban me personally, but declared that in future no political candidate or Member of Parliament could be invited to the annual dinner.

The 1964 election had produced a hung parliament and it was obvious that another election would take place before very long. As my Liberal colleagues prepared enthusiastically for this event, I was becoming increasingly worried about Kit's health. I asked the chairman of my constituency association to find a replacement and wrote to George Mackie, by then MP for Caithness and Sutherland, explaining the situation.

George appeared at Tillychetly without warning one evening just before Christmas. I invited him to stay for supper. Kit was displeased and made it perfectly clear that he was not welcome. Nevertheless he stayed and after supper we moved to the sitting room where I had lit a fire. Kit had disappeared to bed. Over a pot of coffee and a bottle of Glenmorangie we talked – or rather George did. He pointed out the difficulty of finding another suitable candidate at such short notice and the disappointment of those who had worked so hard to build up the organisation, if I did not stand. By 2 a.m. the coffee was cold, the bottle was empty and I had agreed that if the election came before 30 June 1966 I would contest the seat. If it came after that date, a substitute would have to be found. I was not entirely happy about the outcome, but I had now given my word and could only make the best of the situation.

Election

The Election came in May 1966. Shortly before it was called, I went down with what I thought was a severe attack of flu. I had rarely been unwell and never to the point where I had to stay in bed. Our doctor advised me to withdraw my candidature. So did the local minister. I was, however, committed to a carefully pre-arranged plan involving visits to places of work in the morning – auction marts, quarries, schools, factories and even a knacker's yard. Each afternoon I was to spend four hours on house-to-house visits. Each evening there would be three or four meetings to address, sometimes in places several miles apart. Kit had by now told me that she would not vote for me and was indifferent to what I did. I neither expected nor got much attention as I lay in bed feeling horribly unwell. Years later I had a blood test which indicated I was a burnt-out case of brucellosis, transmitted by cattle.

Three weeks before polling day, I forced myself to get up, bathed and shaved rather shakily, put on my warmest clothes, reversed the third-hand Land Rover out of the shed and drove to the organisation offices in Inverurie. There I checked through the programme with my agent Gerald Ritchie and talked briefly to some of my supporters who were stuffing envelopes with my election address* and looking with horror at their pale, haggard candidate. As I set off to visit a paper mill in Bucksburn I was thinking to myself, This is either going to kill or cure me! Fortunately for me, it was the latter.

Everybody was astonished, myself not least, at how very rapidly the hard routine subjugated the virus. By the third or fourth day I was feeling reasonably well. By the end of the first week I was in good form and feeling optimistic. By the end of the second week, my supporters and I were elated. For the first time

---

* See Appendix A.

we felt there was a real chance of winning. We were getting a good press and the sitting member was making some silly mistakes. By the eve of poll meetings in Culter, Bucksburn, Inverurie and Alford I was completely fit again. The meetings were well attended and even Kit had absorbed some of the enthusiasm and appeared at my final meeting. I never found out if she voted for me.

My plan on polling day was to visit every polling station in the 2,000-square-mile constituency, all seventy-two of them. This meant visiting the school in Alford to record my own vote as soon as the polling station opened, then setting off on an irregular anticlockwise circuit finishing on Deeside. I walked into the last polling station – a primary school in a Deeside village – at 9.10 p.m., ten minutes after the ballot boxes legally had to be sealed. Imagine my astonishment to find the Polling Officer – the local headmaster – and the local laird, a retired brigadier, stuffing slips of paper into the unsealed ballot box. Imagine their horror as they saw me. I have never seen two men appear more guilty. Unfortunately there were no witnesses and I realised there was nothing I could do. They had looked at one another and reached the same conclusion. When I asked why the boxes were not sealed, the Polling Officer replied that the van to collect them would not be down from Upper Deeside for another twenty minutes. 'By law the ballot boxes should have been sealed at nine o'clock,' I said. 'I'm going to stay and watch you do it.' Sourly and without another word, the schoolmaster carried out his duty. The Brigadier stumped up and down the room, snorting and coughing.

Inadvertently, I had exposed a real flaw in our supposedly watertight electoral system. In a rural area where the timetable for collecting ballot boxes is known to the Polling Officer, there is nothing to prevent him ticking off the names of any electors who have not voted and casting a few illegal votes for the candidate of his choice before sealing the box. Every party fielding a candidate should have a representative at each polling station to guard against this.

The following morning I drove early to the Assembly Rooms in Aberdeen where the count was due to be held. By the time I arrived, the count had already started and I had accumulated a respectable pile of votes. As the day progressed, I appeared to be overtaking the Tory incumbent and he began to look pale and drawn, with beads of sweat forming on his forehead. I began to feel sorry for him. It was certainly no joke for a member of his party, a well-established Member of Parliament, to lose what was considered to be a safe seat.

I won by 1,195 votes. I was subject to a whole range of mixed emotions: elation because we had achieved what many people considered impossible; sadness because I suspected that my new status would play havoc with my fragile domestic situation; disbelief that I was now actually a Member of Parliament; and determination to do everything within my limited power to justify my election.

I returned to Alford where a party had been organised to celebrate the victory. I even ended up singing for the company. The most satisfying aspect was the intense pleasure which the result was obviously giving to all who had worked hard and long to get me elected. Kit seemed as happy as everybody else in Alford Public Hall at the moment of victory. Perhaps, I thought, the stimulation of being the wife of an MP will help her.

The following evening, I was interviewed by Grampian Television in a post-election programme with two leagues of participants – the first league was for politicians of established reputation such as Jo Grimond and Sir Alec Douglas-Home, and the second for newcomers such as Alick Buchanan-Smith, Donald Dewar and myself. Sir Alec asked me if we had not met before. I told him that I had shouted support for the Liberal candidate at the by-election in his own constituency, West Perthshire, as he went past. 'It didn't make the slightest difference did it?' was his good-humoured reply. There was an honesty and directness about him which is not the commonest of qualities in a politician. I was touched when he recognised me and spoke some words of encouragement on my first day in the House of Commons, despite my not being of his party.

With Harold Wilson's government in power, the Liberals were sharing the Opposition benches with the Conservatives. Not all of them were as gentlemanly as Sir Alec. The very first time I went to take my seat on those benches, somebody put out a foot to trip me up. It was quite deliberate. I turned and looked down at a pale, sour face.

'Did you do that on purpose?'

He ignored my question but said, 'You won't last long in this place.'

'I don't intend to spend a lifetime here. I just want to do a few things that need to be done for Scotland and then I shall go.' He looked surprised and smiled disbelievingly. That was John Biffen, later to become Leader of the House in Mrs Thatcher's government.

On another much later occasion, I took Johnny Bannerman to the House of Commons Smoking Room for a drink. We were halfway through our dram when Willie Whitelaw advanced on us. Ignoring Lord Bannerman, he addressed me contemptuously. 'You appear to be unaware of the rules of the House. Only members or former members of the House of Commons are allowed to drink in the Smoking Room.'

Johnny Bannerman, of course, had gone straight to the Lords without being elected to the Commons. I asked if we could just finish our drinks, but Willie Whitelaw said we could not. Lord Bannerman drained his glass and walked with dignity from the room. I did not mind the rule. I objected to the way Willie Whitelaw had set about enforcing it. To give him his due, he apologised the next time he saw me.

I was not one of those members for whom Westminster is the centre of the universe or the best club in the world. I disliked the smell of the place, the hothouse atmosphere, the enmity of certain members caused by nothing more than the fact that I belonged to a different party. At a personal level, I disliked living in a big city away from my family and from the countryside. I could not afford accommodation any better than a small room in the National Liberal Club, dominated by central heating pipes which clanked all night. In those days MPs earned only £3,000 a year.

I wanted to do things for my constituency and found it appallingly frustrating that there was so little I could do. I like to see results from my work, but at Westminster results were usually imperceptible. Jo Grimond made me the Liberal Party's spokesman in the House on Foreign Affairs and Defence. There were only thirteen of us. Membership of the EEC and of NATO were mainstays of our foreign policy. Over the four years I was in the House I put down 309 written questions, made 183 speeches and contributions to debates, asked 179 oral questions, introduced two Private Member's bills, initiated two debates on the Adjournment and delivered one petition from my constituents. I do not believe I ever left a constituent's letter unanswered and almost every weekend when Parliament was in session, I held clinics in different parts of West Aberdeenshire. I served on several committees and attended almost every debate on Scottish affairs, agriculture, foreign affairs and defence. I was a member of two small Parliamentary delegations: to the United Nations, and to Singapore when the former colony achieved independence.

Of all the speeches I made, few were significant and only two perhaps memorable. One of these was not made in the House of Commons but at the annual conference of the Liberal Party when I was Foreign Affairs spokesman. By the late 1960s the Young Liberal movement was becoming the tail that wagged the party dog, nearly causing it to fall on its left side. Official Liberal defence policy was to maintain membership of NATO, support a NATO-controlled nuclear deterrent – preferably maritime-based, not land-based – but to dispense with the independent British nuclear deterrent. The Young Liberals put down a motion supporting unilateral nuclear disarmament and opting out of NATO.

The credibility of the Liberal Party was on the line. The media were waiting with relish to see if the party would tear itself apart in front of the TV cameras. I decided that this was one situation where attack really would be the best form of defence. I prepared my speech meticulously then tore into the Young Liberals' motion, labelling it 'ill-conceived, based on a total lack of practical knowledge, virtually impossible to implement and so damaging to the credibility of the Liberal Party that it would leave us without the framework for any foreign policy in the future.' I supported my arguments with a battery of well-researched facts and statistics. Support for the motion crumbled. I was given a standing ovation and enjoyed a brief period of television celebrity

– at least with that small part of the general public who watch party political conferences!

In Parliament I spoke several times on the subject of the war in Vietnam, about which I had very strong feelings. I had long been convinced that for the Vietnamese this was a war for national survival, and there was a real danger that the United Kingdom might be dragged into it. I am still convinced that peace talks would have started much sooner if both government and opposition parties in Great Britain had opposed US involvement from the very start.

On 7 July 1966 I spoke at length for the Liberal Party in the debate on Vietnam:

> The quickest way to bring to an end the risk faced by Commonwealth and American troops and airmen in Vietnam is to bring the parties concerned to the conference table ... We cannot support American action in Vietnam, not because we are anti-American in any way. It is simply because there is no genuine political objective in what the Americans are doing. Their action is thoroughly self-defeating. If they achieve a military victory – and this is questionable – although they may obliterate the strong points and occupy the cities and towns, it is unlikely in my view that they will be able to occupy the terrain and eliminate the guerrilla forces they are up against. Even if they do this there will still be the threat of political collapse in South Vietnam. It must be appreciated that there is a wide gulf between the South Vietnam military junta and the South Vietnamese people. In this policy of escalation, the point will be reached, is bound to be reached, when China will hit back...

> Hansard, HC (series 5) vol. 731, cols 781–7

I pointed out that the Vietnamese had faced one long struggle against foreign domination: first against the Chinese, then against the French, then the Japanese, then the French again and now against the Americans. I concluded:

> There seem to be just four points in dispute: the United States will not negotiate with the National Liberation Front; they have also said they want free elections in South Vietnam. If they would agree to negotiate with the National Liberation Front and agree to

free elections throughout Vietnam, the position would be entirely changed. On the other side, the North Vietnamese want United States withdrawal as a preliminary condition and they also want no intervention by the United Nations. If they would be prepared to concede on these two points, I see no reason why a solution should not be found within a reasonably short time.'

Hansard, HC (series 5) vol. 731, cols 781–7

Years and many thousands of deaths later, this is roughly what happened. Sir Alec Douglas-Home walked from the opposition front bench to congratulate me on this speech.

In 1968, I asked the Prime Minister whether he had considered the further expert evidence, details of which I had sent to him, of the permanent damage to the soil and hence to the future of Vietnamese agriculture, caused by the US spraying herbicides from the air. He thanked me for the trouble I had taken to send him the information but added, 'I still, however, have seen no evidence that the use of herbicides in Vietnam is causing lasting harm to the ecology of that country.'

Obviously he had not read the evidence I had sent him.

At that time there was a very respectable organisation called the Great Britain–USSR Association. General Tom Churchill was chairman, with three vice-chairmen – one from each of the three major political parties. I was the Liberal Party nomination for vice-chairman, but the Russians refused to accept me. A Soviet official by name of Chubarov hinted that I had been a spy. The *Evening Express* and *Daily Telegraph* got hold of the story, which was published under banner headlines. I took exception to one of the phrases used in the *Telegraph* – that I had been 'fingered' by Vassall – and got Stephen Tyrrell QC to write to the paper on my behalf. The *Telegraph* then published a full apology and a revised version of the story.

Some twenty years later I was approached in the Press Pavilion at the Royal Highland Show by a careworn journalist who told me I had lost him his job on the *Daily Telegraph*. Apparently he had been sacked because the first story had been inaccurate. I pointed out that this was his fault, not mine, but he maintained that a sub-editor had inserted the phrase I objected to. He asked me how the episode had ended. I told him I continued to act as vice-chairman of the Great Britain-USSR Association, that I was invited to and attended receptions organised by the British, but I was never invited when the Russians were hosts. The subject was resurrected in the press in 1996 when John Vassall died, and a national newspaper misleadingly reported that he had been a naval attaché in the British Embassy in Moscow. I wrote to the press informing them of their mistake, and that he had been a civilian Admiralty clerk and that I had written a report in May 1954, long before he was entrapped by the Russians, recommending that he should be sent back to London from Moscow.

In a Foreign Affairs debate on 20 July, I made the longest speech of my short parliamentary career – twenty-eight minutes. I ranged across the world from the United Nations in New York, and the Middle East to the Far East. I propounded the case, as I had done many times previously, for the United Kingdom to join the Common Market. Towards the end of this long speech I was interrupted more than once. Eventually the Speaker, Dr Horace King, intervened. He was a man for whom I had immense respect and with whom I was on good terms. 'Order, order. Will Honourable Gentlemen please remember that interruptions prolong long speeches and many Honourable Members wish to speak.' I took the hint, wound up and sat down.

Meeting in Copenhagen

During the summer Parliamentary recess of 1966, I led the British delegation to a conference of the Liberal International in Copenhagen. 23 September 1966 turned out to be one of the most important days in my life.

The conference was held in Cristiansslot, the Parliament building. As I walked up to the conference desk to register, I was struck by one of the two girls on duty. She was dark and vivacious with a pretty, intelligent face and an attractive voice. Good humour shone from her large olive green eyes and animated the corners of her mouth. I knew from her accent that she was English. She asked my name but clearly had never heard of me. She was not the least bit impressed that I was a Member of Parliament. She did seem to approve of me, but she looked like the sort of person who approved of most people who were not positively unpleasant.

At the beginning of those two or three days in Copenhagen, I thought it was just coincidence that I was always at the same table or in the same group as Janet, but I discovered later that she had arranged it that way. On the final evening, a group of half a dozen or more delegates and the administrative staff went along to the Tivoli Gardens. We explored that marvellous park, listened to some music, then the others wanted to go into a nightclub. It was horribly noisy and Janet and I decided we would prefer to go somewhere quiet where we could talk.

We found a small café and for the next two or three hours explored each other's lives and attitudes. By now she knew I was married and asked about my children. I told her about them, about the farm and about Kit's illness. She told me that she came from Harrow, was the youngest of a large family, that she currently worked as secretary to Andre Deutsch the publisher, but had been on the permanent staff of the Liberal International before that. She was qualified as a bilingual secretary in French and English and took her holidays to coincide with Liberal International conferences for the chance to travel. She loved Sibelius, Italian opera, Judy Garland and the Beatles and appeared to be a voracious reader.

I had never met anybody with whom I felt more at ease, whose outlook seemed so much in harmony with my own. There was a natural empathy between us which required no effort, no pretence. Well after midnight we left the café and I walked with Janet to her hotel and said what I thought would be a permanent goodbye to her at the door. I still believed that my marriage to Kit should and could be salvaged, if only the doctors could somehow cure her.

I left for London the next day and Janet returned to the UK a day later. After a week, I received a short note from her on the lines that she thought there was something important between us and did not want it to be lost. With some misgivings I agreed to meet her and we spent an afternoon on a boat trip down the Thames, at the end of which I said with great regret that we could not meet again. I was acutely aware of how much the children depended upon me for continuity and consistency, although I had to be away for much of the time. I also clung to the idea that Kit could become again the person she had been ten years earlier. It is traumatic when somebody beloved dies suddenly, or is struck down by a terminal illness, but I believe it is even harder to bear when illness completely changes the personality. When I said goodbye to Janet that evening, I did not intend to see her again.

At home, the situation was becoming desperately worrying. We had taken on a succession of home helps, some living in, some not. Kit was unable to get on with any of them, so the children had constant changes of people coming to look after them either full-time or part-time. Kit had started talking about getting a divorce and returning to her family in Canada. Her sleeping habits were irregular. She would go to bed soon after 8 p.m., having first put Polly to bed, then get up at four or five in the morning to play records, read, or do the washing. The older children were frequently left to their own devices. She was a heavy smoker and, under the influence of sleeping pills which she took in addition to other medication, she risked setting fire to the bed. On one occasion she burned a large hole in the bedding, but thankfully it only smouldered. I worried continually about her driving herself with the children, but I could not restrict her activities when I was away, and she ignored my pleas.

Problems began to build up in 1967. The cousin with whom I had gone into partnership on the farm when I was elected to Parliament told me privately that Kit had accused him of going through my desk. He avoided the house when I was not there. Kit had to go back into hospital at the beginning of April and stayed there for six weeks. Early spring was always a dangerous time for her. It seemed to exacerbate her illness.

In July 1967 I fulfilled a commitment to speak at a Foreign Affairs conference at Nottingham University. I was to be away for a weekend and had given Kit a note with the telephone numbers for the university and where I would be staying. On the Saturday afternoon Sandy, who was only twelve years old, became very worried by his mother's behaviour and wanted to telephone me, but she tore up my note to prevent him from doing so.

Kit had accused the seven-year-old daughter of Rob Riach, our tractorman, of stealing and told her and her mother to leave and not to come back. Rob and his wife Helen had been with us for nine years, living in a tied house on the farm. Their daughter was Polly's great friend and companion. Helen was a pillar of reliability: conscientious, hard-working, cheerful and good-natured with great tact and patience. She had been coming in regularly to help Kit in the house. I had felt that she, at least, was somebody with whom my wife could not quarrel.

Sandy waited until he could telephone his grandparents in Edinburgh. My father, then seventy-four, drove the 125 miles to the farm and arrived the same evening. Kit was truculent and would not agree to his ringing the doctor. My father was finally able to trace me at about 4 p.m. on Sunday. Although I was due in Westminster the following day, I undertook to come straight back home. I was waitlisted for three planes but was unable to get home until 10 p.m. on Monday.

My farming partner met me at the airport. My father had found his time at the farm very difficult and had returned to Edinburgh, feeling that his presence was actually making things worse for the children. At the farm I found Sandy and Ros sitting outside the house in the summer twilight, waiting for me. Polly was asleep in a sleeping bag on top of a bed and Kit had disappeared to bed earlier. Rosalind, aged ten, had cooked supper for Sandy and herself. I got both of them to bed, then had something to eat and went to bed myself.

I was woken at 4 a.m. by the sound of the radiogram blaring out and Barney, the Alsatian which Kit had bought, sniffing round the bed. I found Kit in a familiar pose, cross-legged on the floor in front of an electric heater in the kitchen, smoking. She asked why on earth I had come home and why on earth I had come downstairs. She could see nothing wrong with letting the dog upstairs to see the children. They loved him. She couldn't see why she shouldn't play music whenever she liked. I rang the Royal Cornhill Hospital and asked for the home number of the doctor in charge of her case so that I could ring him first thing. It was arranged that I should take Kit in to Aberdeen at 11 a.m. She refused to go, but finally I persuaded her to speak to the doctor herself, and she agreed to go and, in due course, to stay in hospital.

Before I could return to London for the final few days of the Parliamentary session, there was much to do. I had to make arrangements for someone to come and look after the children; I had to persuade Helen to forgive the insults and come back to help in the house and ask Rob not to give in his notice, which he had threatened to do.

Late in the evening, I went out to the back of the steading and sat on a heap of large boulders in the middle of the field, overlooking the Howe of Alford. Two miles away and 200 feet below me were the lights of the village. Across the Howe the familiar silhouette of Bennachie was still clear against the darkening sky. I knew that I had reached a crossroads, that I had vitally important decisions to take. If I did not take the right ones, at least four lives could be ruined. It was already too late to undo the damage done to the family by Kit's illness and my election to Parliament. It came to me with startling clarity that there were three things I now had to do. The first was to tell the Principal of the Cornhill Hospital I was not prepared to have Kit home until he could state in writing that she was a competent person to be looking after three young children. The second was to inform my Parliamentary colleagues and constituency officials that I would not defend the seat at the next election. The third was to get in touch with Janet again, if I could. Apart from short weekend visits home, when I was there, Kit remained in hospital for the next fifteen months. I helped her with funds to buy a flat in Aberdeen. She was allowed to leave hospital as long as she reported fortnightly to have an injection of the drugs essential to keep her condition reasonably stable.

I informed my local association in confidence of my decision not to stand for re-election. They did not try to dissuade me, knowing the circumstances, but they did ask me not to make any public announcement. One luxury my decision afforded me was to enable me to speak with complete political freedom for the remainder of my time in Parliament.

I had never known Janet's home address, but I rang Andre Deutsch's office, only to be told that she had given notice. Luckily they were able to give me a home telephone number. Janet's father answered and, with some reluctance, gave me a contact number. She was working at a Barnardo's Home in the south of Scotland. I eventually made contact with her and we agreed to meet in Glasgow. The past year evaporated like a bad dream. It was as if we had only been apart for a few days. In fact, it had been a year of intermittent hell for both of us. Janet had been convinced from the start that we had a future together and had been devastated by my refusal to see her. She had left her job as a result. We talked as I drove – three times through the Clyde Tunnel because I was not paying attention – and had lunch on Loch Lomondside. I told her everything that had happened and asked if she would be willing to come and help me. My idea was to advertise for someone to look after the children, and to do my parliamentary correspondence, in return for a salary and board and lodging. Helen would look after the housework. I would place an advertisement in the national papers. To my joy, Janet agreed.

There were two respondents to a carefully worded advertisement: Janet and one other. I arranged to interview them on successive days at the caravan site on the West Coast where I was taking the children on holiday. The other candidate was a very pleasant woman in her middle thirties and there was some hesitation, but no coercion, before there was a decision in favour of Janet. And so, a few weeks later, Janet came to look after us all. She had given up her career, her financial independence, her home and the opportunity of a conventional marriage to somebody nearer her own age. She was convinced it was the right thing to do and nearly forty years on I am thankful she was.

It was six years before Janet and I were able to marry. Although Kit had initiated the idea of a divorce some years before, she now fluctuated between wanting to return to Canada and staying on in Aberdeen. My priority was that I should have custody of the children. I told her that if she wanted to divorce me I would not contest it provided she did not seek custody. There followed endless wrangles between the two sets of solicitors. I would have liked to reach an agreement without having to go to court. Janet was a tower of strength and immensely patient. By 1971, Kit decided to start an action against me for desertion. Counsel advised me that such a case would fail and that I should start proceedings on the grounds of mental cruelty – in essence, that life had been made intolerable...

Looking back, it seems appalling that we all had to go through these legal contortions. Fortunately the law has since been altered to enable divorce on the grounds of the breakdown of a marriage. I was given a divorce in February 1973 with custody of the children and Janet and I were married soon after in a Register Office in Edinburgh with representatives of both our families present.

Kit left for Canada at one point but abandoned the idea of returning there permanently within a few months. She remained in Aberdeen, living quietly and pursuing her interest in antiques and the stock market. She was unable to work regularly. I took the children to visit her weekly in Aberdeen until Polly was sixteen. Thereafter the children made their own arrangements to see their mother, though Janet and I continued to help with transport.

Lords, Insults and the Iron Lady

During the short Christmas recess of 1966 Jo Grimond decided to retire as leader of the Liberal Party. He was a tired man and had not recovered from the tragic death of his elder son Andrew during the election campaign. Early in 1967, the thirteen Liberal MPs had to elect a new leader. The two candidates were Jeremy Thorpe and Emlyn Hooson QC. David Steel was still 'the boy David' and was not a contestant. Jo Grimond asked me privately if I would consider standing. Perhaps he thought of me as a compromise candidate, but I told him emphatically that I could not even think of it in view of my domestic situation.

I found it difficult to decide between Thorpe and Hooson. I knew Emlyn better than Jeremy. A quiet shrewd Welshman with a lot of charm, Emlyn shared my interests in farming and the countryside. He was natural and unaffected, but despite his legally trained mind and experience at the Bar, he cut little ice when he spoke in the House. He was too diffident and too pleasant to make an impression in that strident place. Jeremy, on the other hand, was a born actor with a quicksilver mind, a penetrating sense of humour and a gift for mimicry which would have made most of those who live by impersonation on stage and screen look like inferior amateurs. When he spoke in the House he commanded immediate attention and because of his reputation for wit and humour, when he chose to be serious he could be devastating.

I debated my choice for so long that when there were only two or three hours to go before the closing time for our votes, I was informed by one of the lobby correspondents that not only was I the last to vote, but that the votes so far cast were evenly balanced. He had asked each of the other MPs and, assuming that Jeremy and Emlyn would each vote for himself, it stood at six all. Fate had therefore given me the privilege and responsibility of deciding the next leader of the Liberal Party. Eventually I cast my vote for Jeremy on the basis of what I thought would be most acceptable to the party.

I continued to speak for the party on foreign affairs and defence and, sometimes, on agriculture when Alasdair Mackenzie, our official spokesman, was unavailable. Alasdair, the member for Ross and Cromarty, had been born and bred a crofter and had been in farming all his life. Tory backbenchers were inclined to laugh at his way of speaking. On one occasion I accosted one of these, the member for a semi-rural constituency in the south-east of England. I asked him what he found so funny.

'The man can't even speak the Queen's English,' he replied.

'How many languages do you speak?' I asked. There was no reply.

'Alasdair Mackenzie speaks two languages fluently,' I continued, 'English a little less so than Gaelic. Have you ever made a speech in a foreign language?'

'Don't be ridiculous.'

'Gaelic is Alasdair's native language. He won Ross and Cromarty because of the immense respect in which they hold him there and his first-hand knowledge of the area. I doubt if you could claim the same.'

I knew that the English expert was a carpet-bagger, a London solicitor.

On 16 April 1968 I wrote to Jeremy Thorpe to tell him about my domestic situation, concluding:

> I have told you only the barest outline of the situation but … against this background I would be wrong to contest West Aberdeenshire at the next General Election … I have taken this step for family reasons and with great regret. I think you will agree that, in the difficult circumstances, it is the only possible decision I can take.

A few days later, Jeremy asked me along to his office. I was used to going there once or twice a month when our irrepressible leader held court for a group of lobby correspondents and a few colleagues. These sessions would usually end with everybody helpless with laughter, often with tears trickling down their cheeks. On this occasion, though, he was seriously sympathetic.

Towards the end of the interview he said to me, 'Would you be interested in going to the other place?'

'The House of Lords?'

'Yes,' Jeremy answered. 'Harold said he could let me have one or two seats.'

This was preposterous. I began to laugh. For once Jeremy did not laugh with me. He actually looked offended.

'You're not serious,' I said, 'I couldn't possibly think of it. I'm going to have to work for a living when I leave this place. Besides, you know my opinion of the upper House.'

'No,' he said, somewhat coolly. 'What is your opinion of the upper House?'

I began to wish I had left it at a simple refusal.

'Well, I believe we need a second chamber, somewhere that people are appointed to on merit, but without any element of patronage or heredity. I can't see myself there, and anyway I do not have the income or domestic background to sustain it. Thank you all the same.'

I left Jeremy's office in an atmosphere of slight constraint.

At lunch that day, I recounted what had happened to two of my Liberal colleagues, not expecting them to take it any more seriously than I had myself. Within a day or two I was sent for by Jeremy again. This time he was really angry.

'What do you mean by telling the others something which I asked you in confidence?'

'You didn't tell me it was confidential and I wasn't even sure whether you meant it seriously or as a joke.'

He smiled wryly, conceding that one of his weaknesses was that his own sense of humour sometimes prevented others from taking him seriously, then he continued. 'Frank Byers was livid. He asked me what on earth I was doing offering peerages around my colleagues without first consulting the Liberal Lords.'

Lord Byers, a somewhat self-important individual, was Liberal Leader in the House of Lords. I had always found him irritating.

'You can tell Frank Byers to take a running jump at himself. And if you haven't already done so, you can tell him I don't want a bloody peerage. I've quite enough on my plate already without hanging that millstone round my neck.'

I was appointed to a Parliamentary delegation to the United Nations in New York, where we were given a fascinating insight into the workings of the organisation. I suffered from an air of unreality throughout the fortnight we were there, perhaps because we did not have a job to do, perhaps because my mind was at home with the family and domestic problems.

One evening I was taken out to dinner by the parents of one of the secretaries in the Liberal Whip's office. The husband was a senior man in international insurance. They knew of my farming background and took me to a restaurant reputed to have the best quality beef and lamb in New York. I chose lamb, which was deliciously tender, but with less flavour, I thought, than the Scottish product. My host invited the proprietor to join us for a drink at the end of the meal, and he asked me about beef and lamb rearing techniques in Scotland. I told him I had a flock of North Country Cheviot ewes and used a Suffolk ram for tupping the older ewes. The cross was a lean, quick-growing lamb of high quality which I finished on brassica crops, notably rape, for the late autumn and Christmas market. The restaurateur's eyes lit up. 'Raped Scotch lamb,' he muttered. 'That would look great on my menu!'

On the spot he offered me a price per pound for my lambs which in a year or two would have made me a rich man. It would have paid to send the lambs across the Atlantic sitting up business class in a jet aircraft. I had about 160 ewes. I did a quick calculation. My fortune was made! I went back to my hotel that night in a state of elation and hardly slept. Early the next day, before our first commitment at the UN, I took a taxi to the office of the British Commercial Attaché. Breathlessly, I began to enquire about export permits and import licences. The Attaché looked at me ironically.

'You do know that the United States will not import meat from Europe with the bone in? Your lambs would have to be de-boned and vacuum-packed.'

My vision of a quick fortune evaporated before my eyes. The cost of installing de-boning and vacuum-packaging machinery, veterinary inspections, transport and licensing would eliminate any difference between my costs of production and the end price in New York. I should have known there would be a catch somewhere.

Shortly before we left New York we were invited, by an aristocratic member of the British delegation, to a cocktail party at the home of a wealthy New Yorker with whom he and his wife had been staying. The wife was said to have been a Bluebell girl. She was tall, striking-looking and adept at downing Manhattans. By the time the party had been going for about an hour she was causing both her husband and her host considerable embarrassment. When she grabbed me by the arm and tried to propel me up the stairs, I had to use considerable force to detach myself without causing a fracas. It was the most difficult diplomatic task I performed in the course of my duties as a delegate to the UN.

In May 1968 I participated in a debate on the Scottish aspects of the Transport Bill, an immensely complicated piece of legislation which took many weeks to pass through its various stages in the House. On a certain abstruse clause, we voted with the government when the Tory Opposition apparently expected us to vote with them. It was a close call and indeed the government would have been defeated if we had voted against them, but in political terms it would have been a minor blip. Some of the Tory backbenchers were incandescent with rage. As we returned to our seats from the Division Lobbies, one of them bounced up and down with sweat trickling down his face, repeating over and over again, 'Dirty, filthy, slimy curs! Dirty, filthy, slimy curs!'

I was astonished. I had frequently seen schoolboy behaviour on the floor of the House but never anything quite so puerile. He was seated almost directly behind me. He went on and on with his incantation. Eventually I turned to him. 'Are you calling me a dirty, filthy, slimy cur?'

He changed from the plural to the singular: 'Dirty, filthy, slimy cur! Dirty, filthy, slimy cur!'

The veins were standing out on his forehead and it looked as if his eyes were about to burst out of their sockets.

'If I'm a dirty, filthy, slimy cur,' I said, 'you know what you must be. You're right behind me, hot and steaming.'

On the whole, Labour MPs behaved in a civilised manner and were mostly there to do what they could for their constituents.

Any trouble I had was invariably with members of the official Opposition. I was unpopular with them because I had deprived one of their chums of a seat they had held for thirty years.

Seven MPs were chosen as guinea pigs to undergo a quick reading course in the House of Commons. Tony Buzan, well known as an advocate of original methods of memory training and parallel techniques, was to teach us a method used by President Kennedy. The group was to consist of three Labour, three Conservative and one Liberal MP – me. I do not remember all the participants on the course, but two of the Tories made an impression – Eldon Griffiths because he seemed to find it very difficult, and Margaret Thatcher because she thought she knew better and would not take it seriously.

The technique consisted of hand movements to guide the eyes across the page, coupled with a determination not to 'speak' the words internally. It took great concentration even to master the system, but most of us found that it could be made to work. To this day I still use it for reading reports, legal documents or dull newspaper articles.

At the very beginning of the course Mrs Thatcher decided that it was a waste of time. If John F. Kennedy had been a Republican, she might have thought differently. After one session, I took Tony Buzan down to the House of Commons bar for a pint of beer.

'I wish somebody would take that damned woman off the course,' he said. 'She makes it twice as difficult for me and she's no help to anyone else either.' I had to agree. At that time Margaret Thatcher was shadow Minister of Education. I doubt if anybody then considered her as a future prime minister.

At the end of the course we were expected to take tests, consisting of reading certain documents within preset times – only possible using the quick-reading technique – then answering questions to measure our absorption and comprehension of the information in the documents. Six of the seven of us took the tests, all achieving results between seventy and ninety per cent. Mrs Thatcher did not turn up.

Bills and Petitions

I first encountered the iniquities of feu duties back in the early 1960s during the by-election in West Perth and Kinross, in which Sir Alec Douglas-Home was the Conservative candidate and Alastair Duncan Millar the Liberal, whom I was supporting. A feu was land held in perpetuity, or sometimes for ninety-nine years, in return for a payment of an annual rent or 'feu duty'. More often than not the feu holder no longer had any connection with the land or property concerned and there could be a chain of 'feudal superiorities', each paying a feu duty to his 'feudal superior', going back to the monarch. The worst aspect of this feudal system (now abolished) was that a feudal superior could prevent any sort of development of the land or property over which he held 'feudal superiority'.

Perth and Kinross was the most gentlemanly election campaign in which I was ever involved. However, in the resort town of Pitlochry I came across an example of very ungentlemanly conduct. A Mr MacDonald managed a small hotel on the main street of the town. He had applied for a licence for his expanding hotel business. His 'feudal superior' invoked an old feu charter and prevented him from getting the licence. As Mr MacDonald explained to me when I called, the 'feudal superior' was not only the then-owner of one of the largest and most successful hotels in the town, but simultaneously the chairman of the licensing court – and of the Conservative Association.

It seemed to me a gross injustice that a so-called feudal superior could prevent a potential competitor from expanding his business by invoking the terms of an archaic form of land tenure. It might have been a reasonable system before the planning laws were enacted, but it had become totally unreasonable when used to stifle competition or hinder legitimate development.

Parallel with the feu charter, but much less common and widespread, was a system of multures – mill dues paid by a farm for the use of a local mill which, in the majority of cases, no longer existed! I had come across one case where a small farmer had to pay multures to the owners of two non-existent mills. The multures had become legally established 'burdens' on the farm he occupied and he was obliged to pay them.

I knew of a blacksmith, a constituent of mine, who wished to expand his premises into a light engineering works to serve the farming community over a wide rural area. He was one of the efficient ones who had survived the fierce competition of the age of farm mechanisation. He had plans prepared and had been informed by the Board of Trade that the extension would be eligible for a grant, but the feudal superior withheld permission.

Another constituent had bought one-eighth of an acre to build a house on the false assumption that the land was freehold. Having built the house he discovered that there was a feu to pay. He came to terms to purchase the feu, only to discover that the man he had bargained with was merely the 'mid-superior'. A wrangle then started between the mid-superior and the 'superior', ending in the superior demanding a payment of ten times as much. In that case, the less greedy mid-superior won and the householder gained the freehold of his property.

In February 1967 I was successful in the ballot for Private Member's Bills. I brought in a bill 'Applicable to Scotland to enable vassals under a feu charter, occupiers of agricultural property liable to payment of multures and lessees and sub-lessees occupying residential property under certain long leases to commute their financial obligations and for purposes connected therewith.'

I introduced the Bill by saying:

> We ... consider that the feudal system is not only a relic of an outdated social system but that it is also one of the three main obstacles to development in Scotland. The other two major obstacles ... are the lack of capital investment and the poor system of communications ... The origins of the system are lost in the mists of time. Long ago the sovereign was the owner of all the land. Land was granted to vassals in return for goods or services; military services, sexual services, agricultural services or sometimes part of the crop ... Apart from being an anachronism

in a property-owning democracy and an immense complication
in the legislation relating to conveyancing, the feudal system pro-
vides a second 'planning permission' which may or may not be
wisely used.

Hansard, HC (series 5) vol. 777, cols 64–6

My Bill suffered the fate of virtually all Ten-Minute Rule Bills. It
was talked out, but I continued to pursue the matter. I went to see
Willie Ross, then Secretary of State for Scotland, on more than
one occasion and he gave me a promise that the government
would introduce its own Bill. In due course they did, but I still
thought my proposals better than the legislation contained in the
successful Bill, although my drafting may have been less professional. Private members do not have the assistance of the
professional drafters unless a Bill has official government support.

I can claim to be the first MP ever to propose referenda as a
means of solving problems of nationality and sovereignty.
Following a dispute between Spain and the United Kingdom
regarding the future of Gibraltar, I put down a written question
on 4 August 1966 asking the Secretary of State for the colonies to
'hold a referendum in Gibraltar to establish whether it is the wish
of the majority of the people of Gibraltar to be granted independence to remain in free association with the UK or to be
integrated with the UK or Spain.' My question was answered by
John Stonehouse, later to disappear from the political scene in
strange circumstances; he 'did not believe any form of referendum would be helpful at present...' Yet a few months later
Harold Wilson's government precisely followed my proposal and
the people of Gibraltar decided by a huge majority to remain in
free association with the UK.

Two years on, I presented a Private Member's Bill to give
Scotland and Wales the same opportunity: 'The Scotland and
Wales (Referenda) Bill to authorise referenda in Scotland and in
Wales to enable the Scottish and Welsh peoples respectively to
indicate their views in regard to the government of their
countries.' The Bill was read for the first time on 27 November
1968, and 14 February 1969 was appointed as the date for the
Second Reading. Inevitably the Bill was defeated because the

Labour government would not allocate time for it; it would take them another thirty years – with Mrs Thatcher intervening – to give Scotland and Wales self-government in domestic affairs.

My last campaign in Parliament was an attempt to save the Inverurie Locomotive Works from closure. Inverurie was the biggest town in my constituency. The 580 jobs provided by the Works represented a high proportion of the available employment in the town. The decision to close the Works rested on the assertion that there was excess loco works capacity in the northern half of the British Isles. Inverurie was chosen not because it was inefficient or troublesome, but because it was realised that the British Railways Board and the government would meet powerful opposition from the unions if they tried to reduce the capacity of the enormous St Rollox Works in Glasgow. The Inverurie Loco Works, in a constituency where the Labour candidate had lost his deposit, could be steamrollered.

I knew that all the dice were loaded against us but decided to use every means available to a backbench MP to fight the closure: a petition, a debate on the adjournment, written and oral questions to the Minister, the media, appeals to the British Railways Board and to firms capable of taking over the Works and its labour force.

I asked the President of the Board of Trade if he would make West Aberdeenshire, and in particular the Burgh of Inverurie, a Special Development Area. I presented a petition on behalf of 5,000 constituents and many influential bodies in the north-east of Scotland including the Corporation of the City of Aberdeen.

I opened a Debate on the Adjournment with the aim of making an unanswerable case for the retention of the Inverurie Locomotive Works as an industrial unit. I stressed a few important facts:

> The Works employ about 580 men, one in four of the insured population of the Royal Burgh of Inverurie. Of those men, 224 are skilled and 204 semi-skilled. There are 100 salaried staff and the rest are unskilled, including forty apprentices … When it is appreciated that the population of Inverurie is only 5,267, it can be seen that it is a real railway town. The only other manufacturing is a small paper mill and without the loco works,

Inverurie will be a town without a heart – unless there is a successful transplant from somewhere else. At present, the carriage shop is working at full capacity with occasional pockets of overtime. The wagon shop is in the same position ... The blacksmith shop, too, is very busy and working overtime... The factory is situated only sixteen miles from the freightliner terminal at Aberdeen, on the fast line from Aberdeen to Inverness and only twelve miles from Dyce Airport ... In America, Russia or Australia, 500 miles is nothing, but it seems it is an insurmountable obstacle in this congested little island ... The management of the Inverurie Works claim that for certain types of work costs are less than half those at other works. Surely it must be a very expensive journey to wipe out that advantage...

I asked the Minister not to say in his reply that a final decision rested with the Board of British Railways. The final decision was in the hands of the government and he knew it.

The response from the Joint Secretary to the Ministry of Transport, Neil Carmichael, was flattering to me, and my concern, but he emphasised that it was the British Railways Board, and not the government, which would have to take the decision. I liked Neil Carmichael and felt sorry for him. I knew I would never have to make a speech expressing a view I did not hold, or advocating a policy I did not agree with, just to retain a job in government. I still do not understand to this day how a board set up following the nationalisation of an industry could be considered as not responsible to the government. It was not responsible to any shareholders and, as we were to discover a week or two later, the Board obviously felt no responsibility to the taxpayers who were theoretically the owners of the business.

Once the Board had announced its decision that the workshops were to be closed, in January 1969, I found a firm from the south of England, manufacturing a wide variety of valves for the engineering industry, which was desperately short of skilled labour. The management was genuinely interested in taking over the Inverurie works together with the skilled labour force. All they wanted was bridging finance to tide them over. I had discovered that this was possible under the terms of the Industrial Expansion Act 1968. I was bitterly disappointed when the government declined to help. I am convinced that they were wrong to allow the closure, but the subsequent discovery of North Sea oil saved the area from irreversible economic depression.

In 1969, my last year in Parliament, I decided that if Sandy and Rosalind were to see the inside of the House of Commons while I was still there, it would have to be before the summer recess. They had never been south of the Border in their lives and were enormously excited at the prospect. Polly was too young, so Janet took her to stay with my parents in Edinburgh.

Having the two children in London with me was as much a holiday for me as it was for them. I timed their visit to coincide with a week when I had no major commitments, though I had tabled an oral question to the Prime Minister. I booked seats in the gallery of the Commons so that Sandy and Rosalind could watch while I asked it. More conventional entertainment included Madam Tussaud's, the zoo, and the Post Office tower – subsequently closed because of IRA bombs.

On the Friday, we took a boat trip on the Thames, having left our luggage and travel tickets in the office in St Stephen's Tower which I shared with six other MPs. We got back to Westminster with an hour to spare before our overnight bus was due to leave. The House was deserted and the lobbies echoed to the sound of three pairs of feet of assorted sizes.

I was shocked to find that the door to my office had been locked. I was unaware that it was usual practice over the weekend. Like most Scottish MPs, unless there was business on a Friday directly concerning my constituency, I usually travelled north on Thursday nights. Leaving the children sitting dejectedly at the top of the stair, I searched the lobbies for some official who could tell me where the keys were kept. I had trouble finding anyone at all. The policemen at the entrance did not have the slightest idea where the keys were. I looked at my watch. There was less than half an hour before the bus was due to leave. It was Easter and I had been obliged to book weeks in advance. If we missed the bus I had no accommodation booked and little money. This was before the days of credit cards; the banks were closed and my cheque book was locked in my luggage. The children had already been left alone for twenty minutes when hot, angry and frustrated, I clambered back up the stone staircase.

The door was of solid oak and about two inches thick. I gave it a kick but it did not even shiver. Aiming at the upright nearest to the lock, I charged with my right shoulder. The door withstood my thirteen-and-a-half stones with a slight creak of protest. By now the children were nearly in tears. They were worried that I would be arrested and sent to prison and then, of course, we would miss the bus... I mustered all my anger, frustration and weight, retreated to the top of the stairs and charged the door with the utmost determination. The upright splintered and the door flew open.

'Grab your bags!' I shouted, and we tore down the stairs. By great good fortune we found a taxi and got to the bus station with three minutes to spare.

I reported my break-in to the authorities the following week, expecting to be sent a bill I could ill afford for the repair of the door. Instead I was sent for by the Minister of Works, Bob Mellish, a genial Labour politician of vast experience and placid temperament. He asked what had happened. I told him and asked in turn how much I was going to have to pay. He made some pleasant comment about my having helped to provide employment, but asked me please not to make a habit of it. For a few days, I got the impression that people stepped aside to let me pass.

Perhaps my main claim to fame in the House of Commons was the Aberdeen dinner. I and many other MPs found the House of Commons dining room a very expensive place to eat. It was all right for those with private means or who received directorships or retainers from affluent organisations, but I had to find a way of getting a decent meal at a reasonable cost. I came up with the Aberdeen dinner, consisting of hors d'oeuvre and cheese. With the help of a friendly and co-operative waitress, it was possible to get a good plateful of sardines, tomatoes, rollmop herring, potato salad, gherkins, olives, hard-boiled eggs and other substantial delicacies. The cheese board was good, too, and with half a dozen biscuits and samples of two or three different cheeses, a nourishing meal could be had at an affordable cost. The Aberdeen dinner kept me well-sustained and fit. It is just a pity that more of my battles were not successful.

Country Focus

Having handed over day-to-day management of the farm to my partner, I knew I had to find some other work to do once my time in Parliament came to an end. I had tried to prepare myself and, by taking a three-year correspondence course and by working late at night and early in the morning, I gained graduate membership of the Institute of Export. I had also taken residential courses in management and marketing during the summer recesses. By the spring of 1970, with the General Election imminent, I felt ready to start looking for a job – not just any job but one in Scotland which would cause as little further disruption to the children as possible.

Just before the Election, Charlie Smith, Head of News and Current Affairs at Grampian Television, asked me to present the fortnightly farming and countryside programme *Country Focus*. I was excited at the idea, but cautious. I had experience of being interviewed but not of interviewing other people. I would be following men of the stature of Watson Peat and Mike Joughin, both successful farmers and former presidents of the NFU of Scotland. Watson Peat went on to become a Governor of the BBC and Mike Joughin to become Chairman of the North of Scotland Hydro-Electric Board.

I did not take to television like a duck to water and initially found it a nerve-racking business. I eventually presented *Country Focus* for twelve years but never failed to get butterflies in the stomach as the lights in the studio were adjusted, the seconds ticked away to the start of the programme and the opening bars of the signature tune broke the silence.

Country Focus was a magazine programme and I usually shared the task of linking the component pieces with one of the regular studio presenters – often with Jimmy Spankie. His presence invariably helped to generate an atmosphere of calm and of good humour. The main subject of the programme would be discussed with Charlie Smith a fortnight in advance and anyone I thought appropriate to interview would be invited. Occasionally the programmes went out live, but usually they were recorded. This made little difference to the pressure because Grampian TV was a relatively small company and studio time was so valuable that they could not afford to re-record. Only in an emergency was the programme, or part of it, re-recorded. This happened about twice in the 200 programmes I was involved in, both times due to technical hitches.

On one occasion when we nearly had to go again I was conducting a four-minute interview with a scientist – a specialist in animal husbandry. In our pre-show discussions he had been as knowledgeable and articulate as I expected him to be. I was confident that he knew his subject very thoroughly. However, the atmosphere in a studio is different and four minutes there can seem like eternity.

I started, 'Dr X, you have been conducting these experiments on farrowing sows for two or three years now?'

'Yes.'

'What is the main purpose of your experiments?'

No reply. His face was as pale as suet, beaded with sweat. His mouth was partly open and his jaw rigid. Not a word would come out. I tried to help him.

'I know that you have managed to increase litter size by an average of more than ten per cent. Can you tell me how you've managed to achieve this?'

He emitted a few meaningless words through his ossified mouth. The next three and a half minutes were the most uncomfortable I ever spent in a television studio. Somehow those 210 seconds had to be filled. Never did I do more to earn my fee. I asked the questions, paused for a few grunts from the pig expert, then provided the answers myself, so far as I was able. The most embarrassing moment came after the programme was finished. Suddenly, Dr X became articulate again. He was profusely apologetic and wanted to do the interview again. He was really angry when told it was impossible.

I usually enjoyed *Country Focus*. I liked the studio atmosphere, the relaxed but professional attitude of the studio crews, and I met a great many interesting people. For better or for worse my own face became well known throughout the north of Scotland. I am still called Jim by people I meet for the first time, despite the passing of years and the growing of a beard, all because I was the farmer who presented *Country Focus* at 6.20 p.m. every other Tuesday from 1970 to 1982. This provincial fame gave me many moments of amusement and pleasure. Once I took the children to look round the lighthouse at Ardnamurchan – the most westerly point on the mainland of Great Britain. As my head appeared through the hole in the floor of the lamp-room at the very top, the keeper exclaimed, 'My God, Jim! I thocht you were in Aberdeen.' He had been keeper of the Buchan Ness lighthouse for a number of years and enjoyed the programme because it dealt with an environment so different from his own.

Another time I was waiting with the family in the car at the Gartly Station level crossing, south of Huntly. The gatekeeper was so astonished to see me that instead of opening the gates after the train had passed he came down to make sure it really was the man he had seen on television. He even got his wife to come out and shake my hand. The cars behind had to wait.

By 1982 I was beginning to feel stale. Sadly, Charlie Smith died. A new producer, who had been an agricultural journalist, was given control of the programme and took to it like a dog to a manger. Overnight it became her programme and she would brook no interference. I tried to accept the situation philosophically and decided I would give up at the end of the series in the spring of 1983. One day, however, I found there was an item included in the script which appeared to me to be a straightforward advertisement for a new piece of farm machinery which was neither innovative nor of particular merit. The programme had not previously sunk to blatant advertising and I told the producer I would not present the programme with that piece in it. After I contacted the new Head of News and Current Affairs, Ted Brocklebank, the piece was removed but it became harder for the producer and myself to work together and I gave up at the end of the year.

I applied for three different jobs while still a Member of Parliament and was interviewed for all three. The best paid was with a firm of international business consultants on the personnel selection side, but it would have meant living in the south of England, and although the salary was high and therefore tempting, I refused the post I was offered.

The second option was as the Chief Executive of the Scottish end of a government-financed quango. It had strong links with agriculture and was well paid. I was offered the job but only on condition that I gave up my direct involvement in farming, which I was not prepared to do. Tillychetly was not just a farm, it was my home and had been in my family for 200 years. Furthermore there were rumblings about my simultaneously presenting *Country Focus*. I turned this offer down, too.

There were between seventy and eighty applicants for the third job, as Chief Executive of the Royal Highland and Agricultural Society of Scotland, with offices in Edinburgh. I prepared my application carefully and asked Jo Grimond and George Mackie if they would be referees. I was put on a short leet [shortlist] and three Directors of the Society came down to Westminster to interview me. I took them to the House of Commons Tea Room and ordered a pot of tea. For an hour or more we talked and I answered questions. I ascertained that there would be no objection to my continuing in farming so long as I had a permanent manager and that they were delighted to hear that I would be presenting *Country Focus*. A fortnight later I was invited to the Society's offices in Eglinton Crescent in Edinburgh. The offices were impressive, redolent with history and tradition, but lacking any atmosphere of dynamism or urgency. I was to appear before the entire Board of fifty-two directors, make a fifteen-minute presentation and answer questions. The other short leet candidate, a Scottish-born Professor of Agricultural Engineering from a Canadian university, would follow.

My political experience stood me in good stead and I was not unduly nervous when confronted with fifty-two faces, not all of them unknown to me. I had often addressed audiences of farmers before, but never such a select one. My address seemed to be well received. I set out the plan of action I would follow if appointed, concentrating on maximising the society's assets by broadening its activities and making better use of the showground throughout the year rather than just at the time of the Royal Highland Show. I was questioned for twenty minutes, then the interview was over. Within forty-eight hours I had been offered the job, with a starting date of 1 October 1970, after the General Election.

Laura Grimond had been selected as the able, hard-working and conscientious Liberal candidate for West Aberdeenshire, but she was up against a Tory candidate who had the advantage of being virtually a national figure. Once the Tories knew I was standing down, they dismissed their earlier candidate and looked for someone who would attract national attention. Colonel Mitchell – Mad Mitch – could hardly have picked a more spectacular way of gate-crashing the headlines of the popular press than through his exploits in Aden. He had carried out an ostentatious but fruitless bit of bravado which was popular neither with the army general staff nor with most politicians. A photograph of him in the uniform of the Argyll and Sutherland Highlanders dominated the front page of his election address. His speeches were jingoistic and boastful and contained a variety of personal opinions which bore little resemblance to the Tory manifesto or, indeed, to any recognisable brand of politics. He needed a job and fancied a seat in Parliament. He had flirted with the SNP, then joined the Tories.

Laura Grimond could not have been more different. She came from a traditionally Liberal family whose views were essentially democratic. She had inherited the habit of hard work and her electioneering was tireless and persistent. Face to face with individual electors, she was superb. She would have made a wonderful constituency MP, but for every vote she gained on the doorstep she must have lost two on the platform where she tended to send people to sleep. Scottish Tories will accept a candidate with an upper-class English accent. Laura's was definitely from the drawing rooms of Belgravia and some Labour and Liberal supporters found it difficult to take. I accompanied her canvassing. I chauffeured her, introduced her to key people, went with her on visits to factories and other places of work, including the knacker's yard in Kintore where the stench was indescribable, and preceded her on the rostrum at the agricultural marts and on the platforms every evening when we did three or four meetings in different towns and villages. I held a platform for her in a school or village hall until she arrived from the previous meeting, then went on to the next venue and did the same again.

The involvement of two such well-known names as Laura Grimond and Mad Mitch drew the press to West Aberdeenshire like wasps to a jam jar. One morning I was about to leave Inverurie Auction Mart, where Laura had just arrived, to speak at Huntly Mart pending her arrival, when Leonard Beaton of *The Times* asked if he could come with me. He wanted to get some background information about the constituency. In fact, he ended up giving his own views to me rather than asking mine. I found myself mentally rehearsing what I was going to say in Huntly, not really listening to him. He gave his opinions on Vietnam, the economy, Rhodesian independence and racial riots in parts of London.

'Of course,' I came back to hear him say, 'you don't see many black faces round here.'

'No,' I replied, scanning the sheep grazing on either side of the road. 'Hereabouts it's mostly Cheviots.' The Blackface is the most common breed of sheep in the Highlands.

At first I could not see why he was laughing, then the penny dropped. I apologised for having misunderstood him. He later wrote this up amusingly in *The Times*. I received letters accusing me of ignorance and racism. It was a further reminder of how careful you have to be when speaking to journalists.

Laura lost the election by a few thousand votes and returned to Orkney to continue her conscientious support of her husband. Mad Mitch held the seat for a short time then disappeared, I know not where, and the seat soon reverted to the Liberals.

Royal Highland

My relationship with the Royal Highland and Agricultural Society of Scotland became very much like my relationship with my mother, who died at the age of ninety-six in 1990: a mixture of duty, affection and occasional exasperation. From an early age I had been trained to have a strong sense of duty. I felt affection for the RHASS because it had pursued the promotion of Scottish agriculture and related education and industries for more than two centuries. The exasperation factor stemmed from a variety of causes – the sheer size of the Board of Directors, (fifty-two); the fact that I was not given a clear job specification, so that few directors understood where my responsibilities lay; and the fact that for 180 years the senior member of staff had been the Secretary. It seemed difficult for directors to understand that a new post of Chief Executive had been created, senior to the Secretary and responsible to the Board of Directors for all the activities of the Society.

The members of the board were a group of determinedly independent individuals, most of whom had started their careers at least halfway up the farming ladder. As the years went by I found that my satisfaction and enjoyment of the work were directly related to the attitude and personality of the current chairman. They occupied the chair for only two years and I was treated variously as a clerk, an office manager, a chief executive or a friend. As each one demitted office I had to readjust, sometimes fundamentally, to the new man: eleven times in twenty-one years.

The first chairman I served with was Sir William Young, a man of great ability with a quick and incisive mind, but like most of us he had his blind spots. At the first meeting of the board after my appointment, he declared that there were certain areas of administration outside my responsibility. I was shocked. I rose to my feet and pointed out that this was not the basis on which I had been offered the job.

'If you want me to accept that, you need a chief clerk, not a chief executive,' I said.

Sir William continued urbanely. Only an occasional jerk of the papers he was holding indicated that he was in the least bit put out.

'Of course you will be ultimately responsible to the Board for all the activities of the Society,' he continued, as if nothing had happened. Nevertheless I could feel shock waves emanating from the rows of directors facing us. I made sure the point was minuted.

Other chairmen caused different problems. At one meeting of the Finance Committee the then-incumbent announced without warning that the compulsory retirement age for all members of staff would henceforth be sixty. I was stunned, but managed to ask, 'What about those who are sixty now?' There were several. I had a year to go. For me it could mean uprooting the family again and looking for alternative employment until I reached pensionable age. The Chairman mumbled something about there being no exceptions. The idea had not been discussed with me and had clearly not been thought through. I hardly spoke a word for the remainder of the meeting. Already I had realised that there was a breach of contract involved and I planned to take legal advice. The atmosphere was heavy with embarrassment on one side and anger on the other.

As soon as the meeting finished I got on to a friend in the law department of Edinburgh University and asked for the name of an expert on dismissal and redundancy. Then I rang the man he recommended and made an appointment for the following morning. His advice was clear; it was a case of constructive dismissal. The Chairman had to back down. He saved face by revising his proposal to the effect that any members of staff engaged thereafter would have to retire at the age of sixty. Those already engaged would be offered the option of continuing to sixty-five.

The first thing I wanted to do when I took up my post in 1970 was to close the communication gap between the Society's office staff and those responsible for the showground at Ingliston. By Christmas 1970 the Society's offices were sold and we moved to newly refurbished offices in Ingliston House on the Showground.

I had discovered that the Royal Highland Show was sacrosanct. It had become the whole reason for the Society's existence. The Show was put on once a year, and then work started methodically to organise the next one. The publication of the *Transactions*, which had recorded agricultural innovation and progress for over a century, had ceased in 1968. Through its links with the Scottish agricultural colleges the RHASS nominally still awarded certificates and diplomas in agriculture, but the involvement was peripheral. I was determined to broaden the scope of the Society's activities and reassume some of the roles which had been abandoned.

Over the years we increased the numbers of events between Shows. In most cases we simply let premises and facilities to other organisations who organised events such as trade fairs, dog shows and Formula 2 racing. Other events we began to organise ourselves. In 1972 there was a mediaeval tournament which, despite tropical downpours over its two days, drew a crowd of 21,000 – a good attendance, but not enough to break even financially. The following year there was a successful international clan gathering and a year or two later we were asked to organise the first major horse-driving trials in Scotland with the Duke of Edinburgh as one of the competitors.

This event involved all of us in much extra work for little return except prestige. The trials concluded with a huge parade of horses and ponies in the main ring. At the end of the afternoon Prince Philip was due to leave by car from the back of the grandstand. When I saw him preparing to leave, I called up his car and, with the aid of two policemen, opened the big doors at the rear, which operated on rollers. As the Prince Philip emerged, he said, 'Can't you do something about those damned doors? They make a noise like thunder every time they're moved.' I suppose I had been expecting a friendly nod, or even a word of thanks. There was no time to reply before he got into his limousine and was driven off.

When I first joined the Society, the Show ran from Tuesday to Friday, but we began to consider including at least part of the weekend to get the general public in. The change was eventually made in 1984, the bicentenary of the Society, when a five-day show was held and achieved a record attendance of 185,650. It has now settled at four days: Thursday–Sunday in the third week of June. We first transgressed the Scottish Sabbath in July 1973 by allowing a Sunday Market to operate in the car parks. This grew year by year until by the early 1980s it was drawing average crowds of fifteen or sixteen thousand almost every Sunday.

My attempt to fulfil Sir William Young's exhortation to make the construction of an exhibition hall a priority met an obstacle when in 1973 the City of Edinburgh opposed our plans to build an exhibition complex on the smallholdings east of the showground. The project had been ambitious – nothing less than a national exhibition centre for Scotland. This was the starting point for the concept which finally resulted in a Scottish Exhibition Centre in Glasgow. Our plans had to be revised to allow the building of a large exhibition hall inside the Showground. We were led to believe that this would not be opposed by the City of Edinburgh and it was eventually finished in time for the 1979 Show. Its completion influenced the Scottish National Fatstock Club to bring their annual show to the Hall from Perth and we held the first Scottish Agricultural Winter Fair the same year. This was an immediate success although its appeal did not extend much beyond the professional farming community.

In 1980 membership of the Society peaked at nearly 18,000, show attendances had continued to increase and financial sponsorship had grown until it represented nearly eight per cent of the Society's total revenue. Unfortunately, during the 1980s, signs of recession began to be seen in the agricultural industry, interest rates were high and the Society was paying local authority rates equivalent to ten per cent of its total turnover. The City of Edinburgh regarded the Showground at Ingliston as a cow to be milked rather than a national enterprise to be encouraged.

The exhibition hall was getting fewer bookings. Over and over again I told the directors that although we were doing our best to market it, I had not been given the resources to do so properly. I asked for a member of staff to be dedicated to this, but the proposal was repeatedly rejected. At one point it was suggested that management consultants should be brought in. I was angry.

Our management structure and operations had already been thoroughly investigated twice, by an international financial institution before they offered a loan to build the hall, and then by the Scottish Development Agency.

I was told to look round for a buyer for the hall. I objected strongly and repeated that what was needed was a full-time marketing executive. I also suggested that rather than selling the hall, which was capable of earning revenue, it would be better to sell the twenty-six acres of land on the opposite side of the A8 trunk road from the showground. We had failed to get planning permission to use it for car parking or other developments, or for a footbridge to link it to the showground. The land only earned a few hundred pounds a year for cropping, whereas the hall was capable of earning a six-figure sum or more annually.

On my own initiative, I contacted Murray International Metals who were in the market for development land on the west side of Edinburgh. I made an appointment to see David Murray, the dynamic, genial and decisive Managing Director. Within a matter of days I was able to put very attractive terms before the Board, which allowed us to eliminate the Society's overdraft overnight. One Director called this outcome an act of God. Another commented sarcastically that we had only eliminated our debts by selling off assets. I took some satisfaction in pointing out that while I had been Chief Executive, I had negotiated the purchase of forty-seven acres of land adjoining the showground, on the right side of the A8, at an average cost of under £2,000 per acre. The twenty-six acres on the wrong side of the A8 was sold for £28,000 per acre.

I have recounted a few unhappy moments in the course of more than two decades at the RHASS. There were many proud and happy ones, too. Few sounds are more thrilling to my ears than massed pipes and drums and at Ingliston we only invited the best. On a day of bright sunshine and white cloud, there is no sight more impressive than the parade of prize livestock in the main ring – a huge area, 170 metres long by seventy metres wide. The early afternoon parade stages a snaking column of champion cattle and horses – black, white, grey, gold, chestnut and brindled – adorning the emerald turf from one end to the other.

Of course, there could be problems in the Main Ring too. One year the ground was so dry it was as hard as asphalt, though there was a good sole of grass. There had been no rain for a month. There were rumbles about the state of the ground from the leading show jumpers, all household names. At 10 p.m. on the first evening of the show I was confronted by a delegation of half a dozen of the most renowned names in the business. They were fortified by the divine right that belongs only to royalty and famous show jumpers. The director who was Chief Steward of the Main Ring could not be found. I was told categorically that the famous would not jump the next day unless water – a lot of water – was put on the Main Ring.

I pointed out that they were not the only users of the ring; a wet surface could be dangerous to other participants such as the Royal Signals motor cyclists. If we put a hose on to such a hard surface, the water would probably just lie in pools. Rain was forecast, I said, and I would monitor the situation over the next twenty-four hours. They were adamant, threatening. If it had been my personal choice rather than my responsibility I would have told them to get lost, but I had to consider the paying public. So at 11 p.m. I had fire hoses put out and in the next hour-and-a-half 11,000 gallons of water gushed on to the grass. At 2 a.m. it began to rain and hardly stopped for the next forty-eight hours.

I have to admit to some satisfaction at seeing the members of that delegation spattered with mud, floundering on a surface like a skidpan. They could not clear jumps which in dry conditions would not have deterred a pony club meeting. Neither riders nor horses were damaged, though the grass was, and the Society had to pay for it.

Royal patronage of the Society meant that I had regular opportunities to meet members of the royal family including HM the Queen, the Queen Mother, Princess Anne and Princess Alexandra, and I was generally impressed by their charm, endurance and genuine interest. There was a memorable occasion in 1977 when Janet and I represented the Society at a conference of Royal Agricultural Societies in Jamaica, attended by Prince Philip. I had to admire his forbearance when a red-shirted left-wing politician took advantage of an official reception to harangue the Duke for what seemed like hours. Prince Philip was given no opportunity to respond but appeared to take it all with patient good humour.

Janet and I had more than a week on the island before the conference started. We visited sheep, poultry and cattle units. We went to a sugar plantation and pimento orchard. We saw the cultivation of bananas, coconuts, grapefruit, lemons, oranges, almonds, ginger, yams, ackee and pineapples, and sampled many of them. We went pony-trekking up into the hills behind the hotel. We were taken to a coffee plantation on Blue Mountain and overnight climbed to its top in the hope of watching dawn over the Caribbean. Sadly there was such a heavy mist that we might as well have stayed in a jungle at sea level. We were taken to see open cast mining of bauxite, probably Jamaica's most valuable legal export, marijuana probably being the most valuable illegal one. Late one night, driving back to our hotel, we saw the lights of a small aeroplane taking off from what appeared to be the middle of a sugar cane field and heading in the direction of Florida. As our last adventure, Janet and I arranged a rafting expedition down the Rio Grande. A group of Australians, English and New Zealanders joined us. On bamboo rafts each holding two passengers, we bumped, surged and floated down the river towards the south coast, piloted by expert raftsmen. One unforgettable sight was Lord Swatheling, a rather stout English aristocrat, attired in a dark formal suit and bowler hat, smiling occasionally to indicate his enjoyment, bobbing along in solemn dignity.

Back in Edinburgh we attended a dinner at Holyrood because of my position with the RHASS. The Queen conversed pleasantly with all her guests. The Duke complained to me about the litter at Edinburgh Airport – not exactly my fault. I inadvertently splashed beetroot salad on the spotless white damask tablecloth. Luckily I knew the waitress, who also worked at the showground for Crawford's catering, and she moved a salt cellar over the stain. I have sometimes wondered if the Queen ever managed to wash it out. We have not been asked back.

In 1991 a group with the surname Davidson, of whom I was one, met in Edinburgh to re-form the Clan Davidson Association which had gone into abeyance during the Second World War. Our first president was the distinguished High Court judge, the

Honourable Lord Davidson FRSE. When poor health compelled him to stand down in 1994 I was elected his successor, and continued in that role until 2001. At the last national census Davidson was the thirty-fifth most common surname in Scotland, the majority domiciled in the north and north-east of the country, although the name is also common in the Borders. The chief of Clan Davidson in the direct line of the Davidsons of Tulloch in Ross-shire is now a New Zealander, Alister Davidson, who lives in Auckland.

Flower of Scotland

In my first decade of retirement I was able to pursue and achieve goals not possible during my working life. I had been looking forward to retiring. Twenty-one years is a long time in the same job with no possibility of promotion – a medium-sized fish in a small pond with fifty-two others swimming above me. I was looking forward to spending more time at home with Janet and our son Calum, now fourteen. Sandy, Ros and Polly had all graduated and were busy with their careers; Sandy was married with three children, working in software design, Ros was a freelance journalist based in San Francisco, Polly worked for charities as a fundraiser and administrator. I was looking forward to being my own boss again – being free of the relentless pressure of meeting deadlines, free to choose – subject to domestic commitments and weather – how I spent the day. Yet I also knew I would miss the discipline of daily and monthly routines. I would miss the level of decision-taking to which I had grown accustomed. I knew I would have to set myself some targets and devise a framework combining domestic and outdoor activities.

Early one Monday morning in May 1991 I was lying in bed at our home in Newtonmore, where we had moved after Tillychetly had been sold. Hill farming had been a demanding life and none of the children had been interested in taking it on without financial backing. Although technically an owner-occupier, in practice I had been a tenant of the bank. I was thinking of my impending retirement and was just about to face the 120-mile journey to Edinburgh which I had driven nearly 2,000 times in the past decade. I went downstairs and made a pot of tea. Light poured through the east window of the kitchen. I let out Sheila, our cross-collie bitch and put the kettle on. While I waited for it to boil I looked out to the west to Creag Dubh, which dominates the first five miles of the road to Laggan and Fort William, to Creag na h-Iolaire where Calum and I had stood on the skyline at nearly 3,000 feet and waved, watched through binoculars by Janet. Beyond, a little to the north, loomed A'Chailleach, a Munro of 3,093 feet with a steep eastern face, still surmounted by a snow cornice.

I let in the dog and took my cup of tea through to our sitting room where I looked out at my favourite view: three receding ranges of hills beyond a field where sheep were grazing, and the Eilan where successive generations of shinty players have battled for Newtonmore's honour. Between the River Spey and the nearest range lies the flat ground of Invernahavon where more than 600 years ago men of the Mackintosh, Davidson and Macpherson clans fought and won a battle against marauding Camerons from Lochaber. Beyond the furthest range eighteen miles away rises the other Munro we can see from the house – the 3,400-feet Geal Charn. Its north-east side, which faces us, usually remains snow-clad well into August each year.

A few years ago I climbed Geal Charn after a long walk in and was sitting devouring my sandwiches when two young men appeared. We exchanged greetings and they shared a bar of chocolate before preparing to move on to tackle the next Munro. As they did so, one of them asked me, 'Isn't your name Davidson?'

'Yes, James Davidson.'

'Snap!' he grinned.

He was the son of the provost of Ellon, yet another James Davidson. It is a common enough name, of course, but the likelihood of two unrelated holders of the name meeting on top of a remote Highland peak must be very small. He had remembered me from *Country Focus*.

Back in the kitchen I poured myself a second cup of tea and one for Janet. An idea had occurred to me that I wanted to discuss with her. I wanted to do something for Scotland which did not involve politics and which would allow me personal independence. As a former food producer and athlete I had always been interested in the relationship between diet, exercise and health. As a patriot, I was horrified at Scotland's appalling record for heart disease and cancer – one of the worst in the world.

In 1990 we had watched with excitement as David Sole, to the echoes of 'Flower of Scotland', led the Scottish team to victory and the Grand Slam against England. My idea was to run a Flower of Scotland Campaign to encourage Scots, particularly young Scots, to adopt a healthier lifestyle. Any money it raised could be given for research into the prevention of heart disease and cancer, working through established charities.

Despite the early hour, Janet reacted with enthusiasm and for the next four months much of our time was spent planning the campaign and raising funds to get it off the ground. I approached prominent figures from the worlds of sport, music and the screen in the hope that they would provide inspiration to the man, woman and child in the Scottish street. David Sole became a co-trustee. Sean Connery, Evelyn Glennie, Muriel Gray, Gavin Hastings, Karen Matheson, Donnie Munro and Yvonne Murray all agreed to endorse the campaign. Later support came from the Scottish Council of the British Medical Association and Professor Philip James, Chairman of the World Health Organisation's committee on diet and health.

We put out a leaflet setting out the aims of the campaign and the facts behind it. Supporters were asked to pay two pounds and sign an undertaking not to smoke or take drugs, to eat a varied diet, to reduce their intake of fats, sugar and salt to the minimum, to limit their consumption of alcohol and fizzy drinks to a specified safe level and to take at least two hours' healthy exercise a week. In return they received a certificate of membership and badge.

Over the following five years we developed the campaign by producing a book and video setting out its aims. All our well-known supporters, including Ali McCoist the footballer and Sean Connery, who rang personally from Spain to set up a time for filming, took part in the video *Your Life – Your Choice*. It was distributed free to every secondary school in Scotland along with a copy of the book, *Towards a Healthier Scotland*. I spoke in more than 120 schools from Lerwick to Kirkcudbright, promoting the idea. I also made my first parachute jump, at the age of sixty-six, to raise funds for the campaign, along with David Sole, my solicitor Stuart Jeffray – another of my co-trustees – and three young supporters. We jumped on a flawlessly clear sunny day, but

230

the winds at 2,000 feet were on the limits of safety and, after landing in a field of barley, I found myself having to walk about half a mile back to the airfield in Auchterarder – but we raised more than £10,000! David Sole was instrumental in organising annual Burns Dinners in Edinburgh, which helped to cover the costs of running the campaign and enabled us to make small contributions to the supporting charities.

Throughout the last ten years I have done a lot of walking, sometimes with Janet or my children, sometimes on my own or with a friend. Newtonmore is in a beautiful part of Scotland with endless walking possibilities starting from our front door. An undemanding favourite is up Glen Banchor as far as the Shepherd's Bridge. In the hottest days of summer we bathe in the river pools there. We have walked on Mull and Arran, round the mountains of Sutherland, on the Speyside Way and the length of the West Highland Way, north to south. People doing this great ninety-six-mile walk 'the usual way,' from Bearsden to Fort William, seemed to feel that we were doing the wrong thing by doing it in the opposite direction. We were several times told, 'You can't do that,' but we did and thoroughly enjoyed it.

In a twenty-four-hour spell of perfect weather, at the height of summer, I took in all the Cairngorm summits on the west side of the Lairig Ghru and spent the night in a bivvy bag on the Devil's Point looking across Glen Geusachan to the headwaters of the River Dee, sixty miles west of the river's rendezvous with the North Sea at Aberdeen. In twenty-four hours I only saw four people in the distance, before descending to the Lairig. So much for worries about the Cairngorms being overrun by visitors! More people may be found on the Ben Macdui side of the pass, or walking through it in either direction; the more the better, provided they are properly equipped and dressed and have the requisite experience.

By early 1998 I had become involved as chairman of Newtonmore's newly founded community woodland trust. Since then some 22,000 trees have been planted in sixteen compartments around the village. We have developed a ten-kilometre path – the Wildcat Trail – linking these areas of new trees with older woods and set up an information centre for walkers and other visitors in the village. In 2001, the *Sunday Post* Marafun was held over the Wildcat Trail. Nearly a thousand people took part and thousands of pounds were raised for a variety of charities.

One day in 2000, Polly, by then married and mother of a little boy, rang me from London to suggest that I should apply for a Millennium Award from Earthwatch. They were offering the chance to people over fifty to do conservation work all over the word, expenses paid. I was then seventy-four and didn't think I had a chance, but I have been blessed with good health and was offered the choice of several projects. I chose conservation of river otters in the afforested hills east of Valdivia in Southern Chile, eventually spending three weeks living in a tent studying, tracking and electronically tagging otters. This was a triple bonus for me; South America was the one continent, apart from the Antarctic, I had never visited; I consider the otter one of the most fascinating of animals; and Valdivia has close associations with Thomas, Lord Cochrane, who was one of the greatest Scots of all time, featured in my book *Scots and the Sea*. Before departure I undertook a crash course in Spanish and read what I could about Chile.

I arrived at the campsite in the Tolten Basin of southern Chile, two hours' drive from Valdivia, to meet the other members of the team of volunteers, all considerably younger than me – two Brits, an American and a giant of a West German policeman. Our accommodation consisted of two-man tents and a timber hut for cooking and eating situated on the river bank right next to a small and poorly equipped primary school. Most of the pupils arrived in the morning on horseback, perched on the saddle in front of their fathers.

To begin with I was expected to share a tent with the German policeman. As we were the two largest members of the group, this was a little unfair. I eventually moved out to a spare tent. The whole team got on well together, though the American girl, who was the youngest, was also overweight and not very mobile, so that a greater workload was put on the rest of us. The team was led by Professor Vogel of the University of Southern Chile, with the aid of two veterinary students.

Each day the team was split into two groups of four. One group visited the humane otter traps which could not be left for more than twelve hours without being inspected; the other group tracked the otters' transmissions with hand-held receivers. When not tracking or trapping we were employed constructing timber huts. The day started at 7 a.m. We breakfasted on cereal, powdered milk, bread, honey and fruit. We worked until 6 p.m., and sometimes later, walking many miles over rough terrain, carrying sandwiches and flasks of coffee. The traps were set within a radius of twenty miles and were visited twice every twenty-four hours.

Supper consisted of meat or fish stew, fruit and red wine – lots of red wine. We took it in turns to cook. Our water came straight off the hill and had to be boiled, but some members of the team were less conscientious than others and I came home with a bad dose of cryptosporidium. It took me months to get rid of it, with the help of an antibiotic imported from Italy – and probiotic drinks from the local supermarket. We had the use of the primitive washing and toilet facilities at the school before the children's arrival in the morning and after they left at night.

The award had been described as 'a unique opportunity for those aged fifty and over to take part in conservation research teams around the world, learn about the local environment, and gain new skills, motivation and inspiration.' I did not need more motivation or inspiration. As for learning about the environment and gaining new skills, I had an open mind. I learned something about the forest environment of southern Chile and the threat to it from big timber extraction companies from Japan, Germany and the USA. These corporate giants force their way in and out by rough but well-engineered roads, harvest the valuable native hardwoods, then replant the easier areas with quick-growing non-native pine and eucalyptus. Apart from providing temporary employment, they contribute nothing in the way of social infrastructure. I learned that it can rain very heavily. We were lucky. A later Earthwatch team found the camp site completely flooded.

As for 'gaining new skills,' my Spanish improved – very temporarily; my opening of food tins, drawing of corks from bottles of the excellent local Black Cat wine, sawing and knocking nails into a timber hut we were asked to construct all improved –

and I learned to manipulate a radio receiver so that I could take bearings on the otters we were tracking.

My main, but mostly useless, learning experience happened as I watched very carefully while a vet implanted miniature transmitters in the stomachs of two of the otters we had trapped. I was allowed to pass his instruments to him. The otters were not released back into the wild until their surgical incisions had healed, so we had some opportunities to study them at close quarters. The immediate purpose of the research was to establish their movements, range, feeding and reproductive habits with a view to ensuring that they had the requisite links between river systems to enable them to survive and thrive.

The trip was a unique experience and I left with an affection for the Chilean people, a better knowledge of otters and their habits and a determination never to travel again by Lufthansa. While their male staff were polite and efficient, their air stewardesses seemed to have learned their art from warders at Belsen. On return my obligatory 'community project' was to write and illustrate with line drawings a book about all aspects of the River Spey, intended as a colouring book for children. Copies were distributed to all the primary schools along the Spey.

I researched and wrote my book *Scots and the Sea* over the next two years and its publication in 2003 fulfilled a lifelong ambition. I was concerned at the lack of appreciation among Scots of the achievements of their own countrymen. My book was an attempt to fill this gap in an area where I had some specialist professional knowledge.

When I asked the surgeon for a prognosis following an operation just before Christmas, 2004, and the likelihood of my finishing a new book I was writing, he gave me a sixty per cent chance of complete recovery and said the writing would be just a matter of concentration. He was right about the latter and *Admiral Lord St Vincent, Saint or Tyrant – Nelson's Patron – The Life of Sir John Jervis* was published in 2006. My interest in St Vincent arose out of my research for *Scots and the Sea*. He played a key role in reforming the Navy and defending the country against invasion by Napoleon. It was he who gave Nelson the opportunities which resulted in his status as national hero.

Postscript

This series of autobiographical sketches has been written mainly for the benefit of my family but in the hope that others might enjoy reading about what I believe has been an unusually varied life.

It is my wife's opinion that without a project, target or destination, I am like a boat without helmsman or rudder, or a sheepdog without shepherd or flock. As an octogenarian, I shall just have to wait and see. Life, as my own experience shows, is full of surprises.

Appendix A

1966 Election Address

Telephone: Alford 246.

TILLYCHETLY,
ALFORD, Aberdeenshire.

ELECTORS OF WEST ABERDEENSHIRE:

10th March, 1966.

No doubt somebody will ask, "Which would you rather have— A Tory Government or another Labour one?" In my view there is little to choose between them, provided neither has an overwhelming majority. Naturally, what I want is a Liberal Government. Nothing is more certain to lead to self-satisfied complacency and neglect than a comfortable Tory majority; nothing is more certain to produce government by Socialist formulae, regardless of the consequences, than a large Labour majority; and nothing is so likely to lead to sensible reform and a balanced national outlook than the election of a strong body of Liberal M.P.s who are free to put *people* and *places* before Party, Class, and vested interest.

The history of the Tory and Labour Parties has been of electors' hopes dashed, promises forgotten, and good intentions sacrificed to the sectional interests which pay the piper and therefore call the tune. Every worthwhile reform since the 1830's has originated in the Liberal Party. In the life of the last Parliament, Liberal M.P.s stuck to their principles against every assault—they looked at each issue on its own merits; then supported or opposed it on the basis of justice and common sense. 86 times they voted with the Government; 177 times they voted against it, but usually for reasons different to the Tories'.

Our opponents like to say Liberals are not effective. What they really mean is that it takes time for Liberal ideas to take effect, to percolate through the impervious layers of conservatism and bureaucracy. Liberals consistently opposed Steel Nationalisation—Mr. Wilson relegated it to the bottom of his list. Liberals have supported the Common Market idea since its inception—5 years too late, the Tories suddenly came round to it. Liberals have pressed for a Highland Development Board since 1928—in 1964, after the election of Liberal M.P.s in four of the six constituencies in the area, a Board was set up. In August 1964 a Liberal Committee, of which I was Chairman and Editor, published a "Plan for the North East" —three months later the Scottish Council of Development and Industry set up an office in Aberdeen, and the Government announced it was considering plans for the area—disappointing though these plans have turned out to be.

Look for a moment at the figures for the last two General Elections in West Aberdeenshire:

	1959	1964
Tory	22,937	16,429
LIBERAL	—	11,754
Labour	10,542	7,203

In 1964 Tory support had fallen by 28 per cent. and their candidate was elected on a minority vote. Labour support dropped by 31 per cent. It must be obvious that a Labour candidate in West Aberdeenshire does not have the slightest chance of being elected: Labour only uses the seat as a training ground or a platform for the defence of the party record. The Tories, on the other hand, have habitually regarded West Aberdeenshire as a 'safe seat' for a member who could not win one on his own merits.

If you are a convinced Tory or Socialist I will not be representing your *Political* views in Parliament, but I will be glad to help you over any matters of hardship, injustice—or development for the benefit of the majority. If, on the other hand your outlook is Liberal, radical, progressive, or patriotic, or if you are just a thoughtful citizen, I can ask for your support with confidence. I believe you will find that I speak and vote in the House of Commons as you would speak and vote, and I promise to serve you, and the country you live in, to the utmost of my power and abliity.

Yours sincerely,

James Davidson.

Appendix B

Letter to my sister, Julia, 30 August 2008

My dear Julia,

It was lovely having you with us for a day or two and we hope to see you again soon.

You asked me to give you a breakdown of my mantra comprising the initial letters of qualities I ask for in the prayer which has accompanied my exercises for the last 40+ years – 'Which is the scratched aircraft'.

Before I do so, I feel I should let you know where I am coming from in terms of religious belief. Although we were christened and confirmed and I was, for a short time, an elder of the Church of Scotland, I cannot call myself a Christian. I believe that Jesus lived as a special and exceptional human being, but I do not believe he was the son of God, born of a virgin, or that he was magically resurrected after crucifixion and scooped up to heaven.

The trinity is a concept I cannot grasp, and all the ritual and dogma associated with the Episcopal, Anglican, Roman and Orthodox churches is anathema to me. I believe that religion, or belief in God, or gods, or something else, is entirely a matter for the individual and his or her concept of whatever the spiritual world may be, and that nobody has the right to impose their views on anybody else – persuade, perhaps, but not impose. I am an evolutionist, not a creationist, but the God I believe in and pray to is more of a system or plan that a persona sitting high in majesty.

I wrote recently to Professor Dawkins, the author of *The God Delusion*, suggesting that his thesis is based on semantics – what different people mean by the word 'God' – and that therefore his arguments are not valid. I did not expect to get a reply from somebody so eminent, but scientists who argue that the natural laws disprove the existence of God ignore the possibility that evolution, or laws such as gravity, are simply part of God's plan or system.

When I pray to God, I am addressing a concept too vast for my complete understanding, based on the conviction that there must be a reason for the existence of living creatures and the universe around us.

This is the prayer I offer six days a week, on the conclusion of my twenty-minute exercise regime – the changes to the biblical translation of the Lord's Prayer make it easier for me:

Our father who is in heaven, may your will be done on earth: give us this day our daily bread and forgive us our sins as we forgive those who sin against us and lead us not into temptation but deliver us from evil; for yours is the universe, its power and its glory, and the eternal life force.

Please, God, give me Wisdom, Honesty, Integrity, Courage, Humour and make me Indomitable, Sincere, Trustworthy, Humane, Enterprising, Serene, Confident, Relaxed, Alert, Thorough, Cheerful, Helpful, Enthusiastic, Decisive, Astute, Imaginative, Realistic, Compassionate, Reliable, Altruistic, Friendly and Tolerant. I thank you for the many blessings I have received.

Then I list them, offer a prayer for all those whom I love, including your family, and for those in trouble, sorrow, need, sickness, hunger, thirst, fear, pain, loneliness, depression, distress or any other adversity. I conclude by asking God for help to make the right decisions and to take the right turnings and I ask him to take away my adversities, or, if that is not possible, to give me the strength and courage to bear them. I conclude by asking for God's blessing on all my endeavours (assuming they are approved).

All this sounds a bit heavy! I have never put it all down on paper before, and hope you do not find it embarrassing.

Love,
James

Index

United States, 52, 126, 143,
192, 193, 204
US Navy, 45, 76, 157
US Pacific Fleet, 49

V

Vanguard, HMS, 65, 70, 71, 72,
74, 75, 78, 86, 89
Vassall, John, 154, 179, 193, 194
Vian, Philip, 15, 16
Vietnam, 192, 193, 219
Volga, 122, 147

W

Wales, 85, 209, 210
Watson, Bob, 167, 168
Welsh, 39, 40, 209
Wewack, Operation, 46
Whimbrel, HMS, 49, 50, 51, 76,
87
Wildcat Trail, 231, 232
Wren, HMS, 86, 87, 93, 97, 101,
102, 103, 105, 106, 108

Z

Zermatt, 80, 81, 82

Printed in the United Kingdom by
Lightning Source UK Ltd., Milton Keynes
141355UK00001B/8/P